Nikon® D5100™
FOR
DUMMIES®

by Julie Adair King

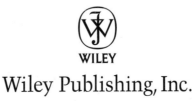

WILEY

Wiley Publishing, Inc.

Nikon® D5100™ For Dummies®

Published by
Wiley Publishing, Inc.
111 River Street
Hoboken, NJ 07030-5774

www.wiley.com

Copyright © 2011 by Wiley Publishing, Inc., Indianapolis, Indiana

Published by Wiley Publishing, Inc., Indianapolis, Indiana

Published simultaneously in Canada

For general information on our other products and services, please contact our Customer Care Department within the U.S. at 877-762-2974, outside the U.S. at 317-572-3993, or fax 317-572-4002.

For technical support, please visit www.wiley.com/techsupport.

Wiley also publishes its books in a variety of electronic formats and by print-on-demand. Not all content that is available in standard print versions of this book may appear or be packaged in all book formats. If you have purchased a version of this book that did not include media that is referenced by or accompanies a standard print version, you may request this media by visiting http://booksupport.wiley.com. For more information about Wiley products, visit us www.wiley.com.

Library of Congress Control Number: 2011932272

ISBN 978-1-118-11819-1 (pbk); ISBN 978-1-118-16003-9 (ebk); ISBN 978-1-118-16004-6 (ebk); ISBN 978-1-118-16005-3 (ebk)

Manufactured in the United States of America

10 9 8 7 6 5 4 3 2 1

WILEY

About the Author

Julie Adair King is the author of many books about digital photography and imaging, including the best-selling *Digital Photography For Dummies*. Her most recent titles include a series of *For Dummies* guides to popular Nikon, Canon, and Olympus cameras. Other works include *Digital Photography Before & After Makeovers, Digital Photo Projects For Dummies, Julie King's Everyday Photoshop For Photographers, Julie King's Everyday Photoshop Elements,* and *Shoot Like a Pro!: Digital Photography Techniques.* When not writing, King teaches digital photography at such locations as the Palm Beach Photographic Centre.

An Ohio native and graduate of Purdue University, she now resides in West Palm Beach, Florida, and does not miss Midwestern winters even a little bit (although she very much misses friends who have not yet made the journey south).

Author's Acknowledgments

I am deeply grateful for the chance to work once again with the wonderful publishing team at John Wiley and Sons. Kim Darosett, Jennifer Webb, Steve Hayes, Jen Riggs, and Katie Crocker are just some of the talented editors and designers who helped make this book possible. And finally, I am also indebted to technical editor Dave Hall, without whose insights and expertise this book would not have been the same.

Publisher's Acknowledgments

We're proud of this book; please send us your comments at http://dummies.custhelp.com. For other comments, please contact our Customer Care Department within the U.S. at 877-762-2974, outside the U.S. at 317-572-3993, or fax 317-572-4002.

Some of the people who helped bring this book to market include the following:

Acquisitions and Editorial

Project Editor: Kim Darosett

Executive Editor: Steven Hayes

Copy Editor: Jennifer Riggs

Technical Editor: David Hall

Editorial Manager: Leah Cameron

Editorial Assistant: Amanda Graham

Sr. Editorial Assistant: Cherie Case

Cover Photo: © iStockphoto.com / Rosemarie Gearhart

Cartoons: Rich Tennant (www.the5thwave.com)

Composition Services

Project Coordinator: Katie Crocker

Layout and Graphics: Claudia Bell, Carl Byers, Samantha K. Cherolis, Corrie Socolovitch

Proofreaders: Jessica Kramer, Susan Moritz, Linda Seifert

Indexer: Potomac Indexing, LLC

Publishing and Editorial for Technology Dummies

Richard Swadley, Vice President and Executive Group Publisher

Andy Cummings, Vice President and Publisher

Mary Bednarek, Executive Acquisitions Director

Mary C. Corder, Editorial Director

Publishing for Consumer Dummies

Kathy Nebenhaus, Vice President and Executive Publisher

Composition Services

Debbie Stailey, Director of Composition Services

Contents at a Glance

Table of Contents

Chapter 11: Ten Special-Purpose Features to Explore on a Rainy Day 327

Introduction

*N**ikon.* The name has been associated with top-flight photography equipment for generations. And the introduction of the D5100 has only enriched Nikon's well-deserved reputation, offering all the control a die-hard photography enthusiast could want while at the same time providing easy-to-use, point-and-shoot features for the beginner.

In fact, the D5100 offers so *many* features that sorting them all out can be more than a little confusing, especially if you're new to digital photography, SLR photography, or both. For starters, you may not even be sure what SLR means or how it affects your picture taking, let alone have a clue as to all the other techie terms you encounter in your camera manual — *resolution, aperture, white balance,* and so on. And if you're like many people, you may be so overwhelmed by all the controls on your camera that you haven't yet ventured beyond fully automatic picture-taking mode. Which is a shame because it's sort of like buying a Porsche and never actually taking it on the road.

Therein lies the point of *Nikon D5100 For Dummies.* Through this book, you can discover not just what each bell and whistle on your camera does, but also when, where, why, and how to put it to best use. Unlike many photography books, this one doesn't require any previous knowledge of photography or digital imaging to make sense of things, either. In classic *For Dummies* style, everything is explained in easy-to-understand language, with lots of illustrations to help clear up any confusion.

In short, what you have in your hands is the paperback version of an in-depth photography workshop tailored specifically to your Nikon picture-taking powerhouse.

A Quick Look at What's Ahead

This book is organized into four parts, each devoted to a different aspect of using your camera. Although chapters flow in a sequence that's designed to take you from absolute beginner to experienced user, I've also tried to make each chapter as self-standing as possible so that you can explore the topics that interest you in any order you please.

Here's a brief preview of what you can find in each part of the book:

  ✔ **Part I: Fast Track to Super Snaps:** Part I contains four chapters to help you get up and running. Chapter 1 offers a tour of the external controls on your camera, shows you how to navigate camera menus to access internal options, and walks you through initial camera setup. Chapter 2 explains basic picture-taking options, such as shutter-release mode and Image Quality settings, and Chapter 3 shows you how to use the camera's fully automatic exposure modes. Chapter 4 explains the ins and outs of using Live View, the feature that lets you compose pictures on the monitor, and also covers movie recording.

✓ **Part II: Working with Picture Files:** This part offers two chapters, both dedicated to after-the-shot topics. Chapter 5 explains how to review your pictures on the camera monitor, delete unwanted images, and protect your favorites from accidental erasure. Chapter 6 offers a look at some photo software options — including Nikon ViewNX 2, which ships free with your camera — and then guides you through the process of downloading pictures to your computer and preparing them for printing and online sharing.

✓ **Part III: Taking Creative Control:** Chapters in this part help you unleash the full creative power of your camera by moving into the advanced shooting modes (P, S, A, and M). Chapter 7 covers the critical topic of exposure, and Chapter 8 explains how to manipulate focus and color. Chapter 9 summarizes all the techniques explained in earlier chapters, providing a quick-reference guide to the camera settings and shooting strategies that produce the best results for portraits, action shots, landscape scenes, and close-ups.

✓ **Part IV: The Part of Tens:** In famous *For Dummies* tradition, the book concludes with two "top ten" lists containing additional bits of information and advice. Chapter 10 covers the photo-editing and effects tools found on the camera's Retouch menu and also shows you how to use the Effects exposure mode to add special effects to movies and photos as you record them. Chapter 11 wraps up the book by detailing some camera features that, although not found on most "Top Ten Reasons I Bought My Nikon D5100" lists, are nonetheless interesting, useful on occasion, or a bit of both.

Icons and Other Stuff to Note

If this isn't your first *For Dummies* book, you may be familiar with the large, round icons that decorate its margins. If not, here's your very own icon-decoder ring:

A Tip icon flags information that will save you time, effort, money, or some other valuable resource, including your sanity. Tips also point out techniques that help you get the best results from specific camera features.

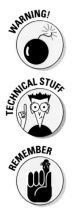

When you see this icon, look alive. It indicates a potential danger zone that can result in much wailing and teeth-gnashing if ignored. In other words, this is stuff that you really don't want to learn the hard way.

Lots of information in this book is of a technical nature — digital photography is a technical animal, after all. But if I present a detail that is useful mainly for impressing your technology-geek friends, I mark it with this icon.

I apply this icon either to introduce information that is especially worth storing in your brain's long-term memory or to remind you of a fact that may have been displaced from that memory by some other pressing fact.

Additionally, I need to point out three additional details that will help you use this book:

- ✏ **Other margin art:** Replicas of some of your camera's buttons and onscreen symbols also appear in the margins of some paragraphs. I include these to provide a quick reminder of the appearance of the button or feature being discussed.

- ✏ **Software menu commands:** In sections that cover software, a series of words connected by an arrow indicates commands that you choose from the program menus. For example, if a step tells you to "choose File⇨Convert Files," click the File menu to unfurl it and then click the Convert Files command on the menu.

- ✏ **Camera firmware:** *Firmware* is the internal software that controls many of your camera's operations. The D5100 firmware consists of three parts, called A and B and L. At the time this book was written, both A and B were version 1.00, and L was version 1.003.

  Occasionally, Nikon releases firmware updates, and it's a good idea to check out the Nikon website (www.nikon.com) periodically to find out whether any updates are available. (Chapter 1 tells you how to determine which firmware version your camera is running.) Firmware updates typically don't carry major feature changes — they're mostly used to solve technical glitches in existing features — but if you do download an update, be sure to read the accompanying description of what it accomplishes so that you can adapt my instructions as necessary.

eCheat Sheet

As a little added bonus, you can find an electronic version of the famous *For Dummies* Cheat Sheet at www.dummies.com/cheatsheet/nikond5100. The Cheat Sheet contains a quick-reference guide to all the buttons, dials, switches, and exposure modes on your D5100. Log on, print it out, and tuck it in your camera bag for times when you don't want to carry this book with you.

Practice, Be Patient, and Have Fun!

To wrap up this preamble, I want to stress that if you initially think that digital photography is too confusing or too technical for you, you're in very good company. *Everyone* finds this stuff a little mind-boggling at first. So take it slowly, experimenting with just one or two new camera settings or techniques at first. Then, each time you go on a photo outing, make it a point to add one or two more shooting skills to your repertoire.

I know that it's hard to believe when you're just starting out, but it really won't be long before everything starts to come together. With some time, patience, and practice, you'll soon wield your camera like a pro, dialing in the necessary settings to capture your creative vision almost instinctively.

So without further ado, I invite you to grab your camera, a cup of whatever it is you prefer to sip while you read, and start exploring the rest of this book. Your D5100 is the perfect partner for your photographic journey, and I thank you for allowing me, through this book, to serve as your tour guide.

Part I
Fast Track to
Super Snaps

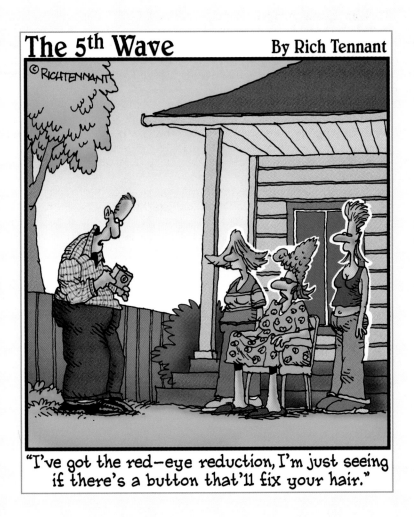

The 5th Wave By Rich Tennant

"I've got the red-eye reduction, I'm just seeing
if there's a button that'll fix your hair."

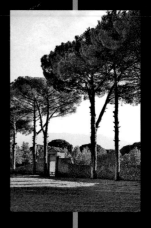

In this part . . .

Making sense of all the controls on your D5100 isn't something you can do in an afternoon — heck, in a week, or maybe even a month. But that doesn't mean that you can't take great pictures today. By using your camera's point-and-shoot automatic modes, you can capture terrific images with very little effort. All you do is compose the scene, and the camera takes care of almost everything else.

This part shows you how to take best advantage of your camera's automatic features and also addresses some basic setup steps, such as adjusting the viewfinder to your eyesight and getting familiar with the camera menus, buttons, and other controls. In addition, chapters in this part explain how to obtain the very best picture quality, whether you shoot in an automatic or manual mode, and how to use your camera's Live View and movie-making features.

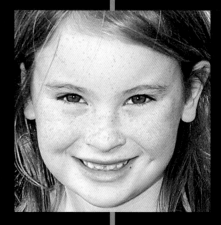

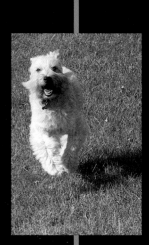

1

Getting the Lay of the Land

1 still remember the day that I bought my first single-lens reflex (SLR) camera. I was excited to finally move up from my one-button point-and-shoot camera, but I was a little anxious, too. My new pride and joy sported several unfamiliar buttons and dials, and the explanations in the camera manual clearly were written for someone with an engineering degree.

You may be feeling similarly insecure if your Nikon D5100 is your first SLR, and doubly so if it's both your first SLR and first digital camera. So to help you get a little more comfortable, this chapter introduces you to each external camera control, explains how to navigate menus, and covers a few other important basics, such as how to work with lenses, memory cards, and the D5100's cool articulating monitor.

Using the Articulating Monitor

When you first take the camera out of its box, the monitor is positioned with the screen facing inward, protecting it from scratches and smudges, as shown on the left in Figure 1-1. It's a good idea to place the monitor in this position when you're not using the camera. When you're ready to start shooting or reviewing your photos, you can lock the monitor in the traditional position on the camera back, as shown on the right in Figure 1-1. Or for more flexibility, you can swing the monitor out and away from the camera body and then rotate it to find the best viewing angle, as shown in Figure 1-2.

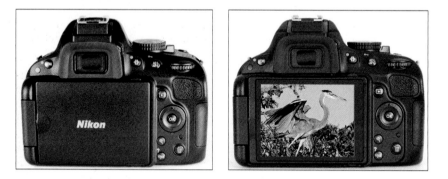

Figure 1-1: Here you see just two of the possible monitor positions.

Because playing with the monitor is no doubt one of the first things you did after unpacking your new camera, I won't waste space walking you through the process of adjusting the screen. (If you need help, the camera manual shows you what to do.) But I do want to offer a few monitor-related tips:

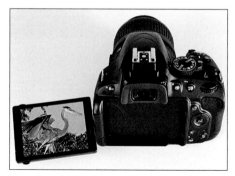

Figure 1-2: You can angle the monitor to get the best view of things.

- ✔ **Don't force things.** Although the monitor assembly is sturdy, treat it with respect as you adjust the screen position. The monitor twists only in certain directions, and it's easy to forget which way it's supposed to move. So if you feel resistance, don't force things — you could break the monitor. Instead, rely on that feeling of resistance to remind you to turn the screen the other way.

- ✔ **Watch the crunch factor.** When positioning the monitor back into the camera (whether face in or face out), take care that nothing gets in the way. Use a lens brush or soft cloth to clean the monitor housing on the camera back so there's nothing in the way that could damage the monitor.

✓ **Clean smart.** It's virtually impossible to keep nose prints and finger-prints off the monitor — well, it is for me, anyway. When you get the urge to clean the screen, use only the special cloths and cleaning solutions made for this purpose. (You can find them in any camera store.) Don't use paper products, such as paper towels, because they can contain wood fibers that can scratch the LCD surface.

One other housekeeping warning: Never use a can of compressed air to blow dust off the camera — the air is cold and can crack the monitor.

✓ **Live View photography has some drawbacks.** The *Live View* feature enables you to compose your photos using the monitor rather than the viewfinder. Live View may feel more comfortable than using the viewfinder if you're stepping up to the D5100 from a point-and-shoot camera that didn't have a viewfinder. But the monitor is one of the biggest drains on battery power, and autofocusing in Live View mode is slower than when you use the viewfinder. For these reasons and a few others you can explore in Chapter 4, I stick with the viewfinder for most regular photography and reserve Live View for movie recording. (You can't use the viewfinder when shooting movies.)

Adjusting the Viewfinder to Your Eyesight

Tucked behind the right side of the rubber eyepiece that surrounds the view-finder is a tiny dial that enables you to adjust the focus of your viewfinder to accommodate your eyesight. Figure 1-3 offers a close-up look at the dial, which is officially known as the *diopter adjustment control.*

Rotate to adjust viewfinder   Autofocus points

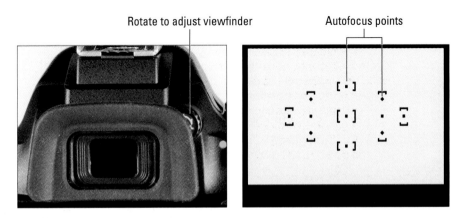

Figure 1-3: Use the diopter adjustment control to set the viewfinder focus for your eyesight.

If you don't adjust the viewfinder, scenes that appear out of focus through the viewfinder may actually be sharply focused through the lens, and vice versa. Here's how to make the necessary adjustment:

1. **Remove the lens cap.**

2. **Look through the viewfinder and concentrate on the little black marks clustered around the center portion of the screen.**

   The marks represent the camera's autofocusing points; the right side of Figure 1-3 shows you what they look like.

3. **Rotate the dial until the viewfinder marks appear sharp.**

   Don't worry about actually focusing the lens on your subject — just pay attention to the sharpness of the autofocus markings.

If you have a hard time making out the autofocus points, give the shutter button a half press and release it. You then see some exposure data at the bottom of the viewfinder display. Some people find it easier to reference that data rather than the autofocus points when adjusting the viewfinder focus.

The Nikon manual warns you not to poke yourself in the eye as you adjust the viewfinder focus. This warning seems so obvious that I laugh every time I read it — which makes me feel doubly stupid the next time I poke myself in the eye as I perform this maneuver.

Looking at Lenses

One of the biggest differences between a point-and-shoot camera and an SLR camera is the lens. With an SLR, you can swap out lenses to suit different photographic needs, going from a *macro lens,* which enables you to shoot extreme close-ups, to a *telephoto lens,* which lets you photograph subjects from a distance, for example. In addition, an SLR lens has a movable focusing ring that lets you focus manually instead of relying on the camera's autofocus mechanism. The next few sections explain the basics of working with this critical part of your camera.

Attaching and removing lenses

You can mount a wide range of lenses on your D5100, but some lenses aren't fully compatible with all camera features. For example, to enjoy autofocusing, you need an AF-S or AF-I lens. (If you bought the so-called "kit lens" — the 18–55mm zoom lens that Nikon offers as a bundle with the camera body — you own an AF-S lens.) Your camera manual offers more details about lens compatibility.

The *AF* in AF-S stands for *autofocus,* and the *S* stands for *silent wave,* a Nikon autofocus technology. AF-I lenses are older, professional-grade (expensive) lenses that are no longer made but may be available on the secondhand market.

Whatever lens you buy, follow these steps to mount it on the camera body:

1. **Turn off the camera and remove the cap that covers the lens mount on the front of the camera.**

2. **Remove the cap that covers the back of the lens.**

3. **Hold the lens in front of the camera so that the little white dot on the lens aligns with the matching dot on the camera body.**

   Official photography lingo uses the term *mounting index* instead of *little white dot.* Either way, you can see the markings in question in Figure 1-4.

   Figures in this book show the D5100 with its kit lens. If you buy a different lens, check your lens manual for complete operating instructions.

4. **Keeping the dots aligned, position the lens on the camera's lens mount.**

   When you do so, grip the lens by its back collar, not the movable, forward end of the lens barrel.

5. **Turn the lens in a counterclockwise direction until the lens clicks into place.**

   To put it another way, turn the lens toward the side of the camera that sports the shutter button, as indicated by the red arrow in the figure.

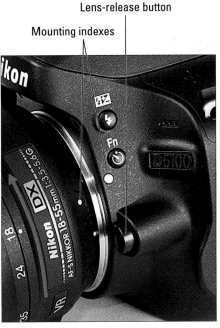

Figure 1-4: When attaching the lens, rotate it in the direction indicated by the arrow.

6. **On a lens that has an aperture ring, set and lock the ring so the aperture is set at the highest f-stop number.**

   Check your lens manual to find out whether your lens sports an aperture ring and how to adjust it. (The D5100 kit lens doesn't.) After locking the aperture on the lens, use the normal camera controls to adjust the f-stop setting. To find out more about apertures and f-stops, see Chapter 7.

To remove a lens, press the lens-release button, labeled in Figure 1-4, and then turn the lens toward that button — that is, the opposite of what the arrow indicates in the figure — until it detaches from the lens mount. Put the rear protective cap onto the back of the lens and, if you aren't putting another lens on the camera, cover the lens mount with its protective cap, too.

Always attach or switch lenses in a clean environment to reduce the risk of getting dust, dirt, and other contaminants inside the camera or lens. Changing lenses on a sandy beach, for example, isn't a good idea. For added safety, point the camera body slightly down when performing this maneuver; doing so helps prevent any flotsam in the air from being drawn into the camera by gravity.

Choosing a focusing method (auto or manual)

To take advantage of the D5100's autofocusing system, you must use an AF-S or AF-I lens. For times when you attach a lens that doesn't support autofocusing or the autofocus system has trouble locking on your subject, you can focus manually. (If you've never used manual focus, don't be intimidated — there's really nothing to it.)

Set the focusing method via the A/M switch, labeled in Figure 1-5. Choose A for autofocusing; M for manual focusing. Again, the figure features the kit lens; if you use a different lens, check the lens instruction guide for information on how to set the focusing method.

Chapter 8 offers complete details on focusing, but here are a few basics on focusing with the kit lens and others that use the same design:

- **To autofocus, press and hold the shutter button halfway.** Whether focus is locked at that point and which area of the frame is used to set the focusing distance depends on two options you can explore in Chapter 8: Focus mode and AF-Area mode. At the default settings, the camera typically focuses on the closest object and locks focus with your half-press of the shutter button. However, for moving subjects, focus may be adjusted up to the time you take the shot.

- **To focus manually, rotate the focusing ring on the lens barrel.** The location of the focusing ring varies from lens to lens; Figure 1-5 shows you where to find the ring on the kit lens.

  Remember to set the lens switch to the M position before you rotate the focusing ring! Otherwise, you can damage the lens.

- **If you have trouble focusing, you may be too close to your subject.** Every lens has a minimum focusing distance, which you can find in your lens manual. For the kit lens, it's about 11".

Focusing ring   Zoom ring   Focal length indicator

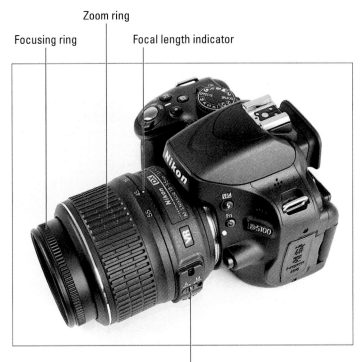

Auto/Manual focus switch

Figure 1-5: Set the focusing method (auto or manual) via the A/M switch.

✔ **Some subjects make autofocusing difficult.** Highly reflective objects, subjects behind fences, scenes that contain little contrast, and dim lighting are just some causes of autofocus problems. The easiest solution when you can't get the camera to target your subject is to focus manually.

✔ **Be sure to adjust the viewfinder to accommodate your eyesight.** Otherwise, you can't accurately gauge focus. The section "Adjusting the Viewfinder to Your Eyesight," earlier in this chapter, provides help with this adjustment.

Zooming in and out

If you bought a zoom lens, it has a movable zoom ring. The location of the zoom ring on the D5100 kit lens is shown in Figure 1-5. To zoom in or out, rotate the ring.

The numbers at the edge of the zoom ring, by the way, represent *focal lengths.* If that term is new to you, Chapter 8 explains it fully. In the meantime, just know that when the kit lens is mounted on the camera, the number that's aligned with the lens mounting index (the white dot) represents the current focal length. In Figure 1-5, for example, the focal length is 45mm. Some lenses use a different marking, so check your lens manual if you use a lens other than the kit lens.

Using a VR (Vibration Reduction) lens

The 18–55mm kit lens, as well as many other Nikon lenses, offers *Vibration Reduction,* indicated by the initials *VR* in the lens name. Vibration Reduction attempts to compensate for small amounts of camera shake that are common when photographers handhold their cameras and use a slow shutter speed (long exposure time), a lens with a long focal length (telephoto lens), or both. That camera movement during the exposure can produce blurry images. Although Vibration Reduction can't work miracles, it enables most people to capture sharper handheld shots in many situations than they otherwise could.

Here's what you need to know about taking best advantage of this feature:

- ✔ **Enabling Vibration Reduction on the kit lens:** Turn Vibration Reduction on or off by using the VR switch, labeled in Figure 1-6.

- ✔ **For other lenses, check the lens manual to find out whether your lens offers a similar feature.** On non-Nikon lenses, it may go by another name: *image stabilization, optical stabilization, anti-shake, vibration compensation,* and so on.

- ✔ **Vibration Reduction is initiated when you depress the shutter button halfway.** If you pay close attention, the image in the viewfinder may appear to be a little blurry immediately after you take the picture. That's a normal result of the Vibration Reduction operation and doesn't indicate a problem with your camera or focus.

- ✔ **With the kit lens, turn off Vibration Reduction when you mount the camera on a tripod.** When you use a tripod, Vibration Reduction can have detrimental effects because the system may try to adjust for movement that isn't actually occurring. This recommendation assumes that the tripod is "locked down" so that the camera is immovable.

- ✔ **With other lenses, check the instruction manuals for recommendations about tripod shooting.** In some cases, the manufacturers may recommend that you leave the system turned on or select a special setting when you use a tripod or *pan* the camera (move it horizontally or vertically as you take the picture). For the kit lens, however, you don't need to disable Vibration Reduction when panning.

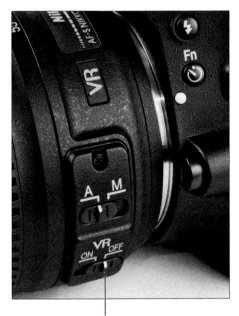

Vibration Reduction switch

Figure 1-6: Turn off Vibration Reduction when you use a tripod.

Working with Memory Cards

Instead of recording images on film, digital cameras store pictures on *memory cards.* Your D5100 uses a specific type of memory card — an *SD card* (for *Secure Digital*).

Most SD cards sold today carry the designation SDHC (for *High Capacity*) or SDXC (for *eXtended Capacity*), depending on how many gigabytes (GB) of data they hold. SDHC cards hold from 4GB to 32GB of data; the SDXC moniker is assigned to cards with capacities greater than 32GB.

The following list offers a primer in the care and feeding of your memory cards:

✓ **Inserting a card:** Turn off the camera and then put the card in the card slot with the label facing the back of the camera, as shown in Figure 1-7. Push the card into the slot until it clicks into place; the memory card access light (labeled in Figure 1-7) blinks for a second to let you know the card is inserted properly.

WARNING!

✓ **Formatting a card:** The first time you use a new memory card or insert a card that's been used in other devices (such as an MP3 player), you need to *format* it. Formatting ensures that the card is properly prepared to record your pictures. Here's what you need to know about this important housekeeping task:

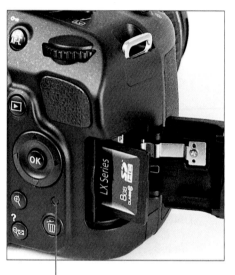

Memory card access light

Figure 1-7: Insert the card with the label facing the camera back.

• *Formatting erases everything on your memory card.* So before formatting, be sure that you have copied any pictures or other data to your computer.

• *Format the card by using the Format Memory Card option on the Setup menu.* (The upcoming section "Ordering from Camera Menus" explains how to use the menus, if you need help.) Some computer programs enable you to format cards as well, but it's not a good idea to go that route. Your camera is better equipped to optimally format cards.

• *The blinking letters* For *in the viewfinder mean that the card requires formatting.* On the monitor, the camera displays a less subtle message: "This card is not formatted. Format the card." Either way, the camera won't let you take any pictures until you give in to its formatting demand.

✓ **Removing a card:** After making sure that the memory card access light is off, indicating that the camera has finished recording your most recent photo, turn off the camera. Open the memory card door, depress the memory card slightly until you hear a little click, and then let go. The card pops halfway out of the slot, enabling you to grab it by the tail and remove it.

REMEMBER

If you turn on the camera when no card is installed, the symbol [-E-] blinks in the lower-right corner of the viewfinder. If the Shooting Information screen is displayed on the monitor, that screen also nudges you to insert a memory card. If you do have a card in the camera and you get these messages, try taking it out and reinserting it.

✓ **Handling cards:** Don't touch the gold contacts on the back of the card. (See the left card in Figure 1-8.) When cards aren't in use, store them in the protective cases they came in or in a memory card wallet. Keep cards away from extreme heat and cold as well.

✓ **Locking cards:** The tiny switch on the side of the card, labeled *lock switch* in Figure 1-8, enables you to lock your card, which prevents any data from being erased or recorded to the card. Press the switch toward the bottom of the card to lock the card contents; press it toward the top of the card to unlock the data. (If you insert a locked card into the camera, you see a message on the monitor alerting you to the fact, and the symbol [d blinks in the viewfinder.)

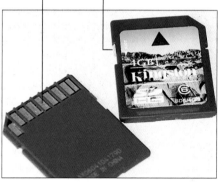

Don't touch   Lock switch

Figure 1-8: Avoid touching the gold contacts on the card.

You also can protect individual images on a card from accidental erasure by using the camera's Protect feature, which I cover in Chapter 5.

✓ **Using Eye-Fi memory cards:** Your camera works with *Eye-Fi memory cards,* which are special cards that enable you to transmit your files wirelessly to other devices. That's a cool feature, but unfortunately, the cards themselves are more expensive than regular cards and require some configuring that I don't have room to cover in this book. For more details, visit www.eye.fi.

Do you need high-speed memory cards?

Secure Digital (SD) memory cards are rated according to *speed classes:* Class 2, Class 4, Class 6, and Class 10, with the number indicating the minimum number of *megabytes* (units of computer data) that can be transferred per second. A Class 2 card, for example, has a minimum transfer speed of 2 megabytes, or MB, per second. Of course, with the speed increase comes a price increase, which leads to the question: Do you really have a need for speed?

The answer is "maybe." If you shoot a lot of movies with the D5100, I recommend a Class 6 or 10 card, as does Nikon — the faster data-transfer rate helps ensure smooth movie-recording and playback performance. For still photography, users who shoot at the highest resolution or prefer the Raw (NEF) file format may also gain

from high-speed cards; both options increase file size and, thus, the time needed to store the picture on the card. (See Chapter 2 for details.)

As for picture downloading, how long it takes files to shuffle from card to computer depends not just on card speed, but also on the capabilities of your computer and, if you use a memory card reader to download files, on the speed of that device. (Chapter 6 covers the file-downloading process.)

Long story short, if you want to push your camera to its performance limits, a high-speed card is worth the expense, especially for video recording. But if you're primarily interested in still photography or you already own slower-speed cards, try using them first — you may find that they're more than adequate for most shooting scenarios.

If you do use Eye-Fi cards, enable and disable wireless transmission via the Eye-Fi Upload option on the Setup menu. When no Eye-Fi card is installed in the camera, this menu option disappears.

Exploring External Camera Controls

Scattered across your camera's exterior are numerous controls that you use to change picture-taking settings, review and edit your photos, and perform various other operations. In later chapters, I discuss all your camera's functions in detail and provide the exact steps to follow to access them. This section provides just a basic road map to the external controls plus a quick introduction to each.

Topside controls

Your virtual tour begins with the bird's-eye view shown in Figure 1-9. There are a number of controls of note here:

- **On/Off switch and shutter button:** Okay, I'm pretty sure you already figured out this combo button. But you may not be aware that you need to press the shutter button in two stages: Press and hold the button halfway and wait for the camera to initiate exposure metering and, if you're using autofocusing, to set the focusing distance. Then press the button the rest of the way to take the picture. See the Chapter 3 section related to the Auto and Auto Flash Off exposure modes for more picture-taking basics.

- **Exposure Compensation button:** This button activates Exposure Compensation, a feature that enables you to tweak exposure when working in three of your camera's autoexposure modes: P (programmed autoexposure), A (aperture-priority autoexposure), and S (shutter-priority autoexposure). Press the button while rotating the Command dial to set the amount of Exposure Compensation. (Chapter 7 explains.) In M (manual exposure) mode, you press this button while rotating the Command dial to adjust the aperture setting.

- **Info button:** Press this button to display the Shooting Information screen on the camera monitor. The screen not only enables you to easily view the current picture-taking settings but also is the pathway to the Quick Settings screen, through which you can adjust some settings more quickly than by using the camera menus. See the upcoming section "Monitoring Shooting Settings" for details. To turn off the screen, press the Info button again.

You also can display the screen by pressing the Information Edit button (described in the next section) or by pressing the shutter button halfway and releasing it. I find these methods easier, so I use the Info button only when I want to turn off the screen.

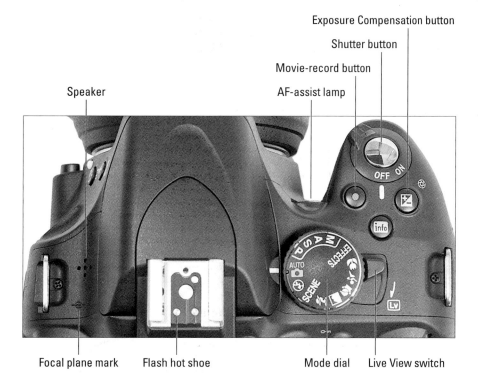

Exposure Compensation button
Shutter button
Movie-record button
AF-assist lamp
Speaker

Focal plane mark   Flash hot shoe   Mode dial   Live View switch

Figure 1-9: The tiny pictures on the Mode dial represent the automatic exposure modes known as Scene modes.

✔ **Live View switch:** As its name implies, this switch turns Live View on and off. As soon as you turn on Live View, the scene in front of the lens appears on the monitor, and you no longer can see anything through the viewfinder. You then can compose a still photo using the monitor or begin recording a movie. Turn off Live View to return to normal, through-the-viewfinder still photography. Chapter 4 details Live View photography and movie recording.

✔ **Movie-record button:** After shifting to Live View mode, press this button to start recording a movie using the default recording settings. (See Chapter 4 to find out how to adjust the settings.) Press again to stop recording.

✔ **Mode dial:** With this dial, labeled in Figure 1-9, you set the camera to fully automatic, semi-automatic, or manual exposure mode. Setting the dial to Effects enables you to apply special effects as the image or movie is captured. Chapter 2 introduces you to all the exposure modes.

✔ **AF-assist lamp:** In dim lighting, the camera may emit a beam of light from this lamp when you use autofocusing. The light helps the camera find its focusing target. If you're shooting in a setting where the light is distracting or otherwise annoying, you can disable it via the Built-In AF-Assist Illuminator option, found in the Autofocus section of the Custom Setting menu. On the flip side, there are some situations in which the lamp is automatically disabled: It doesn't light in Live View mode or during movie recording, for example.

The AF-assist lamp also shoots out light when you use red-eye reduction flash and the Self-Timer shutter-release mode, both covered in Chapter 2. You can't disable the lamp for these two functions.

- **Flash hot shoe:** A *hot shoe* is a connection for attaching an external flash head. When not in use, the contacts on the shoe are protected by a little black cover; remove the cover to expose the contacts, as shown in Figure 1-9. Chapters 3 and 7 discuss flash photography.

- **Speaker:** When you play movies that contain sound, the audio comes wafting through the cluster of little holes labeled *Speaker* in Figure 1-9.

- **Focal plane indicator:** Should you need to know the exact distance between your subject and the camera, the *focal plane mark* labeled in Figure 1-9 is key. The mark indicates the plane at which light coming through the lens is focused onto the negative in a film camera or the image sensor in a digital camera. Basing your measurement on this mark produces a more accurate camera-to-subject distance than using the end of the lens or some other external point on the camera body as your reference point.

Back-of-the-body controls

Traveling over the top of the camera to its back side, as shown in Figure 1-10, you encounter the following controls:

- **Command dial:** After you activate certain camera features, you rotate this dial, labeled in Figure 1-10, to select a specific setting. For example, to choose an f-stop when shooting in aperture-priority (A) mode, you rotate the Command dial. (Chapter 7 explains apertures and f-stops.)

- **AE-L/AF-L button:** Pressing this button initiates autoexposure lock (AE-L) and autofocus lock (AF-L). Chapter 7 explains autoexposure lock; Chapter 8 talks about autofocus lock.

In playback mode, pressing the button activates the Protect feature, which locks the picture file — hence the little key symbol that appears above the button — so that it isn't erased if you use the picture-delete functions. See Chapter 5 for details. (The picture *is* erased if you format the memory card, however.)

You can adjust the performance of the button as it relates to locking focus and exposure, too. Instructions in this book assume that you stick with the default setting, but if you want to explore your options, see Chapter 11.

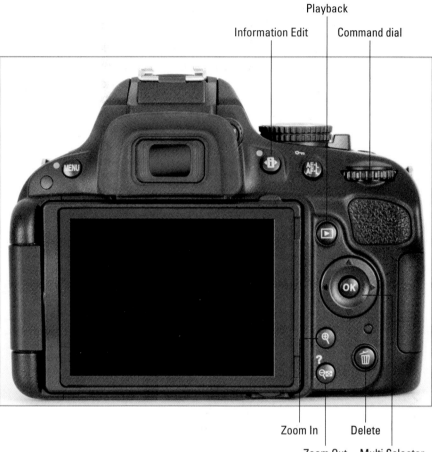

Figure 1-10: Use the Multi Selector to navigate menus and access certain other camera options.

In sections of the Nikon manual that discuss the Protect feature, this button is sometimes referenced just with the little key symbol. To keep things simple, I always refer to it as the AE-L/AF-L button and show the button in the margin to avoid any confusion.

✔ **Multi Selector/OK button:** This dual-natured control, labeled in Figure 1-10, plays a role in many camera functions. You press the outer edges of the Multi Selector left, right, up, or down to navigate camera menus and access certain other options. At the center of the control is OK, which you press to finalize a menu selection or other camera adjustment.

✔ **Delete button:** Sporting a trash can icon, the universal symbol for delete, this button enables you to erase pictures from your memory card. Chapter 5 has specifics.

✔ **Playback button:** Press this button to switch the camera into picture review mode. Chapter 5 details playback features.

✔ **Menu button:** Press this button to access menus of camera options. See the section "Ordering from Camera Menus," later in this chapter, for details on navigating menus.

See that green dot next to the button? It's a clue that you can press the Menu button together with the Information Edit button — also sporting the green dot — to perform a *two-button reset.* This step reverts a batch of camera options to their default settings. See the last section of this chapter for details.

✔ **Zoom Out button:** As you can probably deduce from the three symbols that mark this button, it has not one, but three primary functions:

- *Display help screens:* The little question mark symbol is a reminder that you can press this button to display helpful information about certain menu options. See "Ordering from Camera Menus" later in this chapter, for details.

- *Display thumbnails during playback:* In playback mode, pressing the button enables you display multiple image thumbnails on the screen, thus the little thumbnail grid on the button face. Chapter 5 details picture playback.

- *Reduce image magnification during playback:* If you magnify an image during playback, pressing the button reduces the magnification amount. The magnifying glass with the minus sign tips you off to this button function.

The button also plays various minor roles in other camera operations; I detail these functions later in the book.

✔ **Zoom In:** In playback mode, pressing this button magnifies the currently displayed image and also reduces the number of thumbnails displayed at a time. Note the plus sign in the middle of the magnifying glass — plus for zoom in. Like the Zoom Out button, this one also serves a few minor roles that I explain in later chapters.

✔ **Information Edit button:** Press this button once to display the Shooting Information screen. Press again to shift to the Quick Settings screen, where you can access and adjust some shooting settings more quickly than by using menus or other techniques. See the upcoming section "Using the Quick Settings Screen" for details.

In addition, pressing this button in conjunction with the Menu button performs a two-button reset; again, the last section of this chapter explains that feature.

Front-left buttons

On the front-left side of the camera body, shown in Figure 1-11, you find the following controls:

✔ **Flash button:** In the advanced exposure modes (P, S, A, and M), pressing this button pops up the camera's built-in flash. (In other modes, the camera decides whether the flash is needed.) By holding the button down and rotating the Command dial, you can adjust the Flash mode (fill flash, red-eye reduction, and so on). In advanced exposure modes, you also can adjust the flash power by pressing the button while simultaneously pressing the Exposure Compensation button and rotating the Command dial. The little plus/minus symbol that appears above the button — the same symbol that's on the Exposure Compensation button — is a reminder of the button's role in flash-power adjustment.

See Chapter 3 for an introduction to flash; check out Chapter 7 for the detailed story.

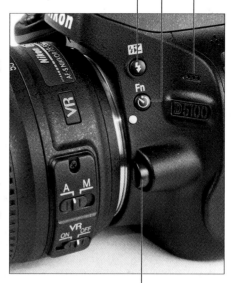

Figure 1-11: Press the Flash button to pop up the built-in flash when you shoot in the P, S, A, or M exposure modes.

✔ **Function (Fn) button:** By default, this button enables self-timer shooting for your next shot. (Chapter 2 has details.) If you don't use that feature often, you can use the button to perform a variety of other operations. Chapter 11 provides the details on changing the button's purpose. (*Note:* All instructions in this book assume that you haven't changed the function.)

✔ **Lens-release button:** Press this button to disengage the lens from the camera's lens mount so that you can remove the lens.

✔ **Lens switches:** Also introduced near the start of this chapter, the A/M switch sets the kit lens to automatic or manual focusing, and the VR switch turns the Vibration Reduction feature on and off.

✔ **Microphone:** The three little holes just above the silver D5100 label lead to the camera's internal microphone. See Chapter 4 to find out how to disable the microphone if you want to record silent movies.

Hidden connections

Hidden under little cover on the left side of the camera, you find the following four connection ports, labeled in Figure 1-12:

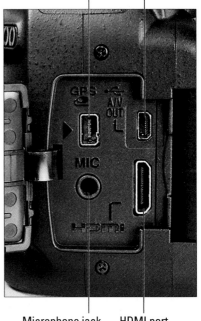

Accessory terminal   USB and A/V port

Microphone jack   HDMI port

Figure 1-12: Open the cover on the side of the camera to reveal these connections.

- ✔ **Accessory terminal:** You can plug in the optional Nikon MC-DC2 remote shutter-release cable or GP-1 GPS (Global Positioning System) unit here. I don't cover these optional accessories in this book, but the manual that comes with the devices can get you up and running. For the GPS unit, also visit the camera manual for information about the GPS option on the Setup menu.

- ✔ **Stereo mini-pin microphone jack:** If you're not happy with the audio quality provided by the internal microphone, you can plug in an external microphone here. The jack accepts a 3.5mm microphone plug. See Chapter 4 for all things movie-related.

- ✔ **USB and A/V port:** Through this port, you can connect your camera to your computer for picture downloading. The same port enables you to cable the camera to a television for picture playback. Nikon supplies the cables you need for both connections in the camera box; see Chapter 5 for information on television connections and Chapter 6 for picture downloading help.

- ✔ **HDMI port:** You can use this port to connect your camera to a high-definition TV, but you need to buy an HDMI cable to do so. Look for a Type C mini-pin cable. Chapter 5 offers more details on HD television playback.

If you turn the camera over, you find a tripod socket, which enables you to mount the camera on a tripod that uses a ¼-inch screw, plus the battery chamber.

Ordering from Camera Menus

Pressing the Menu button on your camera gives you access to a whole slew of options in addition to those you control via the external buttons and dials. When you press the button, you see a screen similar to the one shown on the left in Figure 1-13. The icons along the left side of the screen represent the available menus. (Table 1-1 labels the icons and includes a brief description of the goodies found on each menu.) In the menu screens, the icon that's highlighted or appears in color is the active menu; options on that menu automatically appear to the right. In the figure, the Shooting menu is active, for example.

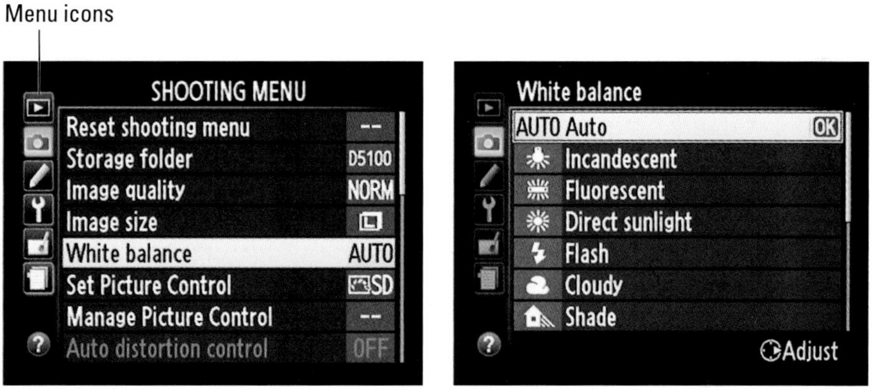

Menu icons

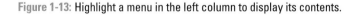

Figure 1-13: Highlight a menu in the left column to display its contents.

Table 1-1		D5100 Menus
Symbol	**Open This Menu . . .**	**To Access These Functions**
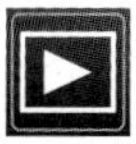 ▶	Playback	Viewing, deleting, and protecting pictures
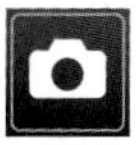 ◉	Shooting	Basic photography settings
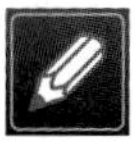 ✎	Custom Setting	Advanced photography options and some basic camera operations

(continued)

Table 1-1 *(continued)*

Symbol	Open This Menu . . .	To Access These Functions
	Setup	Additional basic camera operations
	Retouch	Built-in photo retouching options
	My Menu/ Recent Settings	Your custom menu or 20 most recently used menu options

I explain all the important menu options elsewhere in the book; for now, just familiarize yourself with the process of navigating menus and selecting options therein. The Multi Selector (refer to Figure 1-10) is the key to the game. You press the edges of the Multi Selector to navigate up, down, left, and right through the menus.

In this book, the instruction "Press the Multi Selector left" simply means to press the left edge of the control. "Press the Multi Selector right" means to press the right edge, and so on.

Here's a bit more detail about the process of navigating menus:

✐ **To select a different menu:** Press the Multi Selector left to jump to the column containing the menu icons. Then press up or down to highlight the menu you want to display. Finally, press right to jump over to the options on the menu.

✐ **To select and adjust a function on the current menu:** Again, use the Multi Selector to scroll up or down the list of options to highlight the feature you want to adjust and then press OK. Settings available for the selected item then appear. For example, if you select the White Balance item from the Shooting menu, as shown on the left in Figure 1-13, and press OK, the available White Balance options appear, as shown on the right in the figure. Repeat the old up-and-down scroll routine until the choice you prefer is highlighted. Then press OK to return to the previous screen.

In some cases, you may see a right-pointing arrowhead instead of the OK symbol next to a menu item. That's your cue to press the Multi Selector right to display a submenu or other list of options (Although, most of the time, you also can just press the OK button if you prefer.)

✓ **To select items from the Custom Setting menu:** Displaying the Custom Setting menu, whose icon is a little pencil, takes you to a screen that contains six submenus that carry the labels A through F. Each of the submenus holds clusters of options related to a specific aspect of the camera's operation. Highlight a submenu and press OK to get to those actions.

In the Nikon manual, instructions sometimes reference the Custom Setting menu items by a menu letter and number. For example, "Custom Setting a1" refers to the first option on the a (Autofocus) submenu. I try to be more specific in this book, however, so I use the actual setting names. (Really, we all have enough numbers to remember, don't you think?)

After you jump to the first submenu, you can simply scroll up and down the list to view options from other submenus. You don't have to keep going back to the initial menu screen, selecting the submenu, pressing OK, and so on.

✓ **Create a custom menu or view your 20 most recently adjusted menu items:** The sixth menu is actually two menus bundled into one: Recent Settings and My Menu, both shown in Figure 1-14. The menu icon changes depending on which of these two functions is active; Table 1-1 shows both icons. Each menu contains a Choose Tab option; select this option, as shown in the figures, and press OK to shift between the two menus.

Here's what the two menus offer:

- *My Menu:* Through this screen, you can create a custom menu that contains your favorite options. Chapter 11 details the steps.

- *Recent Settings:* This screen lists the 20 menu items you ordered most recently. So to adjust those settings, you don't have to wade through all the other menus looking for them — just head to the Recent Settings menu instead.

To remove an item from the Recent Settings menu, highlight the item and press the Delete button. Press again to confirm your decision and go forward with trashing the item.

✓ **Display information about the current menu option:** If you see a small question mark in the lower-left corner of a menu, as shown on the left in Figure 1-15, press and hold the Zoom Out button — note the question-mark label above the button — to display information about the current menu option. For example, the right screen in Figure 1-15 shows the help screen associated with the White Balance setting. If you need to scroll the screen to view all the help text, keep the button depressed and scroll by using the Multi Selector. Release the button to close the information screen.

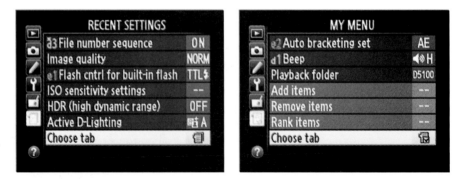

Figure 1-14: The Recent Settings menu offers quick access to the last 20 menu options you selected; the My Menu menu enables you to design a custom menu.

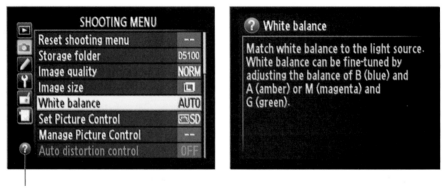

Help screen

Figure 1-15: Press and hold the Zoom Out button to display onscreen help.

Monitoring Shooting Settings

Your D5100 gives you the following ways to monitor the most critical picture-taking settings.

> **Shooting Information display:** If your eyesight is like mine, reading the tiny type in the viewfinder is a tad difficult. Fortunately, the camera offers the Shooting Information screen, which displays the current shooting settings at a size that's a little easier on the eyes and also

provides more detailed data than the viewfinder. Figure 1-16 offers a look at this display. If you rotate the camera to compose a *portrait* shot (the image is taller than it is wide), the Shooting Info display rotates as well.

In this book, I show the screen with the default color scheme, shown in Figure 1-16. Chapter 11 shows you how to switch to a different display option.

To display the Shooting Info screen, use any of these techniques:

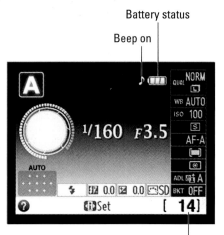

- *Press the Info button.* Press once to display the screen; press again to turn off the monitor.

- *Press the shutter button halfway and release it.* Pressing and holding the button halfway down turns off the screen and fires up the autofocusing and exposure metering systems. Because those two systems use battery power, you may want to avoid this technique when the battery is running low.

Figure 1-16: Press the Info or Info Edit button to view picture-taking settings on the monitor.

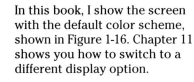

- *Press the Information Edit button.* Note, though, that pressing the button a second time doesn't turn off the display — instead, it toggles the screen to the Quick Settings display, explained in the next section. So to hide the Shooting Information screen, press the Info button.

✔ **Viewfinder:** You can view some camera settings in the viewfinder as well. For example, the data in Figure 1-17 shows (from left to right) the current shutter speed, f-stop, ISO setting, and number of shots remaining. The exact viewfinder information that appears depends on what action you're currently undertaking.

If what you see in Figures 1-16 and 1-17 looks like a confusing mess, don't worry. Many of the settings relate to options that won't mean anything to you until you make your way through later chapters and explore the advanced exposure modes. But do make note of the following bits of data that are helpful even when you shoot in the fully automatic modes:

✔ **Battery status indicator:** A full battery icon like the one in Figure 1-16 shows that the battery is fully charged; if the icon appears empty, look for your battery charger.

Your viewfinder also displays a tiny low-battery icon when things get to the dangerous point. The icon appears just to the right of center in the settings strip at the bottom of the viewfinder. If the icon blinks, the battery is totally kaput, and shutter release is disabled.

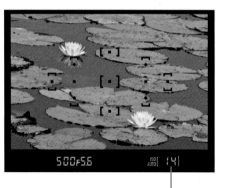

Shots remaining

Figure 1-17: You also can view some camera information at the bottom of the viewfinder.

✔ **Beep on/off indicator:** By default, your camera beeps at you after certain operations, such as after it sets focus when you shoot in autofocus mode. If you're doing top-secret surveillance work and need the camera to hush up, call up the Custom Setting menu, select the Shooting/Display submenu, and then turn off the Beep option. You can also adjust the volume of the beep through the same menu option. On the Shooting Info display, a little musical note icon appears near the top-right corner of the screen when the beep is enabled, as shown in Figure 1-16. Turn off the beep, and the icon appears in a circle with a slash through it.

✔ **Shots remaining:** Labeled in Figures 1-16 and 1-17, this value indicates how many additional pictures you can store on the current memory card. If the number exceeds 999, the value is presented a little differently. The initial K appears above the value to indicate that the first value represents the picture count in thousands. For example, 1.0K means that you can store 1,000 more pictures (*K* being a universally accepted symbol indicating 1,000 units). The number is then rounded down to the nearest hundred. So if the card has room for, say, 1,230 more pictures, the value reads 1.2K.

✔ **Blinking question mark:** A blinking question mark at the right end of the viewfinder or lower-left corner of the Shooting Info screen (not shown in the figures) indicates that the camera wants to alert you to a problem. Again, press the Zoom Out button to display a help screen that contains a suggested solution.

Adjusting automatic shutdown timing

To save battery power, your camera automatically shuts off the monitor and the exposure meter after a period of inactivity. You can specify how long you want the camera to wait before taking that step through Auto Off Timers option, found in the Timers/AE Lock section of the Custom Setting menu. You can specify the auto-off timing for the meter, picture playback, menu displays, and the Live View display. Additionally, you can adjust the length of time the camera displays a picture immediately after you press the shutter button, known as the Image Review period.

When you choose the Auto Off Timers option, you gain access to four settings: Short, Normal, Long, and Custom. If you choose Custom, as shown in the figures here, you can modify the

timing for each component individually. (Be sure to select Done and press OK as the last step.) The Short, Normal, and Long options result in the following shutoff delays:

- Short: meter, 4 seconds; menus/playback, 12 seconds; Image Review, 4 seconds; Live View, 3 minutes

- Normal (default): meter, 8 seconds; menus/playback, 20 seconds; Image Review, 4 seconds; Live View, 3 minutes

- Long: meter, 1 minute; menus/playback, 1 minute; Image Review, 20 seconds; Live View, 10 minutes.

Check out Chapter 5 for details about playback and Image Review. Chapter 4 covers Live View, and Chapter 7 explains the exposure meter.

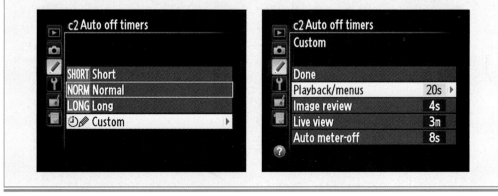

Using the Quick Settings Screen

After you press the Info Edit or Info button to display the Shooting Info screen, press the Info Edit button to toggle to a second screen, the Quick Settings display, shown on the left in Figure 1-18. The Quick Settings display does just what its name implies: It enables you to adjust many picture-taking settings faster than you can by digging through camera menus. In some cases, the *only* way to adjust a setting is to use the Quick Settings screen.

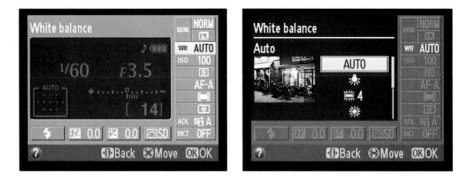

Figure 1-18: Press the Info Edit button to shift from the Shooting Info screen to the Quick Settings display.

After you see the Quick Settings display, follow these steps to adjust the available options:

1. **Use the Multi Selector to highlight the setting you want to change.**

   The available settings are represented by the icons along the right side and bottom of the screen. A little label appears at the top of the screen to tell you the name of the selected setting. For example, in Figure 1-18, the White Balance setting is selected.

2. **Press OK to jump to a screen that contains the available settings for the selected option.**

   For example, the right screen in Figure 1-18 shows the available White Balance options.

3. **Use the Multi Selector to highlight your choice and then press OK.**

   You return to the Quick Settings display.

To exit the Quick Settings display and return to the Shooting Info screen, press the Info Edit button again, or press the shutter button halfway and release it. Or if you're done adjusting settings, just go ahead and take your next picture.

Many of the display screens, including the ones shown in Figure 1-18, include symbols that remind you which controls to use to perform tasks while using the display. For example, at the bottom of the Quick Settings screen, the symbols indicate that you use the Information Edit button to go back to the Shooting Information screen and use the Multi Selector to move the highlight cursor around the screen.

Taking a Few Critical Setup Steps

Your camera offers scads of options for customizing its performance. Later chapters explain settings related to actual picture taking, such as those that affect flash behavior and autofocusing, and Chapter 11 talks about some options that are better left at their default settings until you're fully familiar with your camera. That leaves just a handful of setup options covered in the next two sections that I recommend you consider at the get-go.

Setup menu options

The following important options live on the Setup menu, which is the one marked with the little wrench icon and featured in Figure 1-19:

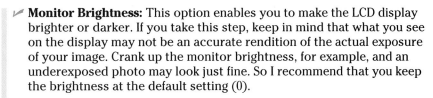

- **Monitor Brightness:** This option enables you to make the LCD display brighter or darker. If you take this step, keep in mind that what you see on the display may not be an accurate rendition of the actual exposure of your image. Crank up the monitor brightness, for example, and an underexposed photo may look just fine. So I recommend that you keep the brightness at the default setting (0).

- **Time Zone and Date:** When you turn on your camera for the very first time, it automatically displays this option and asks you to set the current date and time. Keeping the date and time accurate is important because that information is recorded as part of the image file. In your photo browser, you can then see when you shot an image and, equally handy, search for images by the date they were taken.

- **Language:** You're asked to specify a language along with the date and time when you fire up your camera for the first time. Your choice determines the language of text on the camera monitor.

- **Firmware Version:** Select this option and press OK to view what version of the camera *firmware,* or internal software, your camera runs. You see three firmware items, A, B, and L. At the time this book was written, A and B were version 1.00; L was 1.003. Don't worry about what the A, B, and L mean — they simply relate to different aspects of the camera's operation.

  Keeping your camera firmware up-to-date *is* important, though, so visit the Nikon website (www.nikon.com) regularly to find out whether your camera sports the latest version. You can find detailed instructions on how to download and install any firmware updates on the site.

SETUP MENU	
Format memory card	--
Monitor brightness	0
Info display format	info
Auto info display	ON
Clean image sensor	--
Lock mirror up for cleaning	--
Video mode	NTSC
HDMI	--

SETUP MENU	
Flicker reduction	60Hz
Time zone and date	--
Language	🌐
Image comment	OFF
Auto image rotation	ON
Image Dust Off ref photo	--
GPS	--
Firmware version	--

Figure 1-19: Visit the Setup menu to customize your camera's basic appearance and operation.

Custom Setting options

Also check the status of these Custom Setting menu options before you shoot any more pictures:

✔ **File Number Sequence:** This option, found on the Shooting/Display sub-menu and shown in Figure 1-20, controls how the camera names your picture files. When the option is set to Off, as it is by default, the camera restarts file numbering at 0001 every time you format your memory card or insert a new memory card. Numbering is also restarted if a new image-storage folder is created. (Chapter 11 explains folders.)

Needless to say, this setup can cause problems over time, creating a scenario where you wind up with multiple images that have the same filename — not on the current memory card, but when you download images to your computer. So I strongly encourage you to set the option to On, as shown in Figure 1-20. Note that when you get to picture number 9999, file numbering is still reset to 0001, however, because at that point, the camera automatically creates a new folder to hold your next 9999 images.

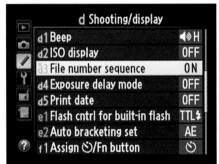

d Shooting/display	
d1 Beep	🔊 H
d2 ISO display	OFF
d3 File number sequence	ON
d4 Exposure delay mode	OFF
d5 Print date	OFF
e1 Flash cntrl for built-in flash	TTL⚡
e2 Auto bracketing set	AE
f1 Assign ⟳/Fn button	⟳

Figure 1-20: Danger, Will Robinson! Change the File Number Sequence to On to avoid winding up with multiple pictures that have the same filename.

As for the Reset option, it enables you to assign the first file number (which ends in 0001) to the next picture you shoot. Then the camera behaves as if you selected the On setting.

Should you be a really, really prolific shooter and snap enough pictures to reach image 9999 in folder 999, the camera will refuse to take another photo until you choose that Reset option and either format the memory card or insert a brand new one.

✔ **Print Date:** Through this option, which lives two doors down from the File Number Sequence option, you can choose to imprint the shooting date, date and time, or the number of days between the day you took the picture and another date that you specify. This feature works only with pictures that you shoot in the JPEG file format; see Chapter 2 for details about file formats.

The default setting, which disables the imprint, is the best way to go, however; you don't need to permanently mar your photos to find out when you took them. Every picture file includes a hidden vat of text data, or *metadata,* that records the shooting date and time, as well as all the camera settings you used — f-stop, shutter speed, and lots more. You can view this data during playback and, after downloading, in the free software provided with your camera as well as in many photo programs. Chapter 6 shows you how.

If you enable the Date Imprint feature, the word *Date* appears in the upper-left corner of the Shooting Info screen. Also remember that applying some Retouch menu options, such as the Trim function, may crop away the date imprint or leave it illegible.

✔ **Slot Empty Release Lock:** This cryptically named feature, found on the Controls section of the Custom Setting menu, determines whether the camera lets you take a picture when no memory card is installed in the camera. If you set it to Enable Release, the camera no longer warns you if a memory card isn't installed. You can take a temporary picture, which appears in the monitor with the word *Demo* but isn't recorded anywhere. The feature is provided mainly for use in camera stores, enabling salespeople to demonstrate the camera without having to keep a memory card installed. I can think of no good reason why anyone else would change the setting from the default, Release Locked.

Restoring Default Settings

Should you ever want to return your camera to its original, out-of-the-box state, the camera manual contains a list of most of the default settings. Look on the pages that introduce each of the menus.

You can also partially restore default settings by taking these steps:

✔ **Reset all Shooting Menu options:** Open the Shooting menu, choose Reset Shooting Menu, and press OK. Note that resetting the menu does not affect the Storage Folder option, which is a concern only if you create custom folders, as outlined in Chapter 11.

✔ **Reset all Custom Setting Menu options:** Choose the Reset Custom Settings option at the top of the Custom Setting menu.

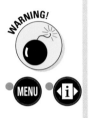

Resetting the Custom Setting menu restores the File Number Sequence option to its default, Off, which is most definitely Not a Good Thing. So if you restore the menu defaults, be *sure* that you revisit that option and return it to the On setting. See the preceding section for details.

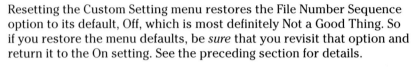

✔ **Restore critical picture-taking settings *without* affecting all options on the Custom Setting menu:** Use the two-button reset method: Press and hold the Menu button and the Info Edit button simultaneously for longer than two seconds. (The little green dots near the buttons are a reminder of this function.) See the camera manual for a list of exactly what settings are restored.

One last tip with regard to Custom Setting menu defaults: When you choose a setting other than the default, an asterisk appears above the number of the menu item. For example, in Figure 1-20, you see an asterisk above the a in a3, the number of the File Number Sequence option, because I changed the setting from the default.

Choosing Basic Picture Settings

*E*very camera manufacturer strives to provide a good *out-of-box* experience — that is, to ensure that your initial encounter with the camera is a happy one. To that end, the camera's default settings are carefully selected to make it as easy as possible for you to take a good picture the first time you press the shutter button. On the D5100, the default settings are designed to let you take a picture the same way you do automatic, point-and-shoot cameras: Just compose the shot, press the shutter button halfway to set focus and exposure, and then press the button the rest of the way to record the image.

Although the default settings deliver nice pictures in many cases, they don't produce optimal results in every shooting situation. You may be able to take a decent portrait using the default setup, for example, but probably need to tweak a few settings to capture action. In fact, adjusting a few settings can help turn that decent portrait into a stunning one, too.

So that you can start fine-tuning camera settings to your subject, this chapter explains the most basic picture-taking options, such as the exposure mode, shutter-release mode, and the image size and quality. They're not the most exciting options to explore (don't think I didn't notice you stifling a yawn), but they make a big difference in how easily you can capture the photo you have in mind.

Choosing an Exposure Mode

The first picture-taking setting to consider is the exposure mode, which you select via the Mode dial, as shown in Figure 2-1. Your choice determines how much control you have over two critical exposure settings — aperture and shutter speed — as well as many other options, including those related to color and flash photography.

Your exposure mode choices break down as follows:

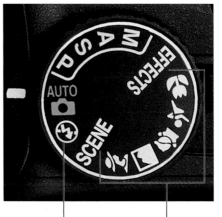

Auto Flash Off   Primary Scene modes

Figure 2-1: The Mode dial determines how much input you have over exposure, color, and other picture options.

✔ **Fully automatic modes:** For people who haven't yet explored photography concepts like aperture and shutter speed — or who just aren't interested in "going there" — the D5100 offers the following point-and-shoot modes:

- *Auto:* The camera analyzes the scene in front of the lens and tries to select the most appropriate camera settings to capture the image.

- *Auto Flash Off:* This mode, represented by the icon labeled in Figure 2-1, works just like Auto but disables the flash.

- *Scene modes:* The D5100 offers 16 automatic modes geared to capturing specific types of scenes: portraits, landscapes, child photos, and such. The five most commonly used modes have their own positions on the Mode dial; they're the ones represented by the pictographs and labeled "Primary Scene modes" in Figure 2-1. You access the others by setting the dial to Scene and then rotating the Command dial to choose the scene type.

- *Effects:* This mode works just like Auto except that the camera applies one of seven special effects to the image as it writes the picture data to the memory card. This mode is the only one that also applies to movie recording; you can use it to add effects to movies as well as to still pictures. (Chapter 4 details movie recording.)

Chapter 3 provides details about using the Auto, Auto Flash Off, and Scene modes; Chapter 10 discusses the Effects mode.

For any of these modes, understand that because they're designed to make picture-taking simple, they prevent you from accessing many of the camera's features. You can't use the White Balance control, for example, to tweak picture colors. Options that are off-limits appear dimmed in the camera menus and Quick Settings screen. And if you press a camera button that leads to an advanced setting, either nothing happens or the monitor displays a message telling you that the option is unavailable.

✔ **Semi-automatic modes:** To take more creative control but still get some exposure assistance from the camera, choose one of these modes:

  • *P (programmed autoexposure):* The camera selects the aperture and shutter speed necessary to ensure a good exposure. But you can choose from different combinations of the two to vary the creative results. For example, shutter speed affects whether moving objects appear blurry or sharp. So you might use a fast shutter speed to freeze action, or you might go the other direction, choosing a shutter speed slow enough to blur the action, creating a heightened sense of motion.

  • *S (shutter-priority autoexposure):* You select the shutter speed, and the camera selects the proper aperture to properly expose the image. This mode is ideal for capturing sports or other moving subjects because it gives you direct control over shutter speed.

  • *A (aperture-priority autoexposure):* In this mode, you choose the aperture, and the camera automatically chooses a shutter speed to properly expose the image. Because aperture affects *depth of field,* or the distance over which objects in a scene remain in sharp focus, this setting is great for portraits because you can select an aperture that results in a soft, blurry background, putting the emphasis on your subject. For landscape shots, on the other hand, you might choose an aperture that keeps the entire scene sharply focused so that both near and distant objects have equal visual weight.

All three semi-automatic modes give you complete access to all the camera's features. So even if you're not ready to explore aperture and shutter speed yet, go ahead and set the mode dial to P if you need to access a setting that's off-limits in the fully automated modes. The camera then operates pretty much as it does in Auto mode but without limiting your ability to control picture settings if you need to do so.

When you're ready to dig into exposure issues and try these exposure modes, head for Chapter 7.

✔ **Manual:** In this mode, represented by the letter M on the Mode dial, you select both the aperture and shutter speed. But the camera still offers an assist by displaying an exposure meter to help you dial in the right settings. See Chapter 7 for details. You have complete control over all other picture settings, too.

One very important and often misunderstood aspect about the exposure modes: Although the Mode dial setting determines your access to exposure and color controls as well as to some other advanced camera features, it has no bearing on your *focusing* method. You can choose from manual focusing or autofocusing in any mode, assuming that your lens offers autofocusing. (Chapter 1 shows you how to set the lens to manual or autofocusing.) However, some options that let you adjust the camera's autofocusing behavior are available only in P, S, A, and M exposure modes.

Choosing the Release Mode

By default, the camera captures a single image each time you press the shutter button. But by changing the Release mode setting, you can vary this behavior. For example, you can set the camera to Self-Timer mode so that you can press the shutter button and then run in front of the camera and be part of the picture. Or you can switch to Continuous mode, which records a burst of images as long as you hold down the shutter button — a great feature for photographing a fast-moving subject.

Why *Release mode?* Well, it's short for *shutter-release mode.* Pressing the shutter button tells the camera to release the *shutter* — an internal light-control mechanism — so that light can strike the image sensor and expose the image. Your choice of Release mode determines when and how that action occurs. (See Chapter 7 for more about the shutter and its role in exposure.)

Upcoming sections detail each Release mode. But first, acquaint yourself with the nuts and bolts of changing the setting: Start by checking the Shooting Information display, which contains an icon representing the current Release mode. Figure 2-2 shows you where to look.

To adjust the setting, you have the following options:

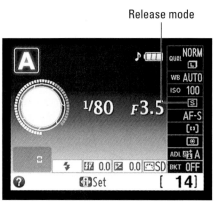

Release mode

Figure 2-2: This S represents the Single Frame mode, which produces one picture for each press of the shutter button.

   ✔ **Quick Settings screen:** Press the Info Edit button once to bring up the Shooting Information screen, if it isn't already visible. Then press again to shift to the Quick Settings screen and highlight the Release mode setting, as shown on the left in Figure 2-3. Press OK to access the available options, as shown on the right. Highlight your choice, press OK to return to the Quick Settings screen, and then press the shutter button halfway to return to shooting.

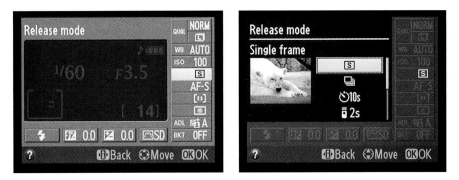

Figure 2-3: Using the Quick Settings screen is the fastest way to change the Release mode setting.

✔ **Shooting menu:** Scroll to the second page of the menu to find the setting, as shown in Figure 2-4. (Chapter 1 explains how to navigate menus, if you need help.)

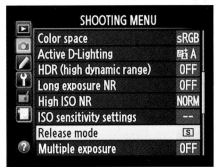

Figure 2-4: The Release Mode option is also found on the second page of the Shooting menu.

Fn

✔ **Fn (Function) button:** By default, pressing the button displays the screen shown in Figure 2-5 and sets the camera to the Self-Timer mode for your next shot. (The symbol on the button is the icon that represents self-timer shooting.) After you take the picture, the camera reverts to whatever Release mode was previously selected.

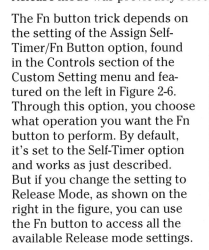

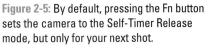

TIP
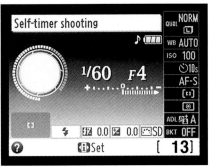

The Fn button trick depends on the setting of the Assign Self-Timer/Fn Button option, found in the Controls section of the Custom Setting menu and featured on the left in Figure 2-6. Through this option, you choose what operation you want the Fn button to perform. By default, it's set to the Self-Timer option and works as just described. But if you change the setting to Release Mode, as shown on the right in the figure, you can use the Fn button to access all the available Release mode settings.

Figure 2-5: By default, pressing the Fn button sets the camera to the Self-Timer Release mode, but only for your next shot.

Just press the button while rotating the Command dial to cycle through the available Release mode settings. While you have the button pressed, the Shooting Information screen appears as shown in Figure 2-7, with the current Release mode setting highlighted.

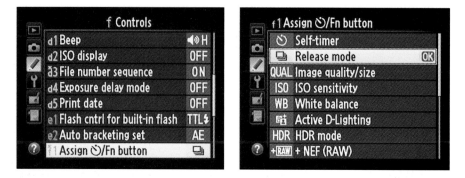

Figure 2-6: Choose these options to use the Fn button to access all the available Release mode settings.

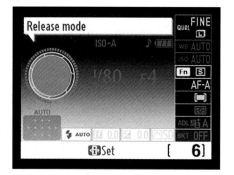

Figure 2-7: After reconfiguring the Fn button, press it while rotating the Command dial to cycle through the available Release mode settings.

Hey, my shutter button isn't working!

You press the shutter button . . . and press it, and press it — and yet nothing happens. Don't panic: This error is most likely related to autofocusing. By default, the camera insists on achieving focus before it releases the shutter to take a picture. You can press the shutter button all day, and the camera just ignores you if it can't set focus.

Try backing away from your subject a little — the focusing issue may be occurring because you've exceeded the minimum focusing distance of the lens. If that doesn't work, the subject itself just may not be conducive to autofocusing. Highly reflective objects, scenes with very little contrast, and subjects behind fences are some of the troublemakers. The easiest solution? Switch the camera to manual focusing and set focus yourself.

Chapter 8 has more information on focusing, including a way to tell the camera to take the picture regardless of whether focus is achieved (this option, called AF-C Priority Selection and found on the Custom Setting menu, is available when you use the AF-C Focus mode setting only).

Single Frame and Quiet Shutter Release modes

At the default Release mode setting, Single Frame, you get one picture each time you press the shutter button. In other words, this is normal-photography mode. The only other thing you need to know is that you must press the shutter button in two stages for autoexposure and autofocusing to work correctly: Press the button halfway, pause to let the camera set focus and exposure, and then press the rest of the way to take the picture.

Quiet Shutter Release mode works just like Single Frame mode but makes less noise as it goes about its business. Designed for situations when you want the camera to be as silent as possible, this mode automatically disables the beep that the autofocus system normally sounds when it achieves focus. (If you prefer, you can disable the beep for all Release modes through the Beep option on the Shooting/Display section of the Custom Setting menu.)

Additionally, Quiet Shutter Release mode affects the operation of the internal mirror that causes the scene coming through the lens to be visible in the viewfinder. Normally, the mirror flips up when you press the shutter button and then flips back down after the shutter opens and closes. This mirror movement makes some noise. So in Quiet Shutter Release mode, you can prevent the mirror from flipping back down by keeping the shutter button fully pressed after the shot. This feature enables you to delay the final mirror movement — and its accompanying clicking sound — to a moment when the noise won't be objectionable.

Continuous (burst mode) shooting

 Sometimes known as *burst mode,* this mode records a continuous series of images as long as you hold down the shutter button, making it easier to capture action. On the D5100, you can capture up to four frames per second.

A few critical details:

- ✔ **Continuous shooting is disabled when you use flash.** You can't use flash in Continuous mode because the time that the flash needs to recycle between shots slows down the capture rate too much. When the flash is enabled, the camera takes only one picture with each shutter-button press, just as it does in Single Frame and Quiet Release modes.

- ✔ **Images are stored temporarily in the memory buffer.** The camera has a little bit of internal memory — a *buffer* — where it stores picture data until it has time to record the images to the memory card. The number of pictures the buffer can hold depends on certain camera settings, such as resolution and file type (JPEG or Raw). The viewfinder displays an estimate of how many pictures will fit in the buffer; see the sidebar "What does [r 24] in the viewfinder mean?" later in this chapter, for details.

  After shooting a burst of images, wait for the memory card access light on the back of the camera to go out before turning off the camera. That's your signal that the camera has successfully moved all data from the buffer to the memory card. Turning off the camera before that happens may corrupt the image files.

- ✔ **Your mileage may vary.** The maximum number of frames per second is an approximation. The actual number of frames you can capture depends on a number of factors, including your shutter speed. At a slow shutter speed, the camera may not be able to reach the maximum frame rate. (See Chapter 7 for an explanation of shutter speed.) Additionally, although you can capture as many as 100 frames in a single burst, the frame rate can drop if the buffer gets full.

Self-timer shooting

 You're no doubt familiar with the Self-Timer Release mode, which delays the shutter release for a few seconds after you press the shutter button, giving you time to dash into the picture. Here's how it works on the D5100: After you press the shutter button, the AF-assist lamp on the front of the camera starts to blink, and the camera emits a series of beeps (assuming that you didn't disable its voice, a setting I cover in Chapter 1). A few seconds later, the camera captures the image.

By default, the camera waits ten seconds after you press the shutter button and then records a single image. But you can tweak the delay time and capture as many as nine shots at a time. Set your self-timer preferences through the Self-Timer option found in the Timers/AE Lock section of the Custom Setting menu, as shown in Figure 2-8. Here's what you need to know:

- ✔ **Self-Timer Delay:** Choose a delay time of 2, 5, 10, or 20 seconds.

- ✔ **Number of Shots:** Specify how many frames you want to capture with each press of the shutter button; the maximum is nine frames. Once again, though, adding flash screws up the works: If you enable flash, the camera records just a single image, regardless of the Number of Shots setting.

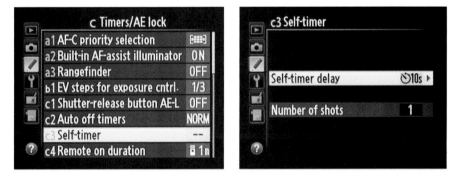

Figure 2-8: You can adjust the self-timer capture delay and the number of frames taken at a time via the Custom Setting menu.

When you use Self-Timer mode or trigger the shutter release with a remote control — that is, any time you take a shot without your eye to the viewfinder — remove the little rubber cup that surrounds the viewfinder and then insert the viewfinder cover that shipped with your camera. Otherwise, light may seep into the camera through the viewfinder and affect exposure. You can also simply use the camera strap or something else to cover the viewfinder in a pinch.

One final note: Turning off the camera automatically resets the Release mode to Single Frame, Quiet, or Continuous mode, depending on which mode you used before Self-Timer mode.

Wireless remote-control modes

The final two Release mode settings relate to the optional Nikon ML-L3 wireless remote-control unit and work as follows:

- ✔ **Delayed Remote:** After you press the shutter-release button on the remote unit, the AF-assist lamp blinks for about two seconds, and then the camera takes the picture.

- ✔ **Quick Response Remote:** The image is captured immediately. In this mode, the AF-assist lamp blinks after the shot is taken.

Remember that in order for the remote control to work, you must aim it at one of the camera's two infrared sensors. One is located on the front of the camera; the other, on the back. Figure 2-9 points out both sensors.

Rear infrared receiver   Front infrared receiver

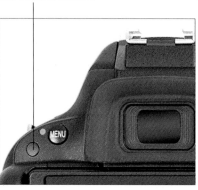

Figure 2-9: When using the optional wireless remote control, aim the unit at one of these two sensors.

Normally, the camera cancels out of the remote control modes if it doesn't receive a signal from the remote after about one minute. You can adjust this timing through the Remote On Duration option, located on the Timers/AE Lock submenu of the Custom Setting menu and shown in Figure 2-10. The maximum delay time is 15 minutes; keep in mind that a shorter delay time saves battery life. After the delay time expires, the camera resets itself to either Single Frame or Continuous

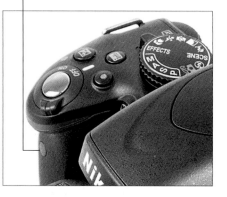

Figure 2-10: Set preferences for wireless-remote shutter release via this menu option.

mode, depending on which mode you last used. The Release mode is also reset to one of those modes if you turn the camera off.

These Release modes are not meant to be used with a remote control that you attach to the camera via the Accessory port (found under the cover on the side of the camera). Select one of the normal Release mode settings and then press the shutter-release button on the remote to trigger the shutter. See your remote's operating guide for details.

Investigating other shutter-release options

In addition to the official Release mode setting, the D5100 offers you two related features, Exposure Delay Mode and Interval Timer Shooting. The first is designed to help eliminate picture-blurring camera shake; the second, to enable automated time-lapse photography. Check 'em out in the next two sections.

Exposure Delay Mode

As I explain earlier in the chapter, one component of the optical system of a dSLR camera is a tiny mirror that moves every time you press the shutter button. The small vibration caused by the mirror action — sometimes referred to as *mirror slap* — can result in slight blurring of the image when you use a very slow shutter speed, shoot with a long telephoto lens, or take extreme close-up shots.

To cope with that issue, many cameras offer mirror-lockup shooting, which delays opening the shutter until after the mirror movement is complete. Although the D5100 doesn't offer mirror-lock up shooting — it's mirror lock-up function is provided solely for the purpose of accessing the sensor for cleaning — it does offer another solution, Exposure Delay Mode. When you enable this feature, the camera waits about one second after the mirror is raised to release the shutter, ensuring that the mirror movement is complete before the image is recorded.

Look for the Exposure Delay Mode option on the Shooting/Display street of the Custom Setting menu, as shown in Figure 2-11. You can use Exposure Delay Mode with any Release mode. Just don't forget you enabled the feature, or you'll drive yourself batty trying to figure out why the camera isn't responding to your shutter-button finger. I say this from experience . . .

d Shooting/display	
d1 Beep	H
d2 ISO display	OFF
d3 File number sequence	ON
d4 Exposure delay mode	ON
d5 Print date	OFF
e1 Flash cntrl for built-in flash	TTL
e2 Auto bracketing set	AE
f1 Assign ⟲/Fn button	

Figure 2-11: Enabling Exposure Delay Mode is a way to make sure that mirror vibrations don't cause blurring.

What does [r 24] in the viewfinder mean?

When you look in your viewfinder to frame a shot, the initial value shown in brackets at the right end of the viewfinder display indicates the number of additional pictures that can fit on your memory card. For example, in the left viewfinder image here, the value shows that the card can hold 856 more images.

As soon as you press the shutter button halfway, which kicks the autofocus and exposure mechanisms into action, that value changes to instead show you how many pictures can fit in the camera's *memory buffer.* In the right image

here, for example, the r 24 value tells you that 24 pictures can fit in the buffer.

So what's the *buffer?* It's a temporary storage tank where the camera stores picture data until it has time to fully record that data onto the camera memory card. This system exists so that you can take a continuous series of pictures without waiting between shots until each image is fully written to the memory card. When the buffer is full, the camera automatically disables the shutter button until it catches up on its recording work.

Interval Timer Shooting

With Interval Timer Shooting, you can set the camera to automatically release the shutter at intervals ranging from seconds to hours apart. This feature enables you to capture a subject as it changes over time — a technique commonly known as *time-lapse photography* — without having to stand around pressing the shutter button the whole time.

Here's how to take advantage of this feature:

1. **Set the Release mode to Single Frame.**

   You can also use the Continuous mode, but the camera still takes one shot at a time, just as if you had selected Single Frame. Quiet mode is also possible; however, the Self-Timer and remote control modes aren't compatible with Interval Timer Shooting.

2. **Display the Shooting menu, highlight Interval Timer Shooting, as shown on the left in Figure 2-12, and press OK.**

   The screen on the right in Figure 2-12 appears.

3. **To begin setting up your capture session, highlight Now or Start Time.**

   - *To start the captures right away,* highlight Now.

   - *To set a later start time,* highlight Start Time.

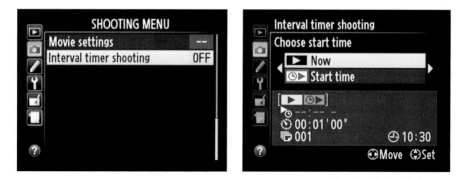

Figure 2-12: The Interval Timer Shooting feature enables you to do time-lapse photography.

4. Press the Multi Selector right to display the capture-setup screen.

If you selected Start Time in Step 3, the screen looks like the one in Figure 2-13. If you selected Now, the Start Time option is dimmed, and the Interval option is highlighted instead.

5. Set up your recording session.

You get three options: Start Time, Interval (time between shots), and Number of Intervals (total number of shots recorded). The current settings for each option appear in the bottom half of the screen, as labeled in Figure 2-13.

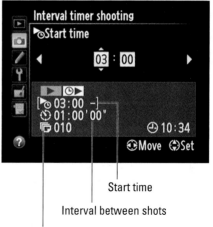

Start time

Interval between shots

Number of intervals

Figure 2-13: Press the Multi Selector right or left to cycle through the setup options; press up or down to change the highlighted value.

At the top of the screen, little value boxes appear. The highlighted box is the active option and relates to the setting that's highlighted at the bottom of the screen. For example, in the figure, the hour box for the Start Time setting is active. Press the Multi Selector right or left to cycle through the value boxes; to change the value in a box, press the Multi Selector up or down.

A few notes about your options:

- The Interval and Start Time options are based on a 24-hour clock. The current time appears in the bottom-right corner of the screen and is based upon the date/time information you entered when setting up the camera.

- For the Interval option, the left column box is for the hour setting; the middle, minutes; and the right, seconds. Make sure that the value you enter is longer than the shutter speed you plan to use.

- For the Start Time option, you can set only the hour and minute values. Again, the Start Time option is available only if you selected Start Time in Step 3.

6. **When you're done setting up the capture options, press the Multi Selector right until you see the On and Off options on the screen, as shown in Figure 2-14.**

7. **Highlight On and press OK.**

   If you selected Now as your interval-capture starting option in Step 3, the first shot is recorded about three seconds later. If you set a delayed start time, the camera displays a "Timer Active" message for a few seconds before returning to the Shooting menu.

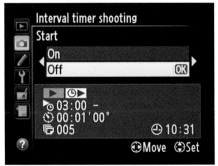

Figure 2-14: Highlight On and press OK to finalize the Interval Timer Shooting setup.

A few final factoids:

- ✔ **Interval Timer Shooting isn't available for Live View photography.** The menu option is disabled any time Live View is active.

- ✔ **The card access light blinks while Interval Timer Shooting is in progress.** It's the little green light just above the Delete button on the back of the camera.

- ✔ **To interrupt Interval Timer Shooting, turn off the camera.** Or move the Mode dial to a different setting.

- ✔ **Menus are disabled while the interval sequence is in progress.** You can't access the Quick Settings screen either. If you display the Shooting Information screen, you see the message Interval Timer Shooting at the top of the screen.

- ✔ **The autobracketing, high dynamic range (HDR), and multiple exposure features are disabled when Interval Timer Shooting is active.** Chapter 7 explains the first two features; Chapter 10 covers the third.

- ✔ **If you're using autofocusing, be sure that the camera can focus on your subject.** It will initiate focusing before each shot. See Chapter 8 for details about autofocusing. Again, remember that if you use the default autofocusing settings, the camera won't release the shutter and take the picture if focus can't be achieved.

✏ **When the interval sequence is complete, the Interval Timer Shooting menu option is reset to Off.** The card access light stops blinking shortly after the final image is recorded to the memory card.

Choosing the Right Quality Settings

Almost every review of the D5100 contains glowing reports about the camera's top-notch picture quality. As you've no doubt discovered, those claims are true: This baby can create large, beautiful images.

What you may *not* have discovered is that Nikon's default Image Quality setting isn't the highest that the D5100 offers. Why, you ask, would Nikon do such a thing? Why not set up the camera to produce the best images right out of the box? The answer is that using the top setting has some downsides. Nikon's default choice represents a compromise between avoiding those disadvantages while still producing images that will please most photographers.

Whether that compromise is right for you, however, depends on your photographic needs. To help you decide, the rest of this chapter explains the Image Quality setting, along with the Image Size setting, which is also critical to the quality of images that you print. Just in case you're having quality problems related to other issues, though, the next section provides a handy quality-defect diagnosis guide.

If you already know what settings you want to use and just need some help finding out how to select the options, skip to the very last section of the chapter.

Diagnosing quality problems

When I use the term *picture quality,* I'm not talking about the composition, exposure, or other traditional characteristics of a photograph. Instead, I mean how finely the image is rendered in the digital sense.

Figure 2-15 illustrates the concept: The first example is a high-quality image, with clear details and smooth color transitions. The other examples show five common digital-image defects.

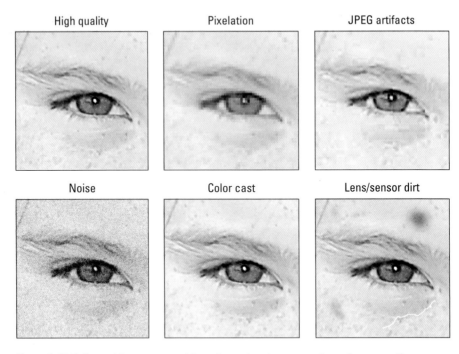

Figure 2-15: Refer to this symptom guide to determine the cause of poor image quality.

Each of these defects is related to a different issue, and only one is affected by the Image Quality setting on your D5100. So if you aren't happy with your image quality, first compare your photos to those in the figure to properly diagnose the problem. Then try these remedies:

- **Pixelation:** When an image doesn't have enough *pixels* (the colored tiles used to create digital images), details aren't clear, and curved and diagonal lines appear jagged. The fix is to increase image resolution, which you do via the Image Size control. See the next section, "Considering image size: How many pixels are enough?" for details.

- **JPEG artifacts:** The "parquet tile" texture and random color defects that mar the third image in Figure 2-15 can occur in photos captured in the JPEG *(jay-peg)* file format, which is why these flaws are referred to as *JPEG artifacts.* This is the defect related to the Image Quality setting; see "Understanding Image Quality options (JPEG or Raw)," later in this chapter, to find out more.

✔ **Noise:** This defect gives your image a speckled look, as shown in the lower-left example in Figure 2-15. Noise can occur with very long exposure times or when you choose a high ISO Sensitivity setting on your camera. You can explore both issues in Chapter 7.

✔ **Color cast:** If your colors are seriously out of whack, as shown in the lower-middle example in the figure, try adjusting the camera's White Balance setting. Chapter 8 covers this control and other color issues.

✔ **Lens/sensor dirt:** A dirty lens is the first possible cause of the kind of defects you see in the last example in the figure. If cleaning your lens doesn't solve the problem, dust or dirt may have made its way onto the camera's image sensor. See the sidebar "Maintaining a pristine view," later in this chapter, for information on safe lens and sensor cleaning.

When diagnosing image problems, you may want to open the photos in ViewNX 2 or some other photo software and zoom in for a close-up inspection. Some defects, especially pixelation and JPEG artifacts, have a similar appearance until you see them at a magnified view. (See Part II for information about using ViewNX 2.)

I should also tell you that I used a little digital enhancement to exaggerate the flaws in my example images to make the symptoms easier to see. With the exception of an unwanted color cast or a big blob of lens or sensor dirt, these defects may not even be noticeable unless you print or view your image at a very large size. And the subject matter of your image may camouflage some flaws; most people probably wouldn't detect a little JPEG artifacting in a photograph of a densely wooded forest, for example.

In other words, don't consider Figure 2-15 as an indication that your D5100 is suspect in the image quality department. First, *any* digital camera can produce these defects under the right circumstances. Second, by following the guidelines in this chapter and the noise and color recommendations that I explore in other chapters, you can resolve any quality issues that you may encounter.

Considering image size: How many pixels are enough?

Pixels are the little square tiles from which all digital images are made. You can see some pixels close up in the right image in Figure 2-16, which shows a greatly magnified view of the eye area in the left image.

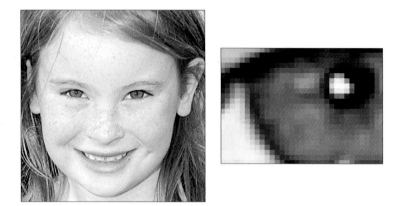

Figure 2-16: Pixels are the building blocks of digital photos.

Pixel is short for *picture element.* The number of pixels in an image is refer-red to as *resolution.* You can define resolution either in terms of the *pixel dimensions* — the number of horizontal pixels and vertical pixels — or total resolution, which you get by multiplying those two values. This number is usually stated in *megapixels,* or MP for short, with one megapixel equal to one million pixels. For example, the D5100 offers a maximum resolution of 4928 x 3264 pixels, which translates to about 16.1 megapixels.

You control resolution on the D5100 via the Image Size setting. You can choose from three settings: Large, Medium, and Small; Table 2-1 lists the resolution values for each setting. (Megapixel values are rounded off.)

Table 2-1	Image Size (Resolution) Options
Setting	*Resolution*
Large	4928 x 3264 (16.1 MP)
Medium	3696 x 2448 (9.0 MP)
Small	2464 x 1632 (4.0 MP)

However, if you select Raw (NEF) as your file format, all images are captured at the Large setting. You can vary the resolution only when choosing JPEG as the file format. The upcoming section "Understanding Image Quality options (JPEG or Raw)" explains file formats.

To choose the right Image Size setting, you need to understand the three ways that pixel count affects your pictures:

✔ **Print size:** Pixel count determines the size at which you can produce a high-quality print. If you don't have enough pixels, your prints may exhibit the defects you see in the pixelation example in Figure 2-15, or worse, you may be able to see the individual pixels, as in the right example in Figure 2-16. Depending on your photo printer, you typically need anywhere from 200 to 300 pixels per linear inch, or *ppi,* of the print. To produce an 8 x 10 print at 200 ppi, for example, you need a pixel count of 1600 x 2000, or just less than 2 megapixels.

Even though many photo-editing programs enable you to add pixels to an existing image, doing so isn't a good idea. For reasons I won't bore you with, adding pixels — known as *upsampling* — doesn't enable you to successfully enlarge your photo. In fact, upsampling typically makes matters worse. The printing discussion in Chapter 6 includes some example images that illustrate this issue.

✔ **Screen display size:** Resolution doesn't affect the quality of images viewed on a monitor, television, or other screen device the way it does for printed photos. Instead, resolution determines the *size* at which the image appears. This issue is one of the most misunderstood aspects of digital photography, so I explain it thoroughly in Chapter 6. For now, just know that you need *way* fewer pixels for onscreen photos than you do for printed photos. In fact, even the Small resolution setting on your camera creates a picture too big to be viewed in its entirety in many e-mail programs.

✔ **File size:** Every additional pixel increases the amount of data required to create a digital picture file. So a higher-resolution image has a larger file size than a low-resolution image.

Large files present several problems:

- You can store fewer images on your memory card, on your computer's hard drive, and on removable storage media, such as a DVD.

- The camera needs more time to process and store the image data on the memory card after you press the shutter button. This extra time can hamper fast-action shooting.

- When you share photos online, larger files take longer to upload and download.

- When you edit your photos in your photo software, your computer needs more resources and time to process large files.

As you can see, resolution is a bit of a sticky wicket. What if you aren't sure how large you want to print your images? What if you want to print your photos *and* share them online?

I take the better-safe-than-sorry route, which leads to the following recommendations about which Image Size setting to use:

- ✏ **Always shoot at a resolution suitable for print.** You then can create a low-resolution copy of the image in your photo editor for use online. In fact, your camera offers a built-in resizing option; Chapter 6 shows you how to use it.

  Again, you *can't* go in the opposite direction, adding pixels to a low-resolution original in your photo editor to create a good, large print. Even with the very best software, adding pixels doesn't improve the print quality of a low-resolution image.

- ✏ **For everyday images, Medium is a good choice.** I find the Large setting (16.1 MP) to be overkill for most casual shooting, which means that you're creating huge files for no good reason. Keep in mind that even at the Small setting, your pixel count (2464 x 1632) is approximately what you need to produce a 12-x-8-inch print at 200 ppi.

- ✏ **Choose Large for an image that you plan to crop, print very large, or both.** The benefit of maxing out resolution is that you have the flexibility to crop your photo and still generate a decent-sized print of the remaining image. Figures 2-17 and 2-18 offer an example. When I was shooting this photograph, I couldn't get close enough to fill the frame with my main interest — the two juvenile herons at the center of the scene. But because I had the resolution cranked up to Large, I could later crop the shot to the composition you see in Figure 2-18 and still produce a great print. In fact, I could have printed the cropped image at a much larger size than fits here.

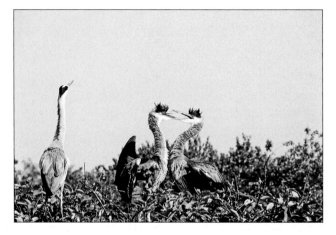

Figure 2-17: I couldn't get close enough to fill the frame with the two juvenile herons, so I captured this image at the Large resolution setting.

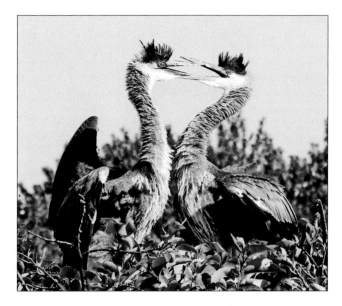

Figure 2-18: A high-resolution original enabled me to crop the photo tightly and still have enough pixels to produce a quality print.

✒ **Reduce resolution if shooting speed is paramount.** If you're shooting action and the shot-to-shot capture time is slower than you want — that is, the camera takes too long after you take one shot before it lets you take another — dialing down the resolution may help. Also see Chapter 9 for other tips on action photography.

After you decide which resolution setting is right for your picture, visit the section "Setting Image Size and Quality," at the end of this chapter.

Understanding Image Quality options (JPEG or Raw)

If I had my druthers, the Image Quality option on the D5100 would instead be called File Type because that's what the setting controls.

Here's the deal: The file type, sometimes also known as a file *format,* determines how your picture data is recorded and stored. Your choice does impact picture quality, but so do other factors, as outlined at the beginning of this chapter. In addition, your choice of file type has ramifications beyond picture quality.

At any rate, your D5100 offers the two file types common on most of today's digital cameras: JPEG and Camera Raw, or just Raw for short, which goes by the specific moniker NEF *(Nikon Electronic Format)* on Nikon cameras.

The next sections explain the pros and cons of each format. If your mind is already made up, skip ahead to "Setting Image Size and Quality," near the end of this chapter, to find out how to make your selection.

Don't confuse *file format* with the Format Memory Card option on the Setup menu. That option erases all data on your memory card; see Chapter 1 for details.

JPEG: The imaging (and web) standard

Pronounced *jay-peg,* this format is the default setting on your D5100, as it is for most digital cameras. JPEG is popular for two main reasons:

- **Immediate usability:** All web browsers and e-mail programs can display JPEG files, so you can share them online immediately after you shoot them. The same can't be said for Raw (NEF) files, which must be processed and converted to JPEG files before you can share them online. And although you can view and print your camera's Raw files in Nikon ViewNX 2 without converting them, many third-party photo programs don't enable you to do that. You can read more about the conversion process in the upcoming section "Raw (NEF): The purist's choice."
- **Small files:** JPEG files are smaller than Raw files. And smaller files consume less room on your camera memory card and in your computer's storage tank.

The downside — you knew there had to be one — is that JPEG creates smaller files by applying *lossy compression.* This process actually throws away some image data. Too much compression leads to the defects you see in the JPEG artifacts example in Figure 2-15.

Fortunately, your camera enables you to specify how much compression you're willing to accept. You can choose from three JPEG settings, which produce the following results:

- **JPEG Fine:** At this setting, the compression ratio is 1:4 — that is, the file is four times smaller than it would otherwise be. In plain English, that means that very little compression is applied, so you shouldn't see many compression artifacts, if any.
- **JPEG Normal:** Switch to Normal, and the compression ratio rises to 1:8. The chance of seeing some artifacting increases as well.
- **JPEG Basic:** Shift to this setting, and the compression ratio jumps to 1:16. That's a substantial amount of compression and brings with it a lot more risk of artifacting.

Note, though, that even the JPEG Basic setting on your D5100 doesn't result in anywhere near the level of artifacting that you see in my example in Figure 2-15. Again, that example is exaggerated to help you be able to recognize artifacting defects and understand how they differ from other image-quality issues. In fact, if you keep your image print or display size small, you aren't likely to notice a great deal of quality difference between the Fine, Normal, and Basic compression levels, although details in the Fine and Normal versions may appear slightly crisper than the Basic one. It's only when you greatly enlarge a photo that the differences become apparent.

Given that the differences between the compression settings aren't that easy to spot until you enlarge the photo, is it okay to stick with the default setting — Normal — or even drop down to Basic in order to capture smaller files? Well, only you can decide what level of quality your pictures demand. For me, the added file sizes produced by the Fine setting aren't a huge concern, given that the prices of memory cards fall all the time. Long-term storage is more of an issue; the larger your files, the faster you fill your computer's hard drive and the more DVDs or CDs you need for archiving purposes. But in the end, I prefer to take the storage hit in exchange for the lower compression level of the Fine setting. You never know when a casual snapshot is going to be so great that you want to print or display it large enough that even minor quality loss becomes a concern. And of all the defects that you can correct in a photo editor, artifacting is one of the hardest to remove.

To make the best decision, do your own test shots, carefully inspect the results in your photo editor, and make your own judgment about what level of artifacting you can accept. Artifacting is often much easier to spot when you view images onscreen. It's difficult to reproduce artifacting here in print because the printing press obscures some of the tiny defects caused by compression. Your inkjet prints are more likely to reveal these defects.

If you don't want *any* risk of artifacting, bypass JPEG altogether and change the file type to Raw (NEF). Or consider your other option, which is to record two versions of each file, one Raw and one JPEG. The next section offers details.

Raw (NEF): The purist's choice

The other picture file type you can create on your D5100 is *Camera Raw,* or just *Raw* (as in uncooked) for short.

Each manufacturer has its own flavor of Raw. Nikon's is NEF, for *Nikon Electronic Format,* so you see the three-letter extension NEF at the end of Raw filenames.

Raw is popular with advanced, very demanding photographers, for three reasons:

✔ **Greater creative control:** With JPEG, internal camera software tweaks your images, adjusting color, exposure, and sharpness as needed to produce the results that Nikon believes its customers prefer. With Raw, the camera simply records the original, unprocessed image data. The photographer then copies the image file to the computer and uses special software known as a *Raw converter* to produce the actual image, making decisions about color, exposure, and so on at that point. The upshot is that "shooting Raw" enables you, not the camera, to have the final say on the visual characteristics of your image.

✔ **Higher bit depth:** *Bit depth* is a measure of how many distinct color values an image file can contain. JPEG files restrict you to 8 bits each for the red, blue, and green color components, or *channels,* that make up a digital image, for a total of 24 bits. That translates to roughly 16.7 million possible colors. On the D5100, a Raw file delivers a higher bit count, collecting 14 bits per channel. (Chapter 8 provides more information about the red-green-blue makeup of digital images.)

Although jumping from 8 to 14 bits sounds like a huge difference, you may not really ever notice any difference in your photos — that 8-bit palette of 16.7 million values is more than enough for superb images. Where having the extra bits can come in handy is if you really need to adjust exposure, contrast, or color after the shot in your photo-editing program. In cases where you apply extreme adjustments, having the extra original bits sometimes helps avoid a problem known as *banding* or *posterization,* which creates abrupt color breaks where you should see smooth, seamless transitions. (A higher bit depth doesn't always prevent the problem, however, so don't expect miracles.)

✔ **Best picture quality:** Because Raw doesn't apply the destructive compression associated with JPEG, you don't run the risk of the artifacting that can occur with JPEG.

But of course, as with most things in life, Raw isn't without its disadvantages. To wit:

✔ **You can't do much with your pictures until you process them in a Raw converter.** You can't share them online, for example, or put them into a text document or multimedia presentation. You can view and print them immediately if you use the free Nikon ViewNX 2 software, but most other photo programs require you to convert the Raw files to a standard format first. Ditto for retail photo printing. So when you shoot Raw, you add to the time you must spend in front of the computer instead of behind the camera lens. Chapter 6 shows you how to process your Raw files using Nikon ViewNX 2 as well as the converter built into the camera.

✔ **Raw files are larger than JPEGs.** Unlike JPEG, Raw doesn't apply lossy compression to shrink files. In addition, Raw files are always captured at the maximum resolution available on your camera, even if you don't really need all those pixels. For both reasons, Raw files are significantly larger than JPEGs, so they take up more room on your memory card and on your computer's hard drive or other picture-storage device.

✔ **To get the full benefit of Raw, you need software other than Nikon ViewNX 2.** The ViewNX 2 software that ships free with your camera does have a command that enables you to convert Raw files to JPEG or to TIFF, another standard imaging format (Chapter 6 has details). However, this free tool gives you limited control over how your original data is translated in terms of color, exposure, and other characteristics — which defeats one of the primary purposes of shooting Raw. The same is true for the Raw converter built into the camera.

Nikon Capture NX 2 offers a sophisticated Raw converter, but it costs about $180. (Sadly, if you already own Capture NX, you need to upgrade to version 2 to open the Raw files from your D5100.) If you own Adobe Photoshop or Photoshop Elements, however, you're set; both include the converter that most people consider one of the best in the industry. Watch the sale ads, and you can pick up Elements for well below $100. You may need to download an update from the Adobe website (www. adobe.com) to get the converter to work with your D5100 files. For additional software options, see Chapter 6.

Whether the upside of Raw outweighs the down is a decision that you need to ponder based on your photographic needs, your schedule, and your computer-comfort level. If you do decide to try Raw shooting, you can select from the following two Image Quality options:

✔ **Raw:** This setting produces a single Raw file at the maximum resolution (16.1 megapixels).

✔ **Raw+JPEG:** This setting produces two files: the standard Raw file plus a JPEG. Both files are captured at the maximum resolution, so remember that creating two files for every image eats up substantially more memory card space than sticking with a single file. However, you can choose whether you want the JPEG version to be captured at the Fine, Normal, or Basic quality level.

I often choose the Raw+JPEG Fine option when I'm shooting pictures I want to share right away with people who don't have software for viewing Raw files. I upload the JPEGs to a photo-sharing site where everyone can view them, and then I process the Raw versions when I have time. Having the JPEG version also enables you to display your photos on a DVD player or TV that has a slot for an SD memory card — most can't display Raw files but can handle JPEGs. Ditto for portable media players and digital photo frames.

My take: Choose JPEG Fine or Raw (NEF)

At this point, you may be finding all this technical goop a bit much — I recognize that panicked look in your eyes — so allow me to simplify things for you. Until you have time or energy to completely digest all the ramifications of JPEG versus Raw, here's a quick summary of my thoughts on the matter:

- If you require the absolute best image quality and have the time and interest to do the Raw conversion, shoot Raw. See Chapter 6 for more information on the conversion process.

- If great photo quality is good enough for you, you don't have wads of spare time, or you aren't that comfortable with the computer, stick with JPEG Fine.

- If you don't mind the added file-storage space requirement and want the flexibility of both formats, choose Raw+JPEG Fine.

- If you go with JPEG only, stay away from JPEG Normal and Basic. The tradeoff for smaller files isn't, in my opinion, worth the risk of compression artifacts. As with my recommendations on image size, this fits the "better safe than sorry" formula: You never know when you may capture a spectacular, enlargement-worthy subject, and it would be a shame to have the photo spoiled by compression defects.

Setting Image Size and Quality

To sum up this chapter:

- The Image Size and Image Quality options both affect the quality of your pictures and also play a large role in image file size.

- Choose a high Image Quality setting — Raw (NEF) or JPEG Fine — and the maximum Image Size setting (Large), and you get top-quality pictures and large file sizes.

- Combining the lowest Quality setting (JPEG Basic) with the lowest Size setting (Small) greatly shrinks files, enabling you to fit lots more pictures on your memory card, but it also increases the chances that you'll be disappointed with the quality of those pictures, especially if you make large prints.

You can view the current Image Size and Image Quality settings on the Shooting Information screen, in the area labeled in Figure 2-19. To adjust the settings, you have the following choices:

✔ **Quick Settings display:** Press the Info Edit button twice — once to bring up the Shooting Info display and then again to shift to the Quick Settings screen. Use the Multi Selector to highlight one of the two options and then press OK to view the screen where you can select the setting you want to use. Figure 2-20 illustrates the process of setting the Image Size option.

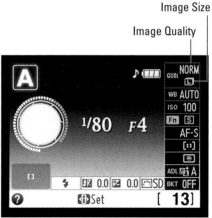

Figure 2-19: The current Image Quality and Image Size settings appear here.

The left side of the screen shows you the file size that will result from your selected setting along with the number of pictures that will fit on the memory card at that size. (Keep in mind that certain other factors also affect file size, such as the level of detail and color in the subject.)

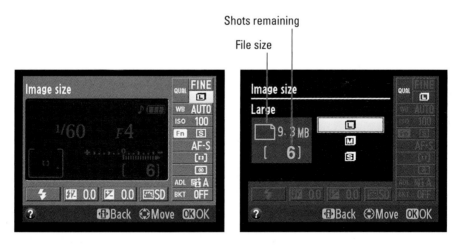

Figure 2-20: You can use the Quick Settings screen to change the Image Size and Quality settings.

✔ **Shooting menu:** As an alternative, you can adjust the settings via the Shooting menu, as shown in Figure 2-21. If you select the Image Size setting from the menu, the options screen shows the pixel counts for each setting.

Maintaining a pristine view

Often lost in discussions of digital photo defects — compression artifacts, pixelation, and the like — is the impact of plain-old dust and dirt on picture quality. But no matter what camera settings you use, you aren't going to achieve great picture quality with a dirty lens. So make it a practice to clean your lens on a regular basis, using one of the specialized cloths and cleaning solutions made expressly for that purpose.

If you continue to notice spots or hair-like defects in your images (refer to the last example in Figure 2-15), you probably have a dirty *image sensor*. That's the part of your camera that does the actual image capture — the digital equivalent of a film negative, if you will.

Your D5100 offers an automated, internal sensor-cleaning mechanism. By default, this automatic cleaning happens every time you turn the camera on or off. You can adjust this behavior or request an immediate cleaning session via the Clean Image Sensor command on the Setup menu.

But if you frequently change lenses in a dirty environment, the internal cleaning mechanism may not be adequate, in which case a manual sensor cleaning is necessary. You can do this job yourself, but . . . I don't recommend it. Image sensors are pretty delicate beings, and you can easily damage them or other parts of your camera if you aren't careful. Instead, find a local camera store that offers this service. In my area (central Indiana), sensor cleaning costs from $35–$75, depending on the level of cleaning that's required.

In addition, the Setup menu offers an option called Image Dust Off Ref Photo, which is tied to an automated dust-removal filter found in Nikon Capture NX 2. After enabling the feature, you take a picture of a piece of white paper and then tell the software to use that image as a reference to the dirty areas of the sensor (areas that show up as specks on the white background are classified as dust). With that information, the software knows where to apply its dust removal filter in your other images. This feature works only with Raw (NEF) photos and isn't a cure-all — it may not always remove dust successfully. Rather, it's designed as a partial remedy until you get your camera cleaned. I don't cover Capture NX 2 in this book, but if you're interested, you can download a 30-day trial from the Nikon website. See Chapter 6 for more information on this program and other imaging software.

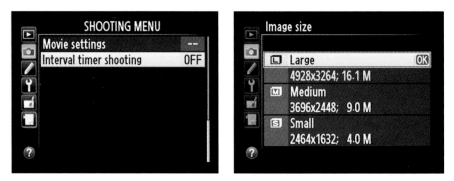

Figure 2-21: You also can set Image Size and Image Quality via the Shooting menu.

✔ **Fn (Function) button:** By default, pressing the Fn button changes the Release mode to the Self-Timer setting for your next shot. But by following the steps laid out in Chapter 11, you can set the button to call up the Image Size and Image Quality settings instead. If you take that step, press the Fn button while rotating the Command dial to cycle through all possible combinations of Image Size and Image Quality settings.

However you adjust the Size and Quality options, remember that when you choose the Raw (NEF) or Raw + JPEG options, you don't need to worry about the Image Size setting. For these formats, all pictures are automatically captured at the Large resolution, and you can't choose a lower resolution setting.

3

Taking Great Pictures, Automatically

*A*re you old enough to remember the Certs television commercials from the 1960s and '70s? "It's a candy mint!" declared one actor. "It's a breath mint!" argued another. Then a narrator declared the debate a tie and spoke the famous catchphrase: "It's two, two, two mints in one!"

Well, that's sort of how I see the Nikon D5100. On one hand, it provides a full range of powerful controls, offering just about every feature a serious photographer could want. On the other, it offers automated photography modes that enable people with absolutely no experience to capture beautiful images. "It's a sophisticated photographic tool!" "It's as easy as 'point and shoot!'" "It's two, two, two cameras in one!"

Now, my guess is that you bought this book for help with your camera's advanced side, so that's what other chapters cover. This chapter, however, is devoted to your camera's easiest shooting modes, showing you how to get the best results in your camera's fully automatic modes, including Auto, Portrait mode, Sports mode, and the other Scene modes.

Note: Information in this chapter assumes that you're using the viewfinder to compose your pictures. Things work a little differently in Live View mode, so Chapter 4 concentrates on that feature.

Setting Up for Automatic Success

Your D5100 offers more than a dozen fully automatic exposure modes, which you access via the Mode dial, as shown in Figure 3-1. Your choices include

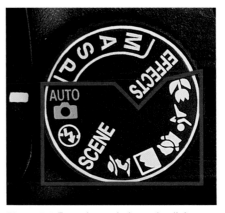

Figure 3-1: For point-and-shoot simplicity, choose from one of these exposure modes.

- ✔ **Auto:** A general purpose point-and-shoot mode.

- ✔ **Auto Flash Off:** The same thing as Auto but without flash.

- ✔ **Scene modes:** Sixteen modes geared to shooting specific types of pictures. Five of the most commonly used Scene modes have their own Mode dial setting; they're the ones represented on the Mode dial by the little pictures between the Scene and Effects settings. To access the others, you set the dial to Scene and then rotate the Command dial to choose a specific scene type. (The upcoming section "Taking Advantage of Scene Modes" provides specifics.)

All these exposure modes are designed for people without any knowledge of photography. You just frame the shot and press the shutter button. But you still have a few ways to control the camera's behavior. On the Shooting Information screen, any settings that aren't dimmed are adjustable. Figure 3-2 labels settings adjustable in Auto and Auto Flash Off modes; in the Scene modes, you can also adjust ISO, an exposure control I cover in Chapter 7. You have access to certain options not displayed on the screen, too.

Here's a quick rundown of the options you can control:

- ✔ **Focusing method:** You can enjoy autofocusing, if your lens supports it, or focus manually. On the D5100 kit

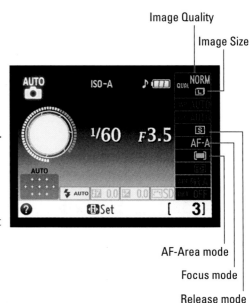

Image Quality

Image Size

AF-Area mode

Focus mode

Release mode

Figure 3-2: Settings that are dimmed in the Shooting Information screen are off-limits, but you can modify these basic options.

lens, select the focusing method via the A/M (auto/manual) switch, shown in Figure 3-3.

✔ **Autofocusing options:** Autofocusing behavior is determined by two settings, the AF-Area mode and the Focus mode. I explain both fully in Chapter 8, but here's the condensed version:

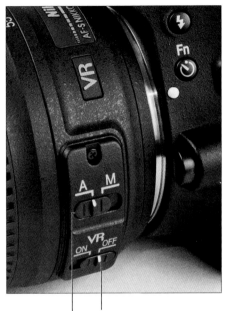

Vibration Reduction switch

Auto/Manual focus switch

Figure 3-3: You can choose automatic or manual focusing in any exposure mode (if your lens supports autofocusing).

- *Focus mode:* For all the automatic exposure modes, this option is set to AF-A, which stands for *auto-servo autofocus.* Here's how it works: If the subject isn't moving, focus is set when you press the shutter button halfway down, and it remains locked as long as you press the button. But if the camera detects motion in front of the lens, it may "unlock" focus and begin continually adjusting focus to track your subject, setting the final focusing distance at the time you press the button fully to record the picture. If your subject is moving, be sure to reframe as needed to keep your subject within the area of the viewfinder covered by the camera's 11 focus points. See Figure 3-5, in the next section, for a look at the focus points.

  Although the Focus mode option is accessible, the only other setting you can use is MF, for manual focusing. With the kit lens and most others, the camera automatically selects that setting when you set the lens focus switch to M. If you want to access to all the Focus mode settings, you must use one of the advanced exposure modes (P, S, A, and M), all detailed in Chapter 7.

- *AF-Area mode:* This option determines which of the 11 focus points is used to establish the focusing distance. You have access to all available settings for this one — you can change it via the Quick Settings screen — but be sure to read the explanations in Chapter 8 first so that you understand how the autofocusing system works at each of the settings. The default setting varies depending on your exposure mode; I spell out the details when discussing the various modes later in this chapter. Also be aware that the setting reverts to the default if you turn the camera off or select a different exposure mode.

✔ **Vibration Reduction:** When enabled, this feature helps produce sharper images by compensating for camera movement that can occur when you handhold the camera. On the kit lens, turn Vibration Reduction on or off via the VR switch, labeled in Figure 3-3. Select On for handheld photography; set the switch to Off when you mount the camera on a tripod. See Chapter 1 for additional details.

✔ **Flash:** In Auto exposure mode, as well as in some Scene modes, the camera automatically raises and fires the built-in flash in dim lighting. In other modes, flash is disabled.

In modes that permit flash, some Scene modes let you alter the behavior of the flash through the Flash mode setting. Chapter 7 provides complete details about Flash modes and other flash settings; here's a quick intro:

- *Checking the current Flash mode:* A symbol representing the current Flash mode appears in the Shooting Information display. For example, in Figure 3-4, the symbol shows that the flash is set to Auto, meaning that the camera will automatically fire the flash if it thinks the ambient lighting is insufficient.

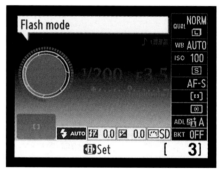

- *Changing the Flash mode:* If the flash is raised, the fastest option is to press and hold the Flash button. As soon as you press the button, you see the Flash mode banner on the Shooting Information screen and the Flash mode setting becomes highlighted, as shown in Figure 3-4. Keep holding the button and rotate the Command dial to cycle through the available settings.

Figure 3-4: Press the Flash button while rotating the Command dial to adjust the Flash mode quickly.

Alternatively, you can use the Quick Settings screen to change the setting. Remember, to access the screen when the Shooting Information screen is displayed, press the Info Edit button once. If the Shooting Information screen isn't displayed, press the button twice.

- *Disabling flash:* Select the Flash Off mode, represented in the displays by the symbol shown in the margin here.

- *Using red-eye reduction flash:* Look for the Flash mode accompanied by the little eye icon, as shown here. The word Auto also appears with the icon. In this mode, the camera still controls whether the flash fires, but if it does see the need for flash, it emits a brief burst of light before the actual flash fires — the idea being that the prelight will constrict the subject's pupils, which helps reduce the chances of red-eye. Warn your subject until after the final flash to stop smiling.

Note that some Scene modes use a variation of red-eye reduction, combining that feature with a slow shutter speed. In that case, you see the little eye icon plus the words Auto Slow. It's important to use a tripod and ask your subject to remain still during the exposure to avoid a blurry picture.

✔ **Release mode:** This setting determines the number of images that are recorded with each press of the shutter button and the timing of each shot. Here's a quick recap of your options, all detailed fully in Chapter 2:

- *Single Frame:* Records a single picture immediately after you depress the shutter button fully. Use this setting for normal photography.

- *Continuous:* Records up to four frames per second for as long as you hold down the shutter button. Try this setting when shooting action shots; just remember that you can't use flash during continuous shooting.

- *Self-Timer:* Captures the image a few seconds after you press the shutter button, enabling the photographer to step from behind the camera and into the shot. The default delay is 10 seconds, but you can shorten it to 2 seconds or extend it as much as 20 seconds via the Self-Timer option on the Timers/AE Lock section of the Custom Setting menu. You also can set the camera to record up to nine shots with each press of the shutter button via the same menu option. If you use flash, though, this multi-shot feature is disabled.

- *Quiet:* Works like Single mode but silences the camera's normal operating sounds as much as possible. Try this mode in situations where camera noise might be disruptive.

The fastest way to change the Release mode is by using the Quick Settings screen. But you also can adjust the setting via the Shooting menu.

✔ **Image Quality and Image Size:** By default, pictures are recorded at the Large Image Size setting, producing a 16.1 MP (megapixel) image, and the Normal Image Quality setting, which creates a JPEG picture file with a moderate amount of compression. Chapter 2 explains both options and offers advice on when you may want to stray from the default settings.

✔ **Exposure:** In the Scene modes, you have access to one exposure-adjustment option, ISO Sensitivity, which determines how much light is needed to properly expose the image. At the default setting, Auto, the camera adjusts the ISO Sensitivity as needed. This option is a little complex, so I save it for Chapter 7; stick with Auto for now. You can view the current setting in the Shooting Information screen. It's located directly above the Release mode setting (refer to Figure 3-2).

⌐ **Advanced Shooting menu options:** You also can control the following more advanced Shooting menu options:

- *Auto Distortion Control:* This feature attempts to correct for the slight distortion that can occur when you shoot with wide-angle or extreme telephoto lenses. Leave this one set to its default, Off, until you explore the details in Chapter 8.

- *Color Space:* Again, stick with the default setting, sRGB, until you delve into the advanced color issues covered in Chapter 8.

- *High ISO NR (Noise Reduction) and Long Exposure NR:* These features try to compensate for image defects that can occur when you use a high ISO setting or a long exposure time, respectively. Chapter 7 explains the pros and cons of enabling the features.

You also have access to a few Custom Setting menu options, but because the mantra of this chapter is "keep it simple," I save those for later chapters, too. In fact, if you're not up to sorting through any of the options in the preceding list, just leave them all at their default settings and skip to the next section to get step-by-step help with taking your first pictures. After all, the defaults are chosen because they're the best solutions for most shooting scenarios. (See the end of Chapter 1 to find out how to restore the default settings if you changed them already.)

As Easy As It Gets: Auto and Auto Flash Off

In Auto mode, the camera analyzes the scene in front of the lens and selects the picture-taking options that it thinks will best capture the image. All you need to do is compose the scene and press the shutter button.

Auto Flash Off mode does the exact same thing, except flash is disabled. This mode provides an easy way to ensure that you don't break the rules when shooting in locations that don't permit flash: museums, churches, and so on.

The following steps walk you through the process of taking a picture in both modes. Remember that these steps assume that you're using the viewfinder, which is the best option in most cases. Chapter 4 explains why and shows you how to take pictures in Live View mode.

Before you work through the steps, adjust the viewfinder to your eyesight so that you get an accurate idea of whether the scene is in focus. (Chapter 1 shows you how.) Also select your focusing method, Release mode, Vibration Reduction setting, and other options as I outline in the preceding section.

1. Set the Mode dial to Auto or Auto Flash Off.

2. **Looking through the viewfinder, frame the image so that your subject appears under one of the 11 focus points, as shown in Figure 3-5.**

The *focus points* are those tiny rectangles surrounded by brackets to make them a little easier to see. I labeled one of the little guys in the figure.

3. **If focusing manually, twist the focusing ring on the lens until the scene appears in focus.**

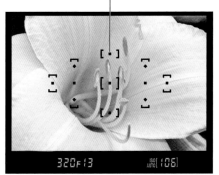

Focus point

Figure 3-5: The markings in the viewfinder indicate autofocus points.

On the kit lens, set the lens switch to M before turning the focusing ring to avoid damaging the lens. The camera then automatically selects the MF (manual focus) setting for the Focus mode option. If you use another lens, check the lens manual for instructions. Either way, also see Chapter 8 for additional information that may help you achieve better results when focusing manually.

4. **Press and hold the shutter button halfway down.**

At this point, the following occurs:

- *Exposure metering begins.* The autoexposure meter analyzes the light and selects initial aperture (f-stop) and shutter speed settings, which are two critical exposure controls. These two settings appear in the viewfinder; in Figure 3-5, the shutter speed is 1/320 second, and the f-stop is f/13. Chapter 7 explains these two options in detail.

- *In Auto exposure mode, the built-in flash may pop up if the camera thinks additional light is needed.* You can set the Flash mode to Auto (normal) or Red-Eye Reduction mode. Or, if you prefer, you can disable the flash by changing the Flash mode to Off; the preceding section has details. (Or just move the Mode dial to the Auto Flash Off exposure setting.)

- *If autofocusing is enabled, the camera's autofocus system begins to do its thing.* In dim light, a little lamp located on the front of the camera, just to the left of the shutter button, may shoot out a beam of light. That lamp, the *autofocus-assist illuminator,* or *AF-assist lamp* for short, helps the camera measure the distance between your subject and the lens so that it can better establish focus.

When the camera has established focus, one or more of the points turns red, as shown in Figure 3-6, for a split second. The red focus points represent the areas of the frame that are now in focus. In the display at the bottom of the viewfinder, the green focus indicator, labeled in the figure, lights to give you further notice that focus has been achieved. Note that if your subject is moving, the light may blink on and off as the camera adjusts focus to track the subject. However, if the focus light blinks continuously, the camera can't achieve focus (and won't let you take the picture). Make sure that you're not too close to your subject; if problems persist, you may need to switch to manual focusing.

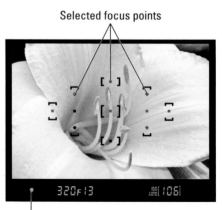

Selected focus points

Focus indicator light

Figure 3-6: The green light indicates that focus is set.

The autoexposure meter continues monitoring the light up to the time you take the picture, so the f-stop and shutter speed values in the viewfinder may change if the lighting conditions change.

5. **Press the shutter button the rest of the way down to record the image.**

While the camera sends the image data to the camera memory card, the memory card access lamp on the back of the camera lights. Don't turn off the camera or remove the memory card while the lamp is lit, or you may damage both camera and card.

When the recording process is finished, the picture appears briefly on the camera monitor. If the picture doesn't appear or you want to take a longer look at the image, see Chapter 5, which covers picture playback.

A few important points about working in the Auto and Auto Flash Off modes:

- **Exposure:** If an exposure meter blinks in the viewfinder or Shooting Information display, the camera can't select settings that will properly exposure the picture. See Chapter 7 for details about reading the exposure meter and coping with exposure problems. If you're shooting in the Auto Flash Off mode, changing to Auto and enabling flash typically provides a solution, however.

- **Autofocusing:** As with all the fully automatic modes, the camera uses the AF-A Focus mode. Focus is locked as long as you hold the shutter button halfway down unless the camera senses motion and adjusts focus as needed to track your subject.

  For the AF-Area mode, the Auto Area setting is selected by default. In that mode, the camera selects which autofocus points to use when establishing focus. Typically, focus is set on the closest object.

Chapter 8 explains how to modify this autofocusing behavior, but if you're having trouble getting the camera to focus on your subject, the easiest solution is often to switch to manual focusing.

I didn't include an example of a photo taken in Auto or Auto Flash Off mode because, frankly, the results that these settings create vary widely depending on how well the camera detects whether you're trying to shoot a portrait, landscape, action shot, or whatever, as well as on lighting conditions. But the bottom line is that both take a one-size-fits-all approach that may or may not take best advantage of your camera's capabilities. So if you want to more consistently take great pictures instead of merely good ones, I encourage you to explore the exposure, focus, and color information found in Part III so that you can abandon this mode in favor of modes that put more photographic decisions in your hands. At the very least, step up to one of the Scene modes, detailed in the next section.

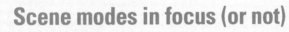

Scene modes in focus (or not)

When you focus the lens, either in autofocus or manual focus mode, you determine only the point of sharpest focus. The distance to which that sharp-focus zone extends from that point — what photographers call the *depth of field* — depends in part on the *aperture setting,* or *f-stop,* which is an exposure control. Some Scene modes are designed to choose aperture settings that deliver a certain depth of field.

The Portrait, Child, and Close Up Scene modes, for example, try to use a wide aperture (low f-stop number) because doing so shortens the depth of field, rendering backgrounds softly focused — an artistic choice that most people prefer for those types of shots. On the flip side, the Landscape mode tries to use a small aperture (high f-stop number), which produces a large depth of field, keeping both foreground and background objects sharp.

However, the range of apertures the camera can select varies depending on the light. In dim lighting, an open aperture is needed to properly expose the picture, and in bright light, a small aperture may be required to avoid overexposing the picture. Additionally, the range of available aperture settings varies from lens to lens,

and the amount of background blurring also increases as the distance between your subject and the background grows. So how much depth of field any Scene mode produces varies from shot to shot.

Another exposure-related control, *shutter speed,* also plays a focus role when you photograph moving objects. Moving objects appear blurry at slow shutter speeds; at fast shutter speeds, they appear sharply focused. In Sports mode, the camera tries to select a shutter speed fast enough to freeze action, but in dim lighting, that may not be possible: The less light, the slower the shutter speed needed to expose the photo. That means that even in Sports mode, a moving subject may appear blurry. Additionally, some Scene modes, such as Night Landscape and Candlelight, purposely choose a slow shutter speed to cope with the dark settings. For these modes, it's critical to use a tripod because any camera movement during the exposure can also blur the image.

To fully understand these issues — and to control focus and depth of field to a greater extent than the automated exposure modes allow — visit Chapters 7 and 8.

Taking Advantage of Scene Modes

In Auto and Auto Flash Off modes, the camera tries to figure out what type of picture you want to take by assessing what it sees through the lens. If you don't want to rely on the camera to make that judgment, check out the *Scene modes,* which are designed to capture specific scenes in ways that are traditionally considered best from a creative standpoint. For example, most people prefer portraits that have softly focused backgrounds. So in Portrait mode, the camera selects settings that can produce that type of background.

Again, because I presume that most people buying this book are more interested in the camera's more advanced options, I don't want to spend pages detailing each Scene mode, but the following sections provide a quick overview and offer some tips to help you get the best results.

Choosing a Scene mode

Scene modes are presented in two ways:

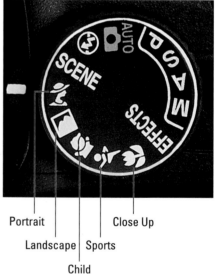

- ✔ **Primary Scene modes:** Five modes are deemed popular enough to have their own address on the Mode dial: Portrait, Landscape, Child, Sports, and Close Up. I labeled these modes in Figure 3-7. Just rotate the Mode dial to the icon representing the scene you want to shoot, and you're good to go.

- ✔ **Secondary Scene modes:** For the remaining modes, set the Mode dial to Scene. The Shooting Information display then shows an icon telling you which of the secondary Scene modes is active. For example, on the left screen in Figure 3-8, the icon indicates that Pet Portrait mode is selected. Rotate the Command dial to display a roulette wheel of Scene modes, as shown on the right in the figure. Keep rotating the dial until the mode you want to use is selected.

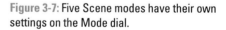

Figure 3-7: Five Scene modes have their own settings on the Mode dial.

Exposure mode icon

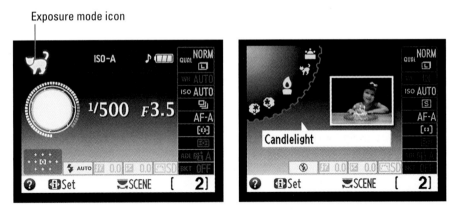

Figure 3-8: To access other Scene modes, set the Mode dial to Scene and rotate the Command dial.

For all Scene modes, you have access to the basic setup options discussed at the beginning of the chapter. The picture-taking process is the same as outlined in the steps I give for shooting in Auto mode, with two exceptions. First, to use flash in the Food mode, you must press the Flash button on the side of the camera to raise the built-in flash. Second, the default AF-Area mode, which determines which focus point the camera uses to establish focus, varies depending on your Scene mode, as follows:

- **Close Up, Candlelight, and Food:** In these modes, the default setting is Single Point AF-Area mode, which bases focus on a single point instead of all 11. Initially, the center focus point is selected as the target, but you can use the Multi Selector to move the point to a different position if necessary. (Sometimes you need to give the shutter button a quick half-press and release it before you can select a new focus point.) Remember to frame the picture with the selected point over your subject before you press the shutter button halfway when autofocusing.

- **Sports and Pet Portrait:** These two modes set the AF-Area mode to Dynamic Area. You start by selecting a single focus point, as with Single Point mode, but if the subject leaves that point, the camera looks to other points for focusing information — it's ideal for focusing on moving subjects. Just make sure to adjust framing as needed to keep your subject within the area covered by the 11 autofocus points.

- **All others:** The rest of the Scene modes use the Auto AF-Area mode, which means that the camera considers all 11 focus points and typically focuses on the closest object.

You can use the Quick Settings screen to change the AF-Area mode setting if you want; Figure 3-2 shows you where to look for the option, and Chapter 8 provides details.

Checking out the Scene modes

And now without further ado, here's a review of all the D5100 Scene modes:

Portrait mode

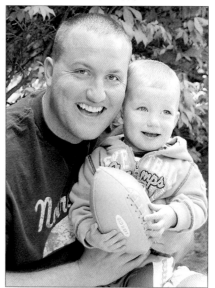

- **Portrait:** Choose this mode to produce the classic portrait look, with the subject set against a softly focused background, as shown in Figure 3-9. Colors are adjusted to produce natural-looking skin tones. You can set the flash to Auto, Auto with Red-Eye Reduction, or Off.

- **Landscape:** In the time-honored tradition of landscape photography, this mode produces crisp images with vivid blues and greens to create that bold, vacation-magazine look (see Figure 3-10). The camera also tries to select a high f-stop setting to extend depth of field, which keeps both foreground and background objects as sharp as possible. Flash is disabled.

Figure 3-9: Portrait mode produces soft backgrounds to help emphasize your subject.

- **Child:** A variation of Portrait mode, Child mode tries to use a slightly faster shutter speed than Portrait mode. The idea is that a faster shutter speed, which freezes action, helps you get a sharp picture of children who aren't sitting perfectly still. In addition, Child mode chooses an f-stop setting that produces a slightly larger zone of sharp focus — the idea being that the child can move a little closer or farther from the camera without going out of focus.

Like Portrait mode, Child mode also aims for a blurry background and natural skin tones. Colors of clothing and other objects, however, are rendered more vividly. That's a picture characteristic I dislike: I don't want background objects or clothing to take the eye away from the face of my subject. But shoot some samples in both Portrait and Child to see which one you prefer. Depending on the subject's attire and the background, you may not see much difference between the two modes. You have the same flash choices as with Portrait mode (Auto, Auto with Red-Eye Reduction, and Off).

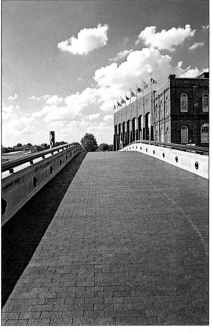

Figure 3-10: Landscape mode features bold colors and a large zone of sharp focus (depth of field).

✔ **Sports:** Select this mode to have a better chance of capturing a moving target without blur, as I did for my furkid in Figure 3-11. To accomplish this outcome, the camera selects a fast shutter speed, if possible. But remember that in dim lighting, it may need to use a slow shutter speed to expose the image — which typically means a shutter speed too low to freeze action. Flash is disabled. Note that in bright lighting, the Pet Portrait mode would produce similar results to what you see in Figure 3-11; that mode is also geared to using a fast shutter speed when possible.

✔ **Close Up:** As with Portrait and Child mode, the camera selects an aperture designed to produce short depth of field, which helps keep background objects from competing for attention with your main subject, as shown in Figure 3-12. You can set the Flash mode to Auto, Auto with Red-Eye Reduction, or Off.

✔ **Night Portrait:** This mode is designed to deliver a better-looking flash portrait at night (or in any dimly lit environment). It does so by constraining you to using Auto Slow-Sync, Auto Slow-Sync with Red-Eye Reduction, or Off Flash modes. In the first two Flash modes, the camera selects a shutter speed that results in a long exposure time. That slow shutter speed enables the camera to rely more on ambient light and less on the flash to expose the picture, which produces softer, more even lighting. If you disable flash, an even slower shutter speed is used.

Sports mode

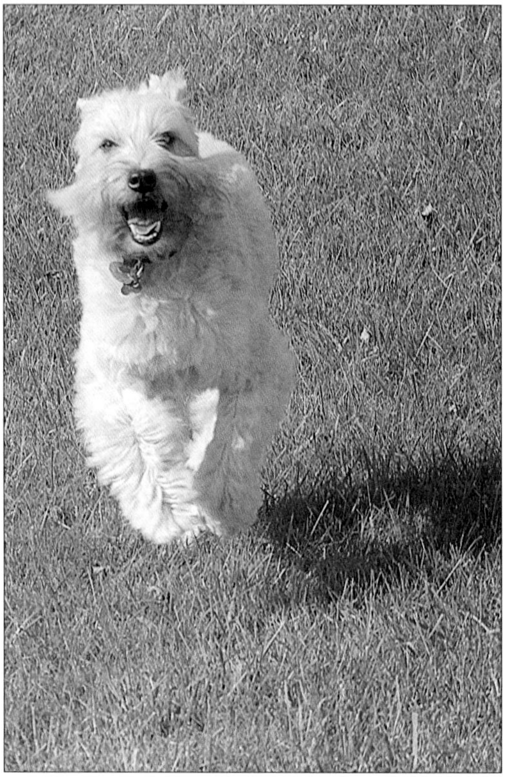

Figure 3-11: Try Sports mode to capture action.

I cover the issue of long exposure and slow-sync flash photography in detail in Chapter 7. For now, the critical thing to know is that the slower shutter speed means that you probably need a tripod. Your subjects also must stay perfectly still during the exposure.

✔ **Night Landscape:** This setting uses a slow shutter speed to capture nighttime city scenes, such as the one in Figure 3-13. Because of the long exposure time, use a tripod to avoid camera shake, which can blur the picture. Note that even when the camera remains perfectly still, any moving objects in the scene appear blurry, as does the fountain water in this example. This mode also is designed to reduce noise and avoid unnatural colors, both of which are common problems in night landscape shots. (See Chapter 7 for more information about noise; refer to Chapter 8 for help with color issues.) Flash is disabled.

✓ **Party/Indoor:** This mode is designed to capture indoor scenes that are lit by room lighting as well as the flash, using settings that produce a nice balance between the two light sources. If the lighting is very dim, the camera may use a slow shutter speed, so use a tripod to avoid blurring. You can set the flash to Auto, Auto with Red-Eye Reduction, or Off.

✓ **Beach/Snow:** Use this mode when you're photographing a scene with lots of bright areas, such as sand or snow, which can fool the camera's autoexposure system into underexposing the image. Flash is disabled.

✓ **Sunset:** Use this mode when photographing sunsets or sunrises and the sun is in the picture; the camera chooses settings designed to preserve the brilliant colors seen at those times of day. And, yep, you guessed it: A tripod produces a better chance of a sharp shot because the light will be dim and the camera will need to use a slow shutter speed.

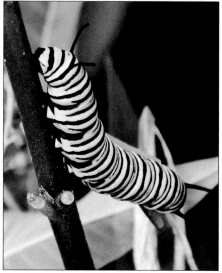

Figure 3-12: Close Up mode helps emphasize the subject by throwing the background out of focus.

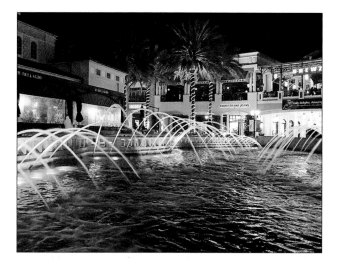

Figure 3-13: To capture this kind of after-dark photo, use Night Landscape mode and a tripod.

When photographing sunsets, don't stare at the sun directly through your viewfinder because this can permanently damage your vision, especially when you're using a telephoto lens. Flash is disabled in this mode.

- **Dusk/Dawn:** Use this mode to better capture the colors of the sky when shooting landscapes just before the sun rises, or just after the sun sets. Flash is disabled. I recommend using a tripod when using this mode as well because the shutter speed the camera selects may be very slow.

- **Pet Portrait:** Despite its name, this mode is just like Sports mode — meaning, you can use it to photograph any moving subject, not just pets — except that in dim lighting, the flash fires unless you set the Flash mode to Off. Note that if flash is required, the camera can raise the shutter speed no higher than 1/200 second, which may not be fast enough to capture a really speedy animal. See Chapter 7 for details about flash and shutter speed. If you do use flash, you can choose from the Auto and Auto with Red-Eye Reduction Flash modes.

- **Candlelight:** Use this mode when shooting subjects lit by candlelight. Flash is disabled, and because the ambient light will be dim, the shutter speed will likely be slow. Again, mount your camera on a tripod to avoid a blurry photo.

- **Blossom:** Use this mode when you're photographing a field of blooming flowers. Flash is disabled; again, use a tripod when photographing in low-light situations.

- **Autumn Colors:** This mode yields pictures with saturated reds and yellows of autumn leaves. The built-in flash is disabled. Mount your camera on a tripod in low-light situations.

- **Food:** This mode increases color saturation to render food more vividly. An important note about flash: Unlike other Scene modes, Food mode requires you to raise the built-in flash yourself if you want to add flash. To do so, press the Flash button; the flash pops up and sets itself to Fill Flash mode, which fires the flash regardless of the ambient light. To go flash-free, just close the flash unit. You can't adjust the Flash mode.

4

Exploring Live View Photography and Movie Making

In This Chapter

▷ Getting acquainted with Live View mode

▷ Customizing the Live View display

▷ Exploring Live View and movie autofocusing options

▷ Taking pictures in Live View mode

▷ Recording, playing, and trimming movies

*L*ike most newer dSLR cameras, the D5100 offers *Live View,* a feature that enables you to use the monitor instead of the viewfinder to compose photos. Turning on Live View is also the first step in recording a movie; using the viewfinder isn't possible when you shoot movies.

In many respects, taking a picture in Live View mode is no different from regular, through-the-viewfinder photography. But a few critical steps, including focusing, work very differently when you switch on Live View. So the first part of this chapter explains everything you need to know about Live View focusing as well as other aspects of the Live View system. Following that, you can find details on taking still photos in Live View mode and shooting, viewing, and editing movies.

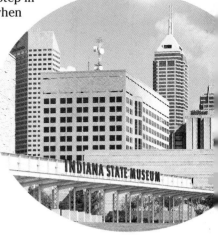

Using Your Monitor as a Viewfinder

The basics of taking advantage of Live View are pretty simple:

- **Switching to Live View:** Rotate the Live View switch, labeled in Figure 4-1, toward the back of the camera and release it. As soon as you take this step, you hear a clicking sound as the internal mirror that normally sends the image from the lens to the viewfinder flips up. The viewfinder goes dark, and the scene in front of the lens appears on the monitor.

- **Monitoring and adjusting camera settings:** During Live View, critical settings appear superimposed atop the live preview instead of on the Shooting Information screen. You can still access the Quick Settings screen by pressing the Info Edit button and adjust other options via external buttons and menus as usual.

- **Shooting photos:** Things work pretty much the same as for viewfinder photography — frame, focus, and press the shutter button. The main difference relates to autofocusing; see the upcoming section "Focusing in Live View Mode" for details.

- **Recording movies:** Press the red movie-record button, also labeled in Figure 4-1, to start and stop recording. Your focusing options are the same as for still photography in Live View mode. The section "Shooting Digital Movies," later in this chapter, explains all your movie-recording options.

Movie-record button

Live View switch

- **Picture playback during Live View:** Nothing different here, either: Just press the Playback button to shift from the Live View preview to playback mode. To return to shooting, press the button again or give the shutter button a quick half-press and release. Chapter 5 details photo playback; the section "Screening Your Movies," near the end of this chapter, explains movie-playback controls.

- **Exiting Live View mode:** Rotate the Live View switch a second time.

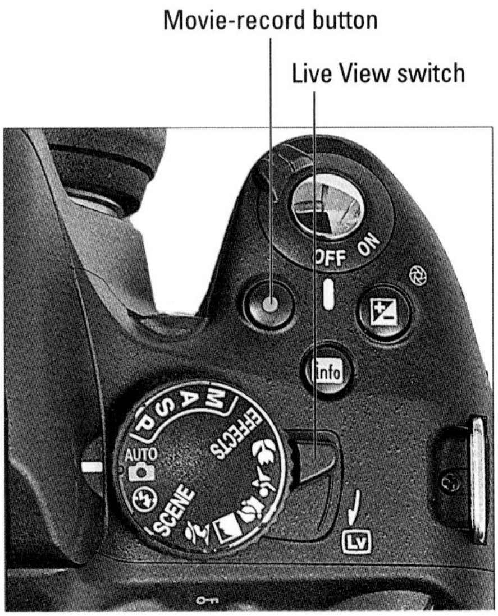

Figure 4-1: Use this switch to toggle Live View on and off; press the red button to start and stop movie recording.

As you may have guessed from the fact that I devote a whole chapter to Live View, these points comprise just the start of the story. The next two sections provide some additional general information that applies to both still photography and movie recording; later sections get into the nitty-gritty of taking pictures in Live View mode and using the movie functions.

Live View safety tips

Whether your goal is a still image or a movie, be aware of the following tips and warnings any time you enable Live View:

✐ **Cover the viewfinder to prevent light from seeping into the camera and affecting exposure.** The camera ships with a little cover designed just for this purpose. To install the cover, first remove the little rubber eyecup that surrounds the viewfinder; just slide the eyecup up and out of the little groove that holds it in place. Then slide the cover down into the groove and over the viewfinder. (Orient the cover so that the Nikon label faces the viewfinder.)

✐ **By default, the monitor turns off after three minutes of inactivity.** When the camera is 30 seconds away from turning off the monitor, a little countdown timer appears in the upper-left corner of the screen, as shown in Figure 4-2.

When you're composing still life images or other shots that require a bit of arranging, the three-minute window can be maddeningly short. Fortunately, you can delay the automatic shutdown if needed. Head for the Custom Setting menu, select the Timers/AE Lock option, and then select the Auto Off Timers option, as shown in Figure 4-3. Press OK to display the screen shown on the left in Figure 4-4, select Custom, and press OK again to display the screen shown on the right. Choose Live View and press OK once more to reveal a screen containing the available timer settings (3, 5, 10, or 15 minutes). Make your selection and press OK. Then highlight Done (toward the top of the right screen in Figure 4-4) and press OK again to lock in your changes.

Countdown warning

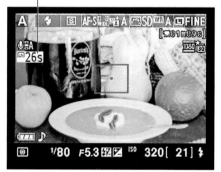

Figure 4-2: The timer tells you how many seconds until auto shutoff.

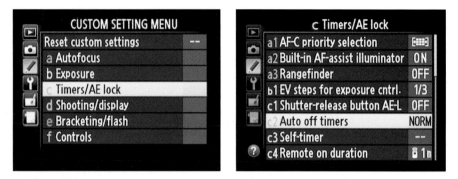

Figure 4-3: Select this menu option to access settings that adjust the timing of the automatic monitor shut down.

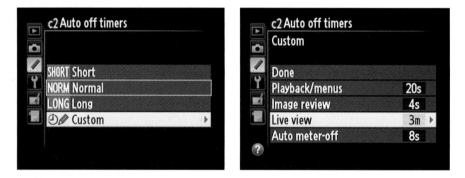

Figure 4-4: Choose Custom to modify the auto shutdown timing for Live View only.

Choosing the Long menu option (see the left screen in Figure 4-4) changes the delay time to ten minutes, but going that route also affects the timing of automatic shutdown for the exposure meter, image review, menu display, and playback display. Both the Short and Normal options set the Live View shutdown at three minutes, by the way. For complete information about the Auto Off Timers option, check out Chapter 1.

✔ **Using Live View for an extended period can harm your pictures and the camera.** When you work in Live View mode, the camera's innards heat up more than usual, and that extra heat can create the right electronic conditions for *noise,* a defect that gives your pictures a speckled look. Chapter 7 contains an illustration of this defect, which also is caused by long exposure times and high ISO Sensitivity settings.

Perhaps more importantly, the increased temperatures can damage the camera itself. For that reason, Live View is automatically disabled if the camera detects a critical heat level. In extremely warm environments, you may not be able to use Live View mode for very long before the system shuts down.

When the camera is 30 seconds or less from shutting down your Live View session to avoid overheating, the countdown timer shown in Figure 4-2 appears to let you know how many seconds you have left before the camera turns itself off. The warning doesn't appear during picture playback or when menus are active, however.

✓ **Aiming the lens at the sun or other bright lights also can damage the camera.** Of course, you can cause problems doing this even during normal shooting, but the possibilities increase when you use Live View. You not only can harm the camera's internal components but also the monitor.

✓ **Some lights may interfere with the Live View display.** The operating frequency of some types of lights, including fluorescent and mercury-vapor lamps, can create electronic interference that causes the monitor display to flicker or exhibit odd color banding.

Changing the Flicker Reduction option on the Setup menu may resolve this issue. You're supposed to match the setting to the frequency of the electrical current being used by the lights, but if you're not sure what that frequency is and an electrical engineer isn't handy, just try changing the setting and see which one works best. You can choose from two options, 50Hz and 60Hz; see Figure 4-5. (In the U.S. and Canada, the standard frequency is 60 Hz, and in Europe, it's 50 Hz.)

Either way, the interference affects only the monitor display; the flicker or banding doesn't show in your pictures or movies.

✓ **Live View puts additional strain on the camera battery.** The monitor is a big consumer of battery juice, so keep an eye on the battery level icon to avoid running out of power at a critical moment.

✓ **The risk of camera shake during handheld shots is increased.** When you use the viewfinder, you can help steady the camera by bracing it against your face. But with Live View, you have to hold

	SETUP MENU	
	Flicker reduction	60Hz
	Time zone and date	--
	Language	🗊
	Image comment	OFF
	Auto image rotation	ON
	Image Dust Off ref photo	--
	GPS	--
	Firmware version	--

Figure 4-5: To reduce display flickering that can occur when you shoot by fluorescent light, try changing the Flicker Reduction setting.

the camera away from your body to view the monitor, making it harder to keep the camera absolutely still. As Chapter 7 explains, any camera movement during the exposure can blur the shot, so using a tripod is the best course of action for Live View photography. If you do handhold the camera, enabling Vibration Reduction can help compensate for a bit of camera shake; Chapter 1 discusses this feature in more detail.

Because of these complications, I don't use Live View for still photography very often. Rather, I think of it as a special-purpose tool geared to situations where framing with the viewfinder is cumbersome. I find Live View most helpful for still-life, tabletop photography, especially in cases that require a lot of careful arrangement of the scene.

For example, I have a shooting table that's about waist high. Normally, I put my camera on a tripod, come up with an initial layout of the objects I want to photograph, set up my lights, and then check the scene through the viewfinder. Then there's a period of refining the object placement, the lighting, and so on. If I'm shooting from a high angle, requiring the camera to be positioned above the table and pointing downward, I have to stand on my tiptoes or get a stepladder to check things through the viewfinder between each compositional or lighting change. At lower angles, where the camera is tabletop height or below, I have to either bend over or kneel to look through the viewfinder, causing no end of later aches and pains to the back and knees. With Live View, I can alleviate much of that bothersome routine (and pain) because I can adjust the articulating monitor so that I can see how things look no matter what the camera position.

Customizing the Live View display

Whether you're shooting movies or still photos, you can choose from the following display styles in Live View mode. Press the Info button to cycle through the different styles.

- ✔ **Show Indicators:** By default, the display uses this mode, which reveals the shooting data shown in Figure 4-6. Later sections of this chapter detail what each of the little symbols represents. Some symbols, such as those representing flash settings, appear only when you have the feature enabled.

- ✔ **Hide Indicators:** To unclutter the screen, press the Info button to cycle from the default display to this mode, which presents only the information shown on the left in Figure 4-7.

In this display mode, as well as in the one described next, you may see four tiny horizontal markers near the corners of the image display area. They appear to show you how much of the vertical image area will not be included in the recorded movie if you set the

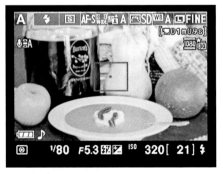

Figure 4-6: In the default Live View mode, you see this shooting data on the monitor.

movie resolution, or frame size, to a setting that produces a 16:9 frame aspect ratio. (The only setting that doesn't produce this ratio is 640 x 424, which captures the same aspect ratio as a still photo, 3:2.) I labeled one of the markers in Figure 4-7.

✔ **Framing Grid:** Press Info one more time to display a grid over the image, as shown on the right in Figure 4-7. The grid is helpful when you need to precisely align objects in your photo. To return to the default display, give the Info button one more push.

Movie frame
height marker

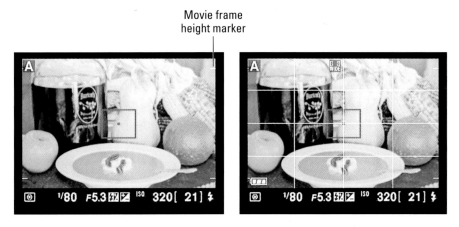

Figure 4-7: Press the Info button to change to one of these other display modes.

 If you connect your camera to an HDMI (High-Definition Multimedia Interface) device, you no longer see the live scene on your camera monitor. Instead, the view appears on your video display. In that scenario, the arrangement of the shooting information on the screen may appear slightly different than in the examples in this chapter. Also note that if you connect the camera to an HDMI-CEC device, you may need to adjust an option on the Setup menu. Select HDMI, press OK, and turn off the Device Control option. Otherwise, you can't record a movie or take a picture in Live View mode. See the Chapter 5 section related to connecting the camera to a television for more HD details.

Focusing in Live View Mode

As with viewfinder photography, you can opt for autofocusing or manual focusing during Live View shooting, assuming that your lens supports both. If you use the kit lens, set the lens switch to A for autofocusing and to M position to focus manually. (With other lenses, check the lens instruction manual for help.)

It's important to understand that the camera typically takes longer to autofocus in Live View mode than it does during viewfinder photography. (The difference is because of the type of autofocusing the camera must use when in Live View.) So for the fastest autofocusing response, take the camera out of Live View mode.

For times when you opt for Live View, you can tweak the camera's focusing performance through two settings: Focus mode and AF-Area mode. You can view the current settings at the top of the screen when you use the default display mode, as shown in Figure 4-8.

The two options affect autofocusing as follows:

Focus mode

AF-Area mode

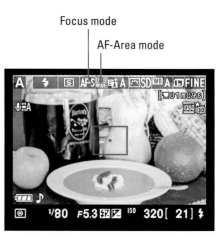

- **Focus mode:** If you use auto-focusing, this option determines whether the camera locks focus when you press the shutter button halfway, or continually adjusts focus up to the moment you take the shot (or throughout your entire movie recording). A third Focus mode option is provided for times when you want to focus manually.

- **AF-Area mode:** With this option, you specify what part of the frame the autofocus system should consider when establishing focus. Note that you can't control this setting in the Auto and Auto Flash Off exposure modes or when you use the Miniature Effects mode (covered in Chapter 10).

Figure 4-8: The current Focus mode and AF-Area mode settings appear here.

You get these same two options for viewfinder photography, but the settings available for Live View are different from those provided for viewfinder photography. See the next two sections to explore the Live View offerings; visit Chapter 8 for information about the Focus mode and AF-Area mode settings available for viewfinder photography.

Choosing a Focus mode: Auto, continuous auto, or manual?

Through the Focus mode setting, you can specify whether you want the auto-focus system to lock focus at the time you press the shutter button halfway or continue to adjust focus until you take the picture. Or you can tell the camera that you prefer to focus manually, by twisting the focusing ring on the lens.

Here's how things work at each of the Focus mode settings:

↙ **AF-S (single-servo autofocus):** The camera locks focus when you depress the shutter button halfway. (This focus setting is one of the few that works the same during Live View shooting as it does during viewfinder photography.) Generally speaking, AF-S works best for focusing on still subjects.

↙ **AF-F (full-time servo AF):** The main purpose of AF-F is to enable continuous focus adjustment throughout a movie recording. To use this option, keep your finger *off* the shutter button. Just switch the camera to the AF-F mode, wait for it to find its focus point, and then press the movie-record button to start recording. Focus is adjusted as needed if your subject moves through the frame or you pan the camera. If you decide to lock focus, you can depress the shutter button halfway. As soon as you release the button, continuous autofocusing begins again.

Unfortunately, there's a downside that makes AF-F less than ideal. If you shoot a movie with sound recording enabled, the camera's internal microphone picks up the sound of the autofocus motor as it adjusts focus. So if pristine audio is your goal, use AF-S mode and lock focus before you begin recording, or abandon autofocus altogether and focus manually. As another option, you can attach an external microphone to the camera and place it far enough away that it doesn't pick up the camera sounds. See the section "Reviewing other movie settings" for more details.

For still photography, focus is locked at the point you press the shutter button halfway, just as with AF-S mode. The only difference between the two modes is that AF-F mode finds a focusing target and keeps adjusting it until you press the shutter button halfway. You might find this option helpful when you're not sure where a moving subject will be when you want to snap the picture: As your subject moves or you pan the camera to keep the subject in the frame, autofocus is adjusted so that when the moment comes to take the shot, you just press halfway, pause, and take the picture. That said, I prefer the continuous autofocusing options available for viewfinder photography for this kind of shot — I find them easier and more reliable than the Live View AF-F option.

↙ **MF (manual focus):** Select this option to focus manually, by twisting the focusing ring on the lens.

With the kit lens and some other lenses, simply moving the switch on the lens from the A (autofocus) to M (manual focus) position automatically selects the MF Focus mode setting. If you're not using the kit lens, check your lens instruction manual for information about whether you need to set the Focus mode to MF to focus manually.

To adjust the Focus mode setting, press the Info Edit button to bring up the Quick Settings screen. Highlight the Focus mode option, as shown on the left in Figure 4-9, press OK to display the second screen in the figure, and then highlight the setting you want to use. Press OK, and then press the Info Edit button again to return to the Live View display (or just press the shutter button halfway and release it).

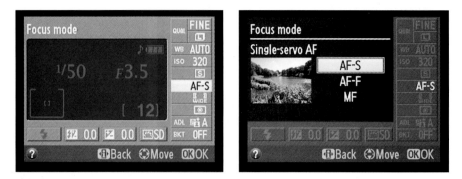

Figure 4-9: Change the Focus mode via the Quick Settings screen.

Selecting a focusing target (AF-Area mode)

Through the AF-Area mode, you give the camera's autofocusing system instructions on what part of the frame contains your subject so that it can set the focusing distance correctly.

 As with the Focus mode, the Live View AF-Area mode options are different than the ones available for viewfinder photography, which I detail in Chapter 8. For Live View photography and movie recording, you can choose from the following settings:

 ✔ **Wide Area:** In this mode, you use the Multi Selector to move a little rectangular focusing frame around the screen to specify your desired focusing spot. The red rectangle you see in Figure 4-8 is the Wide Area focusing frame.

 ✔ **Normal Area:** This mode works the same way as Wide Area autofocusing but uses a smaller focusing frame. The idea is to enable you to base focus on a very specific area. With such a small focusing frame, however, you can easily miss your focus target when handholding the camera. If you move the camera slightly as you're setting focus and the focusing frame shifts off your subject as a result, focus will be incorrect. So for best results, use a tripod in this mode.

 ✔ **Face Priority:** Designed for portrait shooting, this mode attempts to hunt down and focus on faces. Face Detection typically works only when your subjects are facing the camera, however. If the camera can't detect a face, you see a plain red focus frame, and things work as they do in Wide Area mode. In a group shot, the camera typically focuses on the closest face.

 ✔ **Subject Tracking:** This mode tracks a subject as it moves through the frame and is designed for focusing on a moving subject. But subject tracking isn't always as successful as you might hope. For a subject that occupies only a small part of the frame — say, a butterfly flitting through a garden — autofocus may lose its way. Ditto for subjects moving at a face pace, subjects getting larger or smaller in the frame (when moving toward you and then away from you, for example), or scenes in which not much contrast exists between the subject or the background. Oh, and scenes in which there's a great deal of contrast can create problems, too. My take on this feature is that when the conditions are right, it works well, but otherwise, the Wide Area setting gives you a better chance of keeping a moving subject in focus.

In the Auto and Auto Flash Off exposure modes or the Miniature Effects mode, you have no control over this setting; the camera uses the Face Priority setting for Auto and Auto Flash Off and Wide Area for the Miniature mode. In other exposure modes, adjust the setting by pressing the Info Edit button to shift to Quick Settings mode. Then highlight the AF-Area mode icon, as shown on the left in Figure 4-10. The icon represents the currently selected setting; for example, in the figure, the Wide Area mode is active. To change to a different setting, press OK. You then see the four focusing options, as shown on the right in the figure; again, the currently selected one is highlighted initially. Use the Multi Selector to highlight your choice, press OK, and then press the Info Edit button again or give the shutter button a quick half-press to exit the Quick Settings screen.

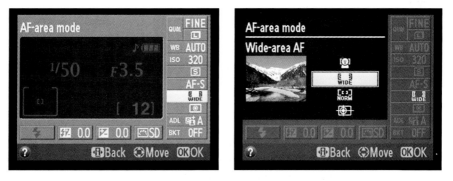

Figure 4-10: Adjust the AF-Area mode through the Quick Settings screen.

Choosing the right focusing pairs

To recap, the way the camera sets focus during Live View and movie shooting depends on your Focus mode and AF-Area mode settings. If you use the kit lens (or a similar lens), you also need to set the switch on the lens barrel to either A for autofocusing or M for manual focusing. For other lenses, check the lens instruction manual for information about this step.

Until you get fully acquainted with all the various combinations of Focus mode and AF-Area mode and can make your own decisions about which pairings you like best, I recommend the following settings:

✔ **For moving subjects:** Set the Focus mode to AF-F and the AF-Area mode to Wide Area. You also can try the Subject Tracking AF-Area mode, but see my comments in the preceding section regarding which subjects may not be well suited to that mode. Either way, remember that in AF-F mode, you don't press the shutter button halfway until you're ready to lock focus and take the picture — focusing begins immediately after you switch the Autofocus mode to AF-F and continues *until* you press the shutter button halfway.

For movie recording, keep your finger off the shutter button if you want the camera to continuously adjust focus during the recording. Just remember that if you use the camera's internal microphone, the sound of the autofocus motor may be audible in the movie. Attach an external microphone or record audio using a separate device to avoid this problem.

✔ **For stationary subjects:** Set the Focus mode to AF-S and the AF-Area mode to Wide Area. Or, if you're shooting a portrait, give the Face Priority AF-Area option a try.

Press the shutter button halfway to initiate focusing; after the camera finds the focusing point, focus is locked. For movie recording, you can then release the shutter button. For still photography, keep your finger on the button — otherwise, focus will be reset when you press the button to take the picture.

✔ **For difficult-to-focus subjects:** If the camera has trouble finding the right focusing point when you use autofocus, don't spend too much time fiddling with the different autofocus settings. Just set the camera to manual focusing and twist the focusing ring to set focus yourself.

Autofocusing in Live View and Movie mode

Having laid out all the whys and wherefores of the Live View autofocusing options, I offer the following summary of the steps involved in choosing the autofocus settings and then actually setting focus:

1. Choose the Focus mode (AF-S or AF-F) and AF-Area mode.

You adjust both settings via the Quick Settings screen. Remember, the button that takes you to that screen is the Info Edit button, shown in the margin here. Refer to Figures 4-9 and 4-10 if you need help locating the two options. Also remember that the camera restricts you to using the Face Priority AF-Area mode in the Auto and Auto Flash Off modes and Wide Area mode in the Miniature Effects mode.

If you set the Focus mode to AF-F, the autofocus system perks up and starts hunting for a focus point immediately.

2. **Locate the focus frame in the Live View display.**

The appearance of the frame depends on the AF-Area mode, as follows:

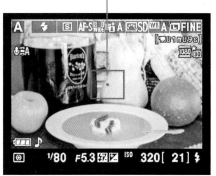

Focusing frame

- *Wide Area and Normal Area:* You see a red rectangular frame, as shown in Figure 4-11. (The figure shows the frame at the size it appears in Wide Area mode; it's smaller in Normal Area mode.)

- *Face Priority:* If the camera locates faces, you see a yellow focus frame around each one, as shown on the left in Figure 4-12. One frame sports corner brackets inside the frame — in the figure, it's the frame on the right. The brackets indicate the face that the camera will use to set focusing distance.

Figure 4-11: The red box represents the focusing frame in Wide Area and Normal Area AF-Area mode.

If you don't see any yellow boxes but instead see a plain red frame, the camera can't detect a face and will set focus as it would if you were using Wide Area mode.

- *Subject Tracking:* A focusing frame like the one shown on the right in Figure 4-12 appears.

In AF-F mode, the frame turns green when the object under the frame is in focus. The frame blinks any time focus is being reset.

Selected frame   Subject Tracking focus frame

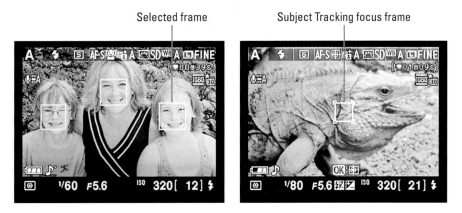

Figure 4-12: The focusing frame appears differently in Face Priority mode (left) and Subject Tracking mode (right).

3. **Use the Multi Selector to position the focusing frame over your subject.**

   For example, I moved the focus frame over the garnish on the soup bowl for my example image, as shown on the left in Figure 4-13.

   In Face Priority mode, you can use the Multi Selector to move the box with the double-yellow border — which indicates the final focusing point — from face to face in a group portrait. In the Wide Area and Normal Area modes, press OK to quickly move the focus point to the center of the frame.

4. **In Subject Tracking AF-Area mode, press OK to initiate focus tracking.**

   If your subject moves, the focus frame moves with it. To stop tracking, press OK again. (You may need to take this step if your subject leaves the frame — press OK to stop tracking, reframe, and then press OK to start tracking again.)

5. **In AF-S autofocus mode, press the shutter button halfway down to start autofocusing.**

6. **Wait for the focus frame to turn green, as shown on the right in Figure 4-13.**

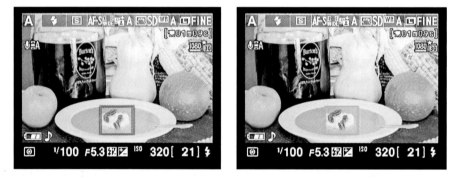

Figure 4-13: The focus frame turns green if the autofocus system was successful.

What happens next depends on your Autofocus mode:

- *AF-S mode:* You also hear a little beep (assuming you didn't disable the beep, which you can do via the Beep option, found on the Shooting/Display section of the Custom Setting menu). Focus is locked as long as you keep the shutter button pressed halfway.

- *AF-F mode:* Focus will be adjusted if the subject moves. The focus frame turns back to red (or yellow or white) if focus is lost; when the frame turns green and stops blinking, focus has been achieved again. You can lock focus by pressing the shutter button halfway. In most cases, the camera will reset focus on your subject when you press the button even if the focus frame is already green.

7. **(Optional) Press the Zoom In button to magnify the display to double-check focus.**

   Each press gives you a closer look at the subject.

   As when you magnify an image when you're viewing photos in playback mode, a small thumbnail appears in the corner of the screen, with the yellow highlight box indicating the area that's currently being magnified, as shown in Figure 4-14. Press the Multi Selector to scroll the display if needed.

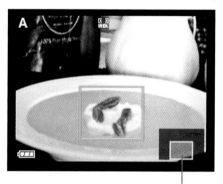

Magnified area

   To reduce the magnification level, press the Zoom Out button. If you're not using Subject Tracking mode, you can also press OK to quickly return to normal magnification.

Figure 4-14: Press the Zoom In button to magnify the display and double-check focus.

Manual focusing for Live View and movie photography

For manual focusing with the kit lens or a similarly featured lens, just set the A/M switch to M. The camera automatically changes the Focus mode setting to MF (manual focus). For other lenses, refer to the lens instruction manual to find out how to set the lens to manual focusing. Then twist the lens focusing ring to bring the scene into focus. But note a few quirks:

✐ Even with manual focusing, you still see the focusing frame; its appearance depends on the current AF-Area mode setting. In Face Priority mode, the frame automatically jumps into place over a face, if it detects one. And if you press OK when Subject Tracking mode is enabled, the camera tries to track the subject under the frame until you press OK again. I find these two behaviors irritating, so I always set the AF-Area mode to Wide Area or Normal Area for manual focusing.

✐ The focusing frame doesn't turn green to indicate successful focusing as it does with autofocusing.

✐ You can press the Zoom In button to check focus in manual mode just as you can during autofocusing. See Step 7 in the preceding section for details. Press the Zoom Out button to reduce the magnification level.

Shooting Still Pictures in Live View Mode

After sorting out the focusing options, the rest of the steps involved in taking a picture in Live View mode are essentially the same as for viewfinder photography. Here's the drill:

1. **Turn the Mode dial (on top of the camera) to select an exposure mode.**

   Chapter 3 introduces you to the fully automatic modes (Auto, Auto Flash Off, and Scene modes). Chapter 7 provides help with the advanced modes (P, S, A, and M). Chapter 10 shows you how to use Effects mode.

   In Auto and Auto Flash Off modes, the camera may shift to the Portrait, Landscape, or Close Up Scene mode if it thinks one of those modes will do a better job of capturing your subject. The Exposure mode icon in the top right corner of the display (refer to Figure 4-15) indicates which mode the camera selected for you.

2. **Enable Live View by rotating the Live View switch and releasing it.**

3. **Review and adjust picture settings.**

   In Live View mode, picture settings appear over the live preview rather than on the Shooting Information screen. Which settings you can access depends on your exposure mode; Figure 4-15 shows the options available in the advanced modes (P, S, A, and M).

   If you don't see the same type of data on your monitor, press the Info button to cycle through the possible Live View display modes. The one shown in Figure 4-15 is the default.

   Some settings, such as Exposure Compensation and Flash Compensation, appear only when those features are enabled. If you enable automatic bracketing, you also see bracketing indicators above the shots remaining value. When AE Lock (autoexposure lock) is engaged, an AE-L symbol appears to the right of the Metering mode symbol. And about that Metering mode symbol: Although the camera lets you change that setting, it always meters using the Matrix setting anyway. See Chapter 7 for details about all these features.

   For some settings, the impact of your selected option is visible in the monitor. Change the White Balance setting, for example, and you can see colors shift in the live preview. But Exposure Compensation adjustments aren't always reflected by the monitor brightness. When you increase or decrease exposure using this feature, the image on the monitor becomes brighter or darker only up to shifts of EV +/–3.0, even though you can select values as high as +5.0 and as low as –5.0. See Chapter 7 to get a primer on Exposure Compensation.

4. **If focusing manually, twist the focusing ring to set focus.**

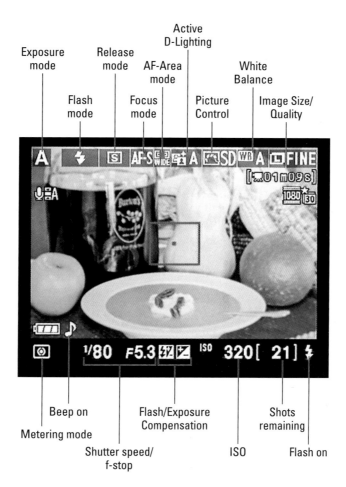

Figure 4-15: You can view these picture settings in the default Live View display mode.

5. **If using autofocusing, position the focus frame over the subject.**

   And if you're using Subject Tracking autofocus, press OK to initiate tracking. See the previous section for details.

6. **In AF-S mode, press the shutter button halfway to initiate autofocusing.**

   Focus is locked when the focus frame turns green.

   Regardless of the Autofocus mode, exposure metering begins when you adjust the shutter button halfway and is adjusted until you take the picture.

7. **Press the shutter button the rest of the way to take the picture.**

Shooting Digital Movies

Your D5100 offers the capability to record high-def movies up to 20 minutes in length, with or without sound. The next two sections explain how to choose recording options; following that, you can find step-by-step instructions for recording, playing, and editing a movie.

Choosing the video type and quality

The first two recording options to consider are Video Mode and Movie Quality.

Video Mode, found on the Setup menu and shown in Figure 4-16, tells the camera whether you want your movies to adhere to the NTSC or PAL video standard. *NTSC* is used in North America; *PAL* is used in Europe and certain other countries. Your camera should already be set to match the country in which it was purchased, but it never hurts to check. (Don't worry about what NTSC and PAL mean — they're just acronyms for the technical names of the standards.)

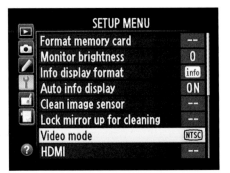

Figure 4-16: The Video Mode determines what Movie Quality settings are available.

Okay, that one's straightforward enough. Now onto the more complex technical soup of the Movie Quality option. This setting determines the resolution (frame size), aspect ratio, and frame rate of the movie, as well as the level of file compression — which all affect the final quality of the movie.

To start looking at your options, choose Movie Settings from the Shooting menu, as shown on the left in Figure 4-17, and then select Movie Quality, as shown on the right. If you chose NTSC for the Video Mode setting, you then see the screen shown in Figure 4-18. (More about how it varies when PAL is selected in a moment.)

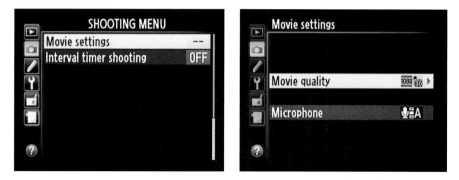

Figure 4-17: The Movie Settings option on the Shooting menu leads to the Movie Quality and Microphone settings.

The first thing to note is that you can choose from various combinations of resolution, or frame size, and frames per second, as follows:

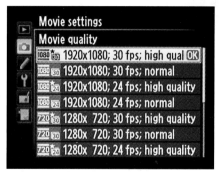

Figure 4-18: The Movie Quality setting determines resolution, aspect ratio, frames per second, and file compression amount.

- **Resolution:** You can choose from three resolution settings, or frame sizes, measured in pixels:
  - *1920 x 1080:* Produces a so-called Full HD (High Definition) movie that has a 16:9 aspect ratio.
  - *1280 x 720:* Standard HD, also 16:9.
  - *640 x 424:* A much smaller frame size with an aspect ratio of 3:2, the same as still images captured by the D5100. (This smaller resolution can be useful for online videos.)
- **Frame rate (fps):** The *frame rate,* measured in *frames per second (fps),* determines the smoothness of the playback. If NTSC is selected as the Video Mode, frame rate options include 24 fps, which is the same frame

rate as film motion pictures, or 30 fps, the NTSC standard for television-quality video. (Well, technically, the NTSC frame rate is 29.97 fps.) If the Video Mode setting is PAL, you can choose from 24 fps and the PAL video standard, 25 fps.

Again, assuming NTSC as the video standard, you can choose from 24 or 30 fps when the resolution is 1920 x 1080 or 1280 x 720. When you select 640 x 424 as the resolution, the only available frame rate is 30 fps.

For each combination, you also can choose a High or Normal setting. Your choice determines how much compression is applied to the video file, which in turn affects the *bit rate,* or how much data is used to represent one second of video, measured in Mbps (megabytes per second). The High setting results in a higher bit rate, which means better quality and larger files. Choose Normal for a lower bit rate and smaller files.

In addition to the High and Normal settings, the resolution and frame rate also affect file size. Table 4-1 shows you the file size of a 20-minute video at each of the Movie Quality settings. Again, the table assumes NTSC as the Video Mode.

Table 4-1		Twenty-Minute Movie File Sizes*		
Frame Size	*FPS*	*Quality*	*Bit Rate*	*File Size*
1920 x 1080	30 or 24	High	18 Mbps	2.9GB
		Normal	10 Mbps	1.7GB
1280 x 720	30	High	10 Mbps	1.7GB
		Normal	6 Mbps	1.1GB
	24	High	8 Mbps	1.4GB
		Normal	5 Mbps	1.0GB
640 x 424	30	High	4 Mbps	0.8GB
		Normal	2 Mbps	0.5GB

Settings available when NTSC is selected as the Video Mode setting.

Reviewing other movie settings

Compared to the mind-numbing intricacies of the video specifications outlined in the preceding section, the rest of the movie settings you can adjust are fairly straightforward. Here's a look at your options:

✓ **Sound recording:** You can record sound using the camera's built-in microphone, labeled in Figure 4-19, or attach an external microphone to the jack labeled on the right. Either way, to enable sound recording and adjust the microphone sensitivity, select the Movie Settings option on the Shooting menu and then select Microphone, as shown on the left in Figure 4-20. Press OK to display the settings shown on the right in the figure.

Microphone   External microphone jack

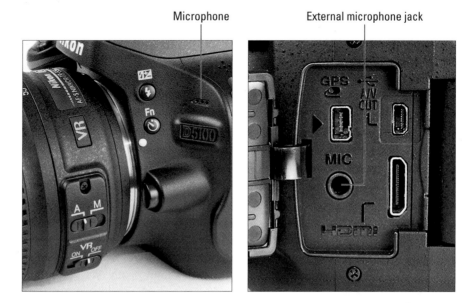

Figure 4-19: You can capture audio using the internal microphone (left) or plug an external microphone into the microphone jack (right).

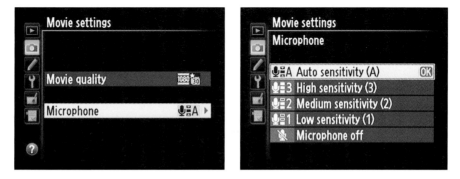

Figure 4-20: Disable audio recording or set the microphone sensitivity level through this menu option.

If you enable sound and choose the Auto Sensitivity option, the camera automatically adjusts the volume according to the level of the ambient noise. Or you can choose one of the other settings to control the microphone sensitivity yourself. Choose Microphone Off to record a silent movie.

When using the built-in microphone, make sure that you don't inadvertently cover it with your finger. And keep in mind that anything *you* say will be picked up by the mike along with any other audio present in the scene. When an external microphone is attached, the internal microphone goes to sleep.

✔ **Exposure:** The camera automatically sets exposure, using matrix metering (whole-frame metering) to choose the proper aperture, shutter speed, and ISO Sensitivity setting. But depending on the setting of the Mode dial, you can take advantage of the following exposure controls:

  - *Aperture:* You can adjust f-stop before recording if you set the Mode dial to A (aperture-priority autoexposure) or M (manual exposure). This option enables you to control depth of field in your movies; Chapter 7 explains the aperture setting's role in depth of field. In A mode, rotate the Command dial to change the f-stop; in M mode, press and hold the Exposure Compensation button while rotating the dial to adjust the f-stop. (See the next point for more about Exposure Compensation.)

  - *Exposure Compensation:* Exposure Compensation enables you to override the camera's autoexposure decisions, asking for a brighter or darker picture. You can apply this adjustment for movies when the Mode dial is set to P, S, A, or M or when you shoot a movie using the Night Vision effect. However, you're limited to an adjustment range of EV +3.0 to –3.0 rather than the usual five steps that are possible during normal photography. See Chapter 7 to find out more about this feature. To adjust the setting, press and hold the Exposure Compensation button while rotating the Command dial *unless* you're using Manual (M) exposure mode. In that mode, you must use the Quick Settings screen to apply Exposure Compensation; pressing the button while rotating the Command dial changes the f-stop in M exposure mode.

Just to head off any possible confusion: For viewfinder photography, Exposure Compensation isn't needed in M exposure mode; if you want a brighter or darker exposure, you just change your aperture, shutter speed, or ISO Sensitivity settings. But because the camera doesn't give you control over shutter speed or ISO during movie recording, you need some way to tell the camera that you want a brighter or darker picture, and Exposure Compensation is it.

• *Autoexposure lock:* In any exposure mode except Auto or Auto Flash Off, you can lock exposure at the current settings by pressing and holding the AE-L/AF-L button. Chapter 7 also tells you more about autoexposure lock.

✔ **Focusing:** You can choose auto or manual focusing and control autofocusing behavior via the Focus mode and AF-Area mode settings. Earlier parts of this chapter provide a primer in focusing.

✔ **White Balance and Picture Control:** The colors in your movie are rendered according to the current White Balance and Picture Control settings. Chapter 8 explains how to adjust these settings, but you have control over the options only when the Mode dial is set to P, S, A, or M.

Want to record a black-and-white movie? Open the Shooting menu, choose Set Picture Control, and select Monochrome. Instant *film noir*.

✔ **Effects:** You can apply any of the Effects filters to your movie as it's recorded. Set the dial to Effects, choose the effect you want to use, and then start and stop recording as usual. Chapter 10 talks more about the Effects mode. One caveat: For movies recorded using the Miniature Effect feature, sound is disabled, and autofocusing during the recording is also not possible. You can record up to 45 minutes of video, but the video is played back at high speed, compressing those 45 minutes into a maximum playback length of three minutes. (The digital magic required to create the effect is to blame for these limitations.)

One more technical point: Movies are created in the MOV format, which means you can play them on your computer using most movie-playback programs. You also can view movies in Nikon View NX2, the free software provided with your camera. If you want to view your movies on a TV, you can connect the camera to the TV, as I explain in Chapter 5. Or if you have the necessary computer software, you can convert the MOV file to a format that a standard DVD player can recognize and then burn the converted file to a DVD disk. You also can edit your movie in a program that can work with MOV files.

Starting and stopping recording

After you establish all the options explained in the preceding section, there's not much left to do to shoot a movie:

1. Rotate the Live View switch and release it to switch to Live View mode.

By default, the shooting information shown in Figure 4-21 appears along with your subject in the monitor. You can view the Movie Quality setting, whether sound is enabled, and the length of the movie that will fit in the remaining space on your memory card.

Microphone setting   Recording time available

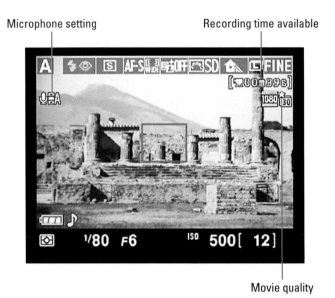

Movie quality

Figure 4-21: These settings relate to options available for movie recording.

2. **Set focus as outlined earlier in this chapter, in the section "Focusing in Live View Mode."**

3. **To begin recording, press the red movie-record button (just behind the shutter button, on top of the camera).**

    Most of the shooting data disappears from the screen, and a red Rec symbol flashes in the top-left corner. As recording progresses, the time remaining value shows you how many more seconds of video you can record. (The length is dependent on the Movie Quality settings you choose and the amount of space on your memory card.) Also note the number found within the brackets in the lower-right corner of the screen — 12, in Figure 4-21. That number indicates how many still photos you can fit in the empty card space if you stop recording, and as each second of recording ticks by and card space is depleted, the value that indicates the number of still shots remaining drops.

4. **To stop recording, press the movie-record button again.**

    You can stop your recording and capture a still image in one fell swoop: Just press and hold the shutter button down until you hear the shutter release.

Screening Your Movies

To play your movie, press the Playback button. In single-image playback mode, you can spot a movie file by looking for the little movie-camera icon in the top-left corner of the screen, as shown on the left in Figure 4-22. Press OK to start playback.

In the Thumbnail and Calendar playback modes, you see little filmstrip dots along the edges of movie files. This time, press OK twice: once to shift to single-image view and again to start movie playback.

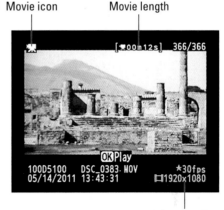

Figure 4-22: The little movie-camera symbol tells you you're looking at a movie file.

After playback begins, the data in the top-right corner shows you how many seconds of the movie have played so far along with the total length of the movie, as labeled in Figure 4-23. In addition, little playback control icons appear at the bottom of the screen to remind you that you can use the Multi Selector, Zoom In, and Zoom Out buttons to control playback, as follows:

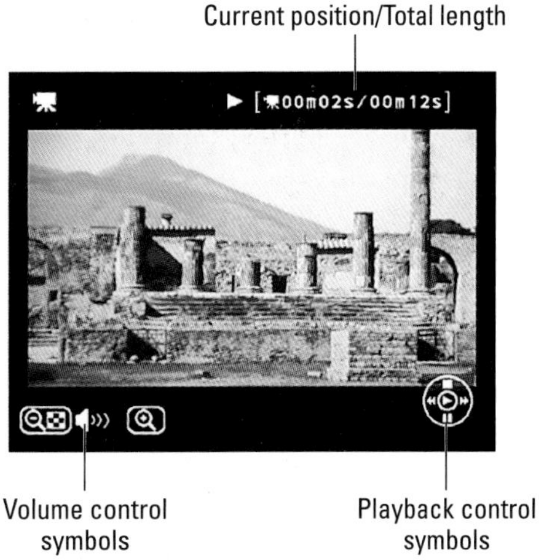

- **Stop playback:** Press the Multi Selector up.

- **Pause/resume playback:** Press down to pause playback; press OK to resume playback.

- **Fast forward/rewind:** Press the Multi Selector right or left to fast-forward or rewind the movie. Press again to double the fast-forward or rewind speed; keep pressing to increase the speed to 8 times or 16 times normal. Hold the button down to fast-forward or rewind all the way to the end or beginning of the movie.

Figure 4-23: The symbols at the bottom of the screen remind you to use the Zoom In and Zoom Out buttons to adjust volume and use the Multi Selector to start, stop, and pause playback.

✔ **Advance frame by frame:** First, press the Multi Selector down to pause playback. Then press the Multi Selector right to advance one frame; press left to go back one frame.

✔ **Adjust playback volume:** See the little markings labeled volume control symbols in Figure 4-23? They remind you that you can press the Zoom In button to increase playback volume. For a quieter playback, press the Zoom Out button.

Chapter 5 explains how to connect your camera to a television so you can play your movies "on the big screen."

Trimming movies

You can do some limited movie editing in camera. I emphasize: *limited* editing. You can trim frames from the start of a movie and clip off frames from the end, and that's it.

To eliminate frames from the beginning of the movie, take these steps:

1. **Display your movie in full-frame view.**

2. **Press OK to begin playback.**

3. **When you reach the first frame you want to keep, press the Multi Selector down to pause the movie.**

    The playback screen looks similar to the one on the left in Figure 4-24.

4. **Press the AE-L/AF-L button.**

    Note the symbols centered under the picture frame in the left image in Figure 4-24: They're the same ones on the face of the AE-L/AF-L button, cluing you into the fact that you use the button to access the trimming feature. After you press the button, you see the Edit Movie screen, as shown on the right in Figure 4-24.

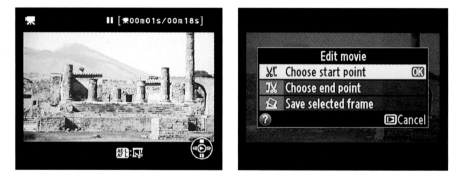

Figure 4-24: After pausing playback, press the AE-L/AF-L button to access the movie-editing tools.

5. Highlight Choose Start Point and press OK.

The screen appears similar to the one in Figure 4-25. Notice that in the Multi Selector icon, the up arrow now sports a little scissors icon. That's your cue about how to take the next step . . .

6. Press the Multi Selector up to lop off all frames that came before the current frame.

Don't worry that you'll lose your original movie — the trimmed version is saved as a separate file.

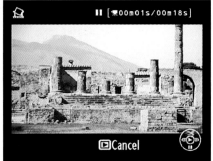

Figure 4-25: Press the Multi Selector up to proceed with the edit.

After you press the Multi Selector up, you see a confirmation screen asking for permission to proceed.

7. Highlight Yes and press OK.

A message appears telling you that the trimmed movie is being saved. During playback, edited files are indicated by a little scissors icon that appears in the area noted in Figure 4-26.

To instead trim footage from the end of a film, take the same steps, but this time pause playback on the last frame you want to keep in Step 3. Then, in Step 5, select Choose End Point instead of Choose Start Point.

Trimmed movie icon

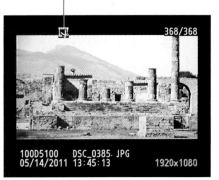

Saving a movie frame as a still image

In addition to trimming frames from the beginning and end of a movie, you can do a *screen grab* — that is, save a single frame of the movie as a regular image file. Here's how:

Figure 4-26: The scissors tell you that you're looking at an edited movie file.

1. **Begin playing your movie.**

2. **When you reach the frame you want to capture, press the Multi Selector down to pause playback.**

3. **Press the AE-L/AF-L button to bring up the Edit Movie screen.**

4. **Choose Save Selected Frame, as shown in Figure 4-27, and press OK.**

   The selected frame appears on the screen.

5. **Press the Multi Selector up to initiate the screen grab.**

6. **On the confirmation screen that appears, select Yes and press OK.**

   Your frame is saved as a JPEG photo.

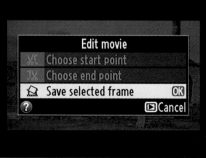

Figure 4-27: Through this option, you can save a single movie frame as a still photo.

Remember a few things about pictures you create this way:

✓ When you view the image, it's marked with a little movie-snip icon in the upper-left corner, as shown in Figure 4-28.

✓ The resolution of the picture depends on the resolution of the movie. For example, if the movie resolution is 1280 x 720, the picture has that same number of pixels. The resolution appears in blue, in the lower-right corner of the playback screen, as shown in Figure 4-28.

✓ You can't apply editing features from the Retouch menu to the file, and you also can't view all the shooting data that's normally associated with a JPEG picture.

Movie-snip icon

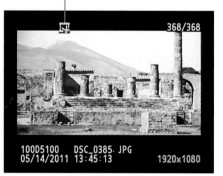

Figure 4-28: This icon marks pictures snipped from a movie.

For more about JPEG and picture resolution, visit Chapter 2.

Part II
Working with Picture Files

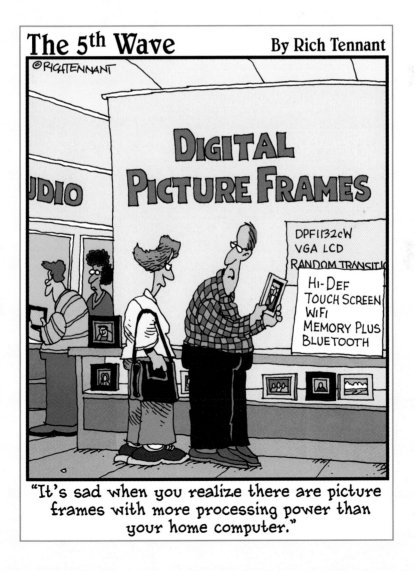

The 5th Wave   By Rich Tennant

DIGITAL PICTURE FRAMES

DPF1132cW
VGA LCD
RANDOM TRANSIT

HI-DEF
TOUCH SCREEN
WIFI
MEMORY PLUS
BLUETOOTH

"It's sad when you realize there are picture
frames with more processing power than
your home computer."

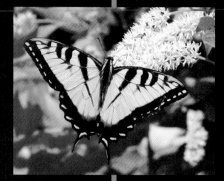

In this part . . .

You have a memory card full of pictures. Now what? Now you turn to the first chapter in this part, Chapter 5, which explains all your camera's picture-playback features, including options that help you evaluate exposure and zoom the display so that you can check small details. The same chapter shows you how to delete lousy pictures and protect great ones from accidental erasure.

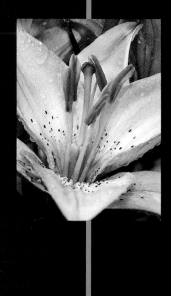

When you're ready to move pictures from the camera to your computer, Chapter 6 shows you the best ways to get the job done. In addition, Chapter 6 offers step-by-step guidance on printing your pictures and preparing them for online sharing.

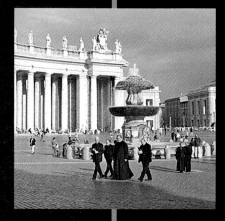

5

Playback Mode: Viewing, Erasing, and Protecting Photos

*W*ithout question, my favorite thing about digital photography is being able to view my pictures on the monitor the instant after I shoot them. No more guessing whether I captured the image I wanted or I need to try again; no more wasting money on developing and printing pictures that stink. In fact, this feature alone was reason enough for me to turn my back forever on my closetful of film photography hardware and all the unexposed film remaining from my predigital days.

But seeing your pictures is just the start of the things you can do when you switch your D5100 to playback mode. You also can review all the camera settings you used to take the picture, display graphics that alert you to serious exposure problems, and add file markers that protect the picture from accidental erasure.

This chapter tells you how to use all these playback features and also explains how to connect your camera to a television so that you can view your photos and movies on a bigger screen. (Note that the on-camera playback information in this chapter deals with still pictures, however; see Chapter 4 for help with movie playback.)

Customizing Basic Playback Options

You can control many aspects of picture playback on the D5100. Later sections show you how to choose what type of data appears with your pictures, how to display multiple images at a time, and how to magnify an image for a close-up look. But first, the next few sections explain options that affect overall playback performance, including how long your pictures appear onscreen and how they're oriented on the monitor.

Adjusting playback timing

By default, the camera monitor turns off after 20 seconds of inactivity during picture playback to save battery power. If you want a longer or shorter interval before the playback cutoff, you can adjust the timing through the Auto Off Timers option, found on the Timers/AE Lock section of the Custom Setting menu and shown on the left in Figure 5-1. Choose Custom, press OK, and then select Playback/Menus to access the shutdown options, which range from eight seconds to ten minutes. Press OK, highlight Done, and press OK again to wrap up.

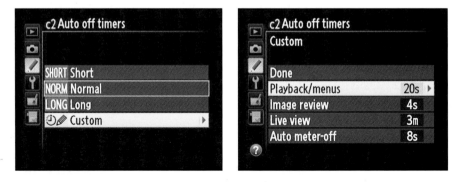

Figure 5-1: Choose Custom to adjust the monitor shutdown time for playback and menu display only.

The Short, Normal, and Long options (see the left screen in Figure 5-1) enable you to set the shutdown timing for playback and menu display as well, but those options also affect how long the camera displays a picture immediately after you capture the image — known as the *image-review period* — as well as the automatic shutoff timing of the exposure meters and Live View display. I prefer to set these timing options separately, but in case you're interested, Chapter 1 spells out the various shutdown intervals produced by the Short, Normal, and Long settings.

Adjusting and disabling instant image review

After you take a picture, it automatically appears briefly on the camera monitor. By default, this review period lasts four seconds. But you can customize this behavior in two ways:

✔ **Adjust the length of the instant-review period.** Take the same steps as outlined in the preceding section, but choose Image Review, as shown in Figure 5-2, instead of Playback/Menus. Press OK to display the timing intervals; you can choose settings ranging from four seconds to ten minutes.

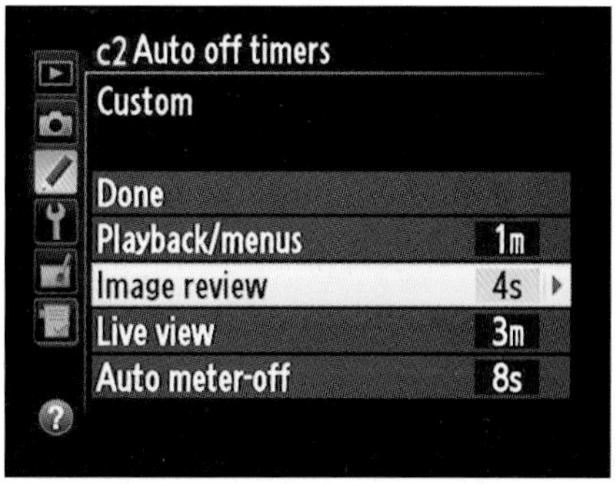

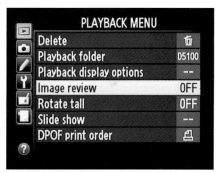

Figure 5-2: You also can adjust the length of the instant-review period through the Auto Off Timers option.

✔ **Disable instant review.** Because any monitor use is a strain on battery power, consider turning off instant review altogether if your battery is running low. Just call up the Playback menu and set the Image Review option to Off, as shown in Figure 5-3. You can still view your pictures by pressing the Playback button at any time.

Figure 5-3: To disable instant image review altogether, set this Playback menu option to Off.

Enabling automatic picture rotation

When you take a picture, the camera can record the image *orientation* — whether you held the camera normally, creating a horizontally oriented image, or turned the camera on its side to shoot a vertically oriented photo. During playback, the camera can then read the orientation data and automatically rotate the image so that it appears in the upright position, as shown on the left in Figure 5-4. The image is also automatically rotated when you view it in Nikon ViewNX 2, Capture NX 2, and other photo programs that can interpret the data. If you disable rotation, vertically oriented pictures appear sideways, as shown on the right in Figure 5-4.

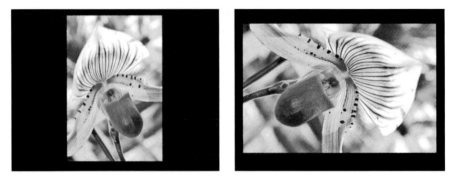

Figure 5-4: You can display vertically oriented pictures in their upright position (left) or sideways (right).

Official photo lingo uses the term *portrait orientation* to refer to vertically oriented pictures and *landscape orientation* to refer to horizontally oriented pictures. The terms stem from the traditional way that people and places are captured in paintings and photographs — portraits, vertically; landscapes, horizontally.

On the D5100, set up your rotation wishes through the following two menu options, both shown in Figure 5-5:

- **Auto Image Rotation:** This option, on the Setup menu, determines whether the orientation data is included in the picture file. The default setting is On; select Off to leave out the data.

- **Rotate Tall:** Found on the Playback menu, this option controls whether the camera pays attention to the orientation data. The default setting is Off. Select On, as shown in the figure, if you want the camera to rotate the image during playback.

SETUP MENU	
Flicker reduction	60Hz
Time zone and date	--
Language	🗺
Image comment	OFF
Auto image rotation	ON
Image Dust Off ref photo	--
GPS	--
Firmware version	--

PLAYBACK MENU	
Delete	🗑
Playback folder	D5100
Playback display options	--
Image review	OFF
Rotate tall	ON
Slide show	--
DPOF print order	🖨

Figure 5-5: Visit the Setup and Playback menus to enable or disable image rotation.

Regardless of these settings, your pictures aren't rotated during the instant-review period. Also, be aware that shooting with the lens pointing directly up or down sometimes confuses the camera, causing it to record the wrong data in the file. Rotating the camera while shooting a burst of images in the Continuous Release mode also causes a playback glitch: The camera tags all files with the orientation of the first image, so some may not be rotated properly during playback. Chapter 2 explains the Release mode setting.

Viewing Images in Playback Mode

To review your photos, take these steps:

1. **Press the Playback button, labeled in Figure 5-6.**

   By default, the camera displays the last picture you took, along with some picture data, such as the filename of the photo and the date it was taken, as shown in Figure 5-6. To find out how to interpret the picture information and specify what data you want to see, see the upcoming section "Viewing Picture Data."

Playback   Multi Selector

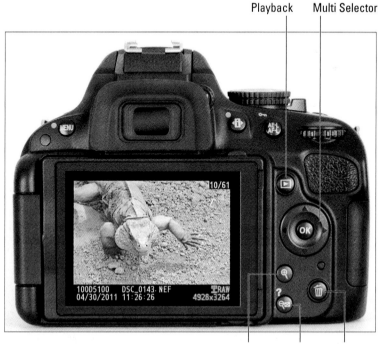

Zoom In   Zoom Out   Delete

Figure 5-6: These buttons play the largest roles in picture playback.

2. **To scroll through your pictures, press the Multi Selector right or left.**

   Just as a reminder: The Multi Selector is the four-way rocker pad that surrounds the OK button. I labeled it in Figure 5-6.

   If some pictures appear to be missing, the problem could be that your memory card contains multiple image folders and the camera isn't set to display all folders. For help sorting out this issue, see the section "Choosing which images to view" later in this chapter.

3. **To return to picture-taking mode, press the Playback button again or press the shutter button halfway and then release it.**

These steps assume that the camera is currently set to display a single photo at a time, as shown in Figure 5-6. You can also display multiple images at a time, as explained next.

Viewing multiple images at a time (thumbnails view)

Along with viewing images one at a time, you can display 4 or 9 thumbnails, as shown in Figure 5-7, or even a whopping 72 thumbnails. Use these techniques to change to thumbnails view and navigate your photos:

Selected photo

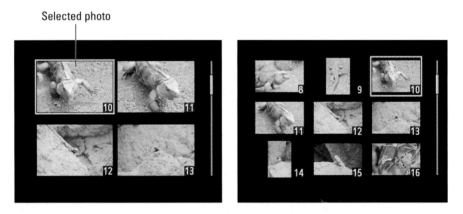

Figure 5-7: You can view multiple image thumbnails at a time.

✔ **Display thumbnails.** Press the Zoom Out button, labeled in Figure 5-6, to cycle from single-picture view to 4-thumbnail view; press again to shift to 9-picture view; and press once more to bring up 72 itty-bitty thumbnails. One more press takes you to Calendar view, a nifty feature explained in the next section.

✔ **Display fewer thumbnails.** Pressing the Zoom In button, also labeled in Figure 5-6, takes you from Calendar view back to the standard thumbnails display or, if you're already in that display, reduces the number of thumbnails so you can see each one at a larger size. Again, your first press takes you from 72 thumbnails to 9, your second press to 4 thumbnails, and your third press returns you to single-image view.

Notice the icons on these two buttons: The Zoom Out button sports a magnifying glass with a minus sign, the universal symbol for zoom out, plus a little grid that resembles a screen full of thumbnails. And the Zoom In button's magnifying glass has a plus sign, reminding you that you use this button to increase the image size.

✔ **Scroll the display.** Press the Multi Selector up and down to scroll to the next or previous screen of thumbnails.

✔ **Select an image.** To perform certain playback functions, such as deleting a photo or protecting it, you first need to select an image. A yellow box surrounds the currently selected image, as shown in Figure 5-7. To select a different image, use the Multi Selector to move the highlight box over the image.

✔ **Jump from any thumbnail display to full-frame view.** Instead of pressing the Zoom Out button multiple times, you can just press OK. After you return to full-frame view, pressing OK again displays the Retouch menu. Now you can select a retouch option and apply it to the image. See Chapter 10 for a look at the tools found on the Retouch menu.

Displaying photos in Calendar view

In Calendar display mode, you see a little calendar on the screen, as shown on the left in Figure 5-8. By selecting a date on the calendar, you can quickly navigate to all pictures you shot on that day. A thumbnail-free date indicates that your memory card doesn't contain any photos from that day.

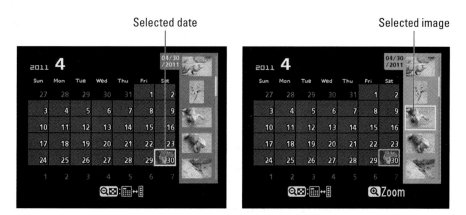

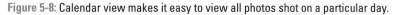

Figure 5-8: Calendar view makes it easy to view all photos shot on a particular day.

The key to navigating Calendar view is the Zoom Out button:

1. **Press the Zoom Out button as needed to cycle through the Thumbnail display modes until you reach Calendar view.**

   If you're currently viewing images in full-frame view, for example, you need to press the button four times to get to Calendar view.

2. **Using the Multi Selector, move the yellow highlight box over a date that contains an image.**

   In the left example in Figure 5-8, the 30th day of April is selected. (The number of the month appears in the top-left corner of the screen.) After you select a date, the right side of the monitor displays a vertical strip of thumbnails of pictures taken on that date.

3. **To view all thumbnails from the selected date, press the Zoom Out button again.**

   As a reminder of what button to press, the little icon underneath the calendar displays the symbols that appear on the Zoom Out button.

   After you press the button, the vertical thumbnail strip becomes active, as shown on the right in Figure 5-8, and you can scroll through the thumbnails by pressing the Multi Selector up and down. A second highlight box appears in the thumbnail strip to indicate the currently selected image.

4. **To temporarily display a larger view of the selected thumbnail, hold down the Zoom In button.**

   Again, note the reminder icon in the bottom-right corner of the screen; it shows the plus-sign magnifying glass that appears on the face of the Zoom In button.

   In the zoomed view, the image filename appears under the larger preview, as shown in Figure 5-9. When you release the Zoom In button, the large preview disappears, and the calendar comes back into view.

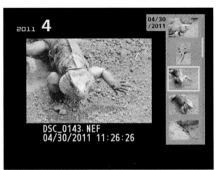

Figure 5-9: Highlight a photo in the thumbnail strip and press the Zoom In button to temporarily display it at a larger size.

5. **To jump from the thumbnail strip back to the calendar and select a different date, press the Zoom Out button again.**

   You can just keep pressing the button to jump between the calendar and the thumbnail strip as much as you want.

6. **To exit Calendar view and return to single-image view, press OK.**

Choosing which images to view

Your D5100 organizes pictures automatically into folders that are assigned generic names: 100D5100, 101D5100, and so on. You can see the name of the current folder by looking at the Storage Folder option on the Shooting menu. (The default folder name appears as just D5100 on the menu.) You also can create custom-named folders through a process outlined in Chapter 11. During playback, which folder's photos appear depend on the Playback Folder option on the Playback menu, as shown in Figure 5-10.

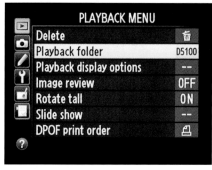

Figure 5-10: Specify which folder you want to view through this option.

Because a folder can contain up to 9999 images, you probably don't need to worry about this setting — all your photos likely are contained in one folder on your memory card, and the camera selects that folder by default. But if you use a gargantuan memory card that contains zillions of images (and therefore may contain multiple folders), or you created custom folders, or your card contains pictures taken on another camera, tell the camera which folder you want to view by choosing one of the following options:

- **Current:** Displays images contained in the folder selected as the Storage Folder option on the Shooting menu. This setting is the default. Again, unless your card contains multiple folders, all your pictures will be contained in that folder.

- **All:** Displays all pictures in all folders, even those taken with other cameras (as long as they're in a format the camera can display — JPEG or NEF — the Nikon version of the Raw image format).

Zooming in for a closer view

After displaying a photo in single-frame view, as shown on the left in Figure 5-11, you can magnify it to get a close-up look at important details, as shown on the right. Here's the scoop:

- **Zoom in.** Press the Zoom In button. You can magnify the image to a maximum of 15 to 31 times its original display size, depending on the resolution (Image Size) of the photo. Just keep pressing the button until you reach the magnification you want.

- **Zoom out.** To zoom out to a reduced magnification, press the Zoom Out button — the one that sports the minus-sign magnifying glass.

Magnified area

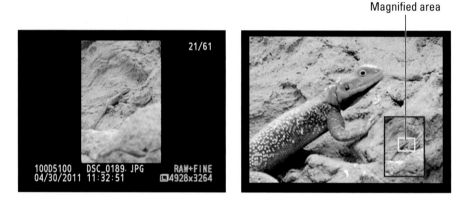

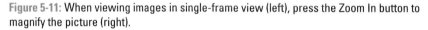

Figure 5-11: When viewing images in single-frame view (left), press the Zoom In button to magnify the picture (right).

▸ **View another part of the magnified picture.** When an image is magnified, a little navigation thumbnail showing the entire image appears briefly in the lower-right corner of the monitor, as shown on the right in Figure 5-11. The yellow outline in this picture-in-picture image indicates the area that's currently consuming the rest of the monitor space. Use the Multi Selector to scroll the yellow box and display a different portion of the image. After a few seconds, the navigation thumbnail disappears; just press the Multi Selector in any direction to redisplay it.

▸ **Inspect faces.** Try this trick to inspect each face in a group shot: Press the Zoom In button once to magnify the image slightly. The picture-in-picture thumbnail then displays a white border around each detected face, as shown on the left in Figure 5-12. (Typically, subjects must be facing the camera for faces to be detected.) Now press the Info Edit button and then press OK to fill the frame with a single face, as shown on the right in the figure. Then press the Multi Selector right or left to jump from face to face and examine each one at a magnified view. Press the Info Edit button again to return to the normal playback zoom behavior.

▸ **View more images at the same magnification.** Here's another neat trick: While the display is zoomed, you can rotate the Command dial to display the same area of the next photo at the same magnification. So if you shot the same subject several times, you can easily check how a particular detail appears in each one.

▸ **Return to full-frame view.** When you're ready to return to the normal magnification level, you don't need to keep pressing the Zoom Out button until you're all the way zoomed out. Instead, just press OK.

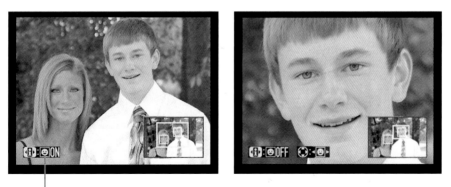

Face Detection symbol

Figure 5-12: The Face Detection feature enables you to quickly inspect faces.

Viewing Picture Data

In single-picture view, you can choose from the six display modes shown in Figure 5-13. If you attach the optional GPS unit to the camera, the Shooting Data display contains an extra screen to present the GPS data.

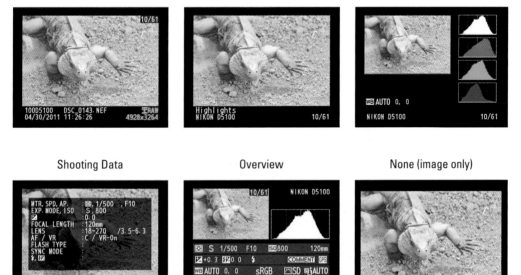

Figure 5-13: You can choose from six playback display modes.

By default, however, only the File Information display mode is available. If you want to use any of the other display options, you must enable them from the Playback menu, as follows:

1. **Open the Playback menu and highlight Playback Display Options, as shown on the left in Figure 5-14.**

2. **Press OK.**

   A menu listing all the hidden display modes appears, as shown on the right in Figure 5-14. A check mark in the box next to a display mode means the mode is enabled; by default, all the modes are turned off.

3. **To toggle a display mode on, highlight it and then press the Multi Selector right.**

   A check mark appears in the box for that mode.

4. **After turning on the options you want to use, highlight Done and press OK.**

After enabling the additional display modes, press the Multi Selector up or down to cycle from one display to the next.

The next sections explain exactly what details you can glean from each display mode, save for the image-only mode. I present them here in the order they appear if you cycle through the modes by pressing the Multi Selector down. You can spin through the modes in the other direction by pressing the Multi Selector up.

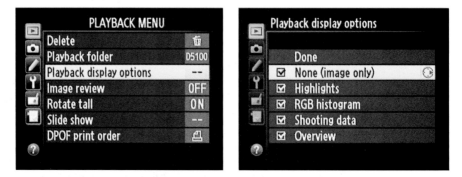

Figure 5-14: You must enable these display modes via the Playback menu.

File Information mode

In the File Information display mode, the monitor displays the data shown in Figure 5-15. Here's the key to what information appears, starting at the top of the screen and working down:

Folder and Filename   Frame Number/Total Pictures

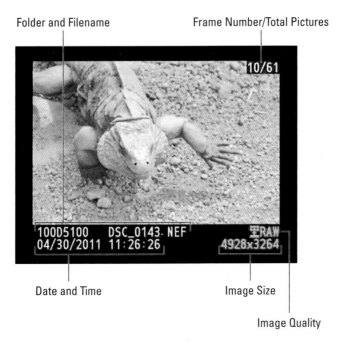

Date and Time   Image Size

Image Quality

Figure 5-15: In File Information mode, you can view these bits of data.

- ✔ **Frame Number/Total Pictures:** The first value here indicates the frame number of the currently displayed photo; the second tells you the total number of pictures in the same folder. In Figure 5-15, for example, the image is number 10 out of 61.

- ✔ **Folder name:** Folders are named automatically by the camera unless you create custom folders, an advanced trick you can explore in Chapter 11. The first camera-created folder is 100D5100. Each folder can contain up to 9999 images; when you exceed that limit, the camera creates a new folder and assigns the next folder number: 101D5100, 102D5100, and so on.

- ✔ **Filename:** The camera also automatically names your files. Filenames end with a three-letter code that represents the file format, which is either JPG (for JPEG) or NEF (for Raw) for still photos. Chapter 2 discusses these formats. If you record a movie (a project you can explore in Chapter 4), the file extension is MOV, which represents a digital-movie file format. If you create a dust-off reference image file, an advanced feature designed for use with Nikon Capture NX 2, the camera instead uses the extension NDF. (Because this software must be purchased separately, I don't cover it or the dust-off function in this book.)

The first four characters of filenames also vary. Here's what the possible codes indicate:

- *DSC_:* This code means you captured the photo at the default Color Space setting, sRGB. You can investigate this option in Chapter 8.

- *_DSC:* If you change the Color Space setting to Adobe RGB, the underscore character comes first.

- *CSC_:* When you create an edited copy of a photo by using one of the Retouch menu features, the copy's filename begins with these characters. If the underscore precedes the letters, you captured the original in the Adobe RGB color space.

- *SSC_:* These letters indicate a lower-resolution copy of a photo that you created by using the Resize option on the Retouch menu; Chapter 6 details that option. If the Color Space was set to Adobe RGB at the time you created the copy, the filename begins with _SSC instead.

Each image is also assigned a four-digit file number, starting with 0001. When you reach image 9999, the file numbering restarts at 0001, and the new images go into a new folder to prevent any possibility of overwriting the existing image files. For more information about file numbering, see the Chapter 1 section that discusses the File Number Sequence option, found on the Custom Setting menu.

- **Date and Time:** Just below the folder and filename info, you see the date and time that you took the picture. Of course, the accuracy of this data depends on whether you set the camera's date and time values correctly, which you do via the Setup menu. Chapter 1 has details.

- **Image Quality:** Here you can see which Image Quality setting you used when taking the picture. Again, Chapter 2 has details, but the short story is this: Fine, Normal, and Basic are the three JPEG recording options, with Fine representing the highest JPEG quality. Raw refers to the Nikon Raw format, NEF (for Nikon Electronic Format).

- **Image Size:** This value tells you the image resolution, or pixel count. See Chapter 2 to find out about resolution.

In the top-left corner of the screen, you may see the following two symbols, labeled in Figure 5-16:

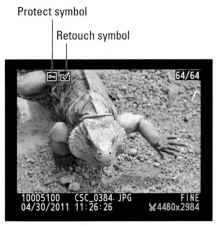

Protect symbol

Retouch symbol

Figure 5-16: These symbols indicate a protected photo and a retouched photo.

- **Protect symbol:** A little key icon indicates that you used the file-protection feature to prevent the image from being erased when you use the camera's Delete function. See the "Protecting Photos" section, later in this chapter, to find out more. (*Note:* Formatting your memory card, a topic discussed in Chapter 1, *does* erase even protected pictures.) This area appears empty if you didn't apply protection.

- **Retouch symbol:** This icon appears on images that you created by applying one of the Retouch menu features to a photo. (The camera preserves the original and applies your alterations to a copy of the image.) For example, the image shown in Figure 5-16 is a cropped version of my original iguana photo; I used the Trim feature to clip away some excess background. Chapter 10 explains this feature and other Retouch menu options.

Highlights display mode

One of the most difficult photo problems to correct in a photo-editing program is known as *blown highlights* in some circles and *clipped highlights* in others. In plain English, both terms mean that *highlights* — the brightest areas of the image — are so overexposed that areas that should include a variety of light shades are instead totally white. For example, in a cloud image, pixels that should be light to very light gray become white due to overexposure, resulting in a loss of detail in those clouds.

Highlights display mode alerts you to clipped highlights by blinking the affected pixels on and off. For example, Figure 5-17 shows you an image that contains some blown highlights. I captured the screen at the moment the highlight blinkies blinked "off" — the black areas in the figure indicate the blown highlights. (I labeled a few of them in the figure.) But as this image proves, just because you see the flashing alerts doesn't mean that you should adjust exposure — the decision depends on where the alerts occur and how the rest of the image is exposed. In my candle photo, for example, it's true that there are small white areas in the flames and the glass vase. Yet exposure in the majority of the photo is fine. If I reduced exposure to darken those spots, some areas of the reddish flower petals floating in the glass would be underexposed. In other words, sometimes you simply can't avoid a few clipped highlights when the scene includes a broad range of brightness values.

Along with the blinking highlight warning, Highlights display mode presents the Protect and Retouch symbols, if you used those features. In the lower-left corner, you see the frame number and total number of images — 3 and 64, in Figure 5-17. The label *Highlights* also appears to let you know the current display mode.

Blown highlights

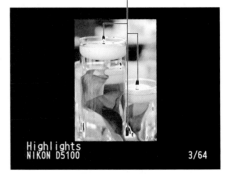

Figure 5-17: In Highlights mode, blinking areas indicate blown highlights.

Like all other playback display modes except File Information, the Highlights mode is disabled by default. Follow the instructions in the "Viewing Picture Data" section, earlier in this chapter, to enable it.

RGB Histogram mode

Press the Multi Selector down to shift from Highlights mode to this mode, which displays your image in the manner shown in Figure 5-18. Again, you can view your picture in this mode only if you enable it via the Display Mode option on the Playback menu. (See "Viewing Picture Data," earlier in this chapter, for help.)

Underneath the image thumbnail, you see just a few pieces of data. As with File Information mode, you see the Protect Status and Retouch Indicator icons if you used those features. Beneath that, you see the White Balance settings used for the shot. In the figure, the data shows that the

Brightness Histogram

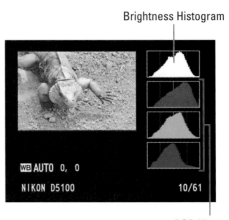

RGB Histogram

Figure 5-18: RGB Histogram mode presents exposure and color information in chart-like fashion.

picture was captured using the Auto White Balance with zero adjustment along the blue-to-amber axis and zero adjustment along the green-to-magenta axis. (Chapter 8 details White Balance options.) Along the bottom row of the display, you see the camera name along with the Frame Number/Total Pictures data, also part of the standard File Information display data.

The core of this display mode, though, are those chart-like thingies called *histograms.* You get two types of histograms: The top one is a Brightness histogram; the three others are collectively an RGB (red, green, blue) histogram.

The next two sections explain what you can discern from the histograms. But first, here's a cool trick to remember: If you press the Zoom In button while in this display mode, you can zoom the thumbnail to a magnified view. The histograms then update to reflect only the magnified area of the photo. Use the Multi Selector to scroll the display to see other areas of the picture. To return to the regular view and once again see the whole-image histogram, press OK.

Reading a Brightness histogram

You can get an idea of image exposure by viewing your photo on the camera monitor and by looking at the blinkies in Highlight mode. But the Brightness histogram provides a way to gauge exposure that's a little more detailed.

A Brightness histogram indicates the distribution of shadows, highlights, and *midtones* (areas of medium brightness) in your image. Figure 5-19 shows you the histogram for the iguana image featured in Figure 5-18, for example.

The horizontal axis of the histogram represents the possible picture brightness values — the maximum *tonal range,* in photography-speak — from the darkest shadows on the left to the brightest highlights on the right. And the vertical axis shows you how many pixels fall at a particular brightness value. A spike indicates a heavy concentration of pixels at that brightness value.

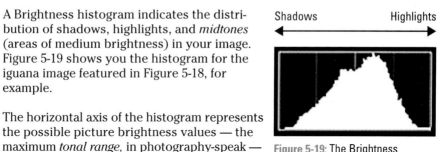

Figure 5-19: The Brightness histogram indicates tonal range, from shadows on the left to highlights on the right.

Keep in mind that there is no one "perfect" histogram that you should try to achieve. Instead, interpret the histogram with respect to the distribution of shadows, highlights, and midtones that comprise your subject. You wouldn't expect to see lots of shadows, for example, in a photo of a polar bear walking on a snowy landscape. Pay attention, however, if you see a very high concentration of pixels at the far right or left end of the histogram, which can indicate a seriously overexposed or underexposed image, respectively. To find out how to resolve exposure problems, visit Chapter 7.

Understanding RGB histograms

When you view your images in RGB Histogram display mode, you see two histograms: the Brightness histogram, covered in the preceding section, and an RGB histogram. Figure 5-20 shows you the RGB histogram for the iguana image.

Less saturated ←———————→ More saturated

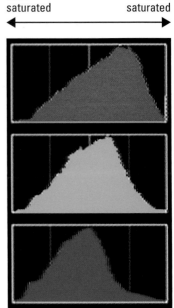

To make sense of an RGB histogram, you first need to know that digital images are known as *RGB images* because they're created from three primary colors of light: red, green, and blue. Whereas the Brightness histogram reflects the brightness of all three color channels rolled into one, RGB histograms let you view the values for each channel.

When you look at the brightness data for a single channel, though, you glean information about color saturation rather than image brightness. (*Saturation* refers to the purity of a color; a fully saturated color contains no black or white.) I don't have space in this book to provide a full lesson in RGB color theory, but the short story is that when you mix red, green, and blue light, and each component is at maximum brightness, you create white. Zero brightness in all three channels creates black. If you have maximum red and no blue or green, though, you have fully saturated red. If you mix two channels at maximum brightness, you also create full saturation. For example, maximum red and blue produce fully saturated magenta. And, wherever colors are fully saturated, you can lose picture detail. For example, a rose petal that should have a range of tones from medium to dark red may instead be a flat blob of pure red.

Figure 5-20: The RGB histogram can indicate problems with color saturation.

The upshot is that if all the pixels for one or two channels are slammed to the right end of the histogram, you may be losing picture detail because of overly saturated colors. If all three channels show a heavy pixel population at the right end of the histogram, you may have blown highlights — again, because the maximum levels of red, green, and blue create white. Either way, you may want to adjust the exposure settings and try again.

A savvy RGB histogram reader can also spot color balance issues by looking at the pixel values. But frankly, color balance problems are fairly easy to notice just by looking at the image on the camera monitor. See Chapter 8 to find out how to correct any color problems that you spot during picture playback.

Shooting Data display mode

Before you can access this mode, you must enable it via the Playback Display Options setting on the Playback menu. See the earlier section "Viewing Picture Data" for details. After turning on the option, press the Multi Selector down to shift from RGB Histogram mode to Shooting Data mode.

In this mode, you can view three screens of information, which you toggle among by pressing the Multi Selector up and down. Figure 5-21 shows you the first two screens.

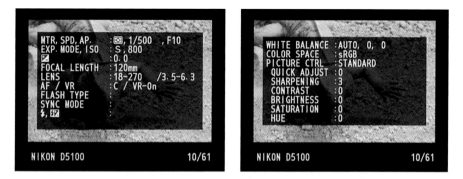

Figure 5-21: You can view the camera settings used to capture the image in Shooting Data display mode.

Most of the data here won't make any sense to you until you explore Chapters 7 and 8, which explain the exposure, color, and other advanced settings available on your camera. But I want to call your attention to a couple of factoids now:

- The top-left corner of the monitor shows the Protect and Retouch icons, if you used these features. Otherwise, the area is empty. (See the earlier section "File Information mode" for details about these particular features.)

- The current folder and frame number appear in the lower-right corner of the display.

- The Comment item, which is the final item on the third screen, contains a value if you use the Image Comment feature on the Setup menu. I cover this option in Chapter 11.

- If the ISO value on Shooting Data Page 1 (the first screen in Figure 5-21) appears in red, the camera overrode the ISO Sensitivity setting that you selected in order to produce a good exposure. This shift occurs only if you enable automatic ISO adjustment in the P, S, A, and M exposure modes; see Chapter 7 for details.

GPS Data mode

This display mode is available only if the image you're viewing was shot with the optional Nikon GPS (Global Positioning System) unit attached. And technically, GPS Data display mode isn't really its own, independent mode, although the camera manual describes it as such. Instead, if you took a picture with the GPS unit enabled, you see a fourth screen of data when you set the display mode to Shooting Data (detailed in the preceding section.)

The data screen shows you the latitude, longitude, and other GPS information recorded with the image file.

Overview Data mode

In this mode, the playback screen contains a small image thumbnail along with scads of shooting data — although not quite as much as Shooting Data mode — plus a Brightness histogram. Figure 5-22 offers a look.

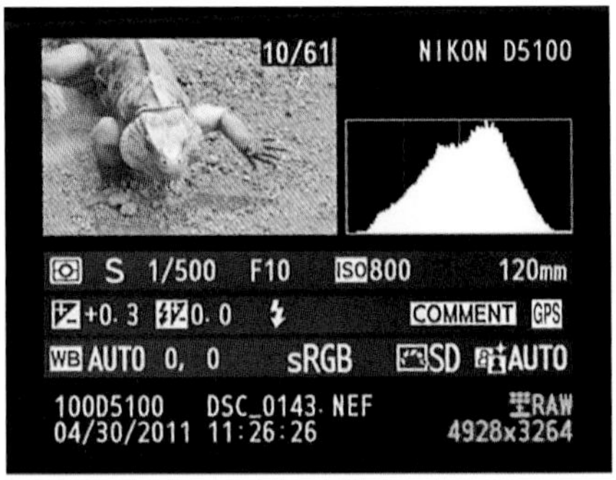

The earlier section "Reading a Brightness histogram" tells you what to make of that part of the screen. Just above the histogram, you see the Protect and Retouch symbols, if you used those features, while the Frame Number/Total Pictures data appears at the upper-right corner of

Figure 5-22: In Overview Data mode, you can view your picture along with the major camera settings you used to take the picture.

the image thumbnail. For details on that data, see the earlier section "File Information mode."

To sort out the maze of other information, the following list breaks down things into the five rows that appear under the image thumbnail and histogram. In the accompanying figures as well as in Figure 5-22, I include all possible data simply for the purpose of illustration; if any of the items don't appear on your screen, it simply means that the relevant feature wasn't enabled when you captured the shot.

> ✔ **Row 1:** This row shows the exposure-related settings labeled in Figure 5-23, along with the focal length of the lens you used to take the shot. As in Shooting Data mode, the ISO value appears red if you had auto ISO override enabled in the P, S, A, or M exposure modes and the camera adjusted the ISO for you. Chapter 7 details the exposure settings; Chapter 8 introduces you to focal length.

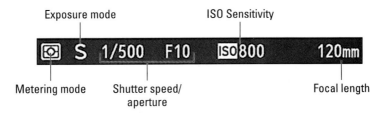

Figure 5-23: Here you can inspect major exposure settings along with the lens focal length.

✏ **Row 2:** This row contains a few additional exposure settings, labeled in Figure 5-24. On the right end of the row, the Comment and GPS labels appear if you took advantage of those options when recording the shot. (You must switch to the Shooting Data mode to view the actual comment and GPS data.)

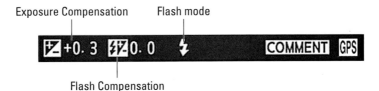

Figure 5-24: This row contains additional exposure information.

✏ **Row 3:** The first three items on this row, labeled in Figure 5-25, relate to color options explored in Chapter 8. Again, the second White Balance value shows the amount of blue-to-amber fine-tuning adjustment; and the third, the amount of green-to-magenta adjustment (both values are 0 in the figure). The last item indicates the Active D-Lighting setting, another exposure option discussed in Chapter 7.

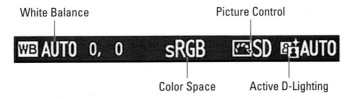

Figure 5-25: Look at this row for details about advanced color settings.

✏ **Rows 4 and 5:** The final two rows of data (refer to Figure 5-22) show the same information you get in File Information mode, explained earlier in this chapter.

Deleting Photos

You have three options for erasing pictures from a memory card when it's in your camera. The next sections give you the lowdown. (Or is it the down low? I can't seem to keep up.) One tip before you start: However you delete a photo, remember that deleting an image that you recorded using one of the Raw+JPEG settings erases both files.

Deleting images one at a time

The Delete button is key to erasing single images. But the process varies a little depending on which playback display mode you use, as follows:

- ✔ In single-image view, you can erase the current image by pressing the Delete button.

- ✔ In Thumbnail view (displaying 4, 9, or 72 thumbnails), use the Multi Selector to highlight the picture you want to erase and then press the Delete button.

- ✔ In Calendar view, first highlight the date that contains the image. Then press the Zoom Out button to jump to the scrolling list of thumbnails, highlight a specific image, and press the Delete button.

After you press Delete, you see a message asking whether you really want to erase the picture. If you do, press the Delete button again. Or, to cancel out of the process, press the Playback button.

See the earlier section, "Viewing Images in Playback Mode," for more details about displaying thumbnails and Calendar view.

You can also press the Delete button during the instant image-review period if you know right away that the picture's a bust. But you have to be quick or the camera returns to shooting mode.

Deleting all photos

To erase all pictures, take these steps:

1. **Display the Playback menu and highlight Delete, as shown in the left image in Figure 5-26.**

2. **Press OK to display the second screen in the figure.**

3. **Highlight All and press OK.**

   You then see a screen that asks you to verify that you want to delete all your images.

4. **Select Yes and press OK.**

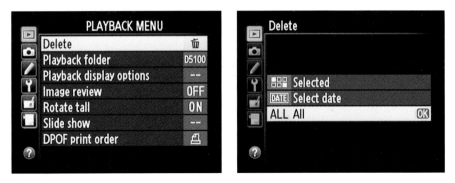

Figure 5-26: To delete all photos, use the Delete option on the Playback menu.

If your memory card contains multiple image folders, these steps delete only pictures in the folder that is currently selected via the Playback Folder option on the Playback menu. See the section "Choosing which images to view," earlier in this chapter, for information. Remember, too, that pictures that you tag with the Protect feature, explained later in this chapter, aren't erased by the Delete function.

Deleting a batch of selected photos

When you want to get rid of more than a few photos — but not erase all pictures on the card — don't waste time erasing each picture, one at a time. Instead, you can tag multiple photos for deletion and then take them all out to the trash at one time.

To start, display the Playback menu and highlight Delete, as shown on the left in Figure 5-27. Press OK to display the second screen in the figure.

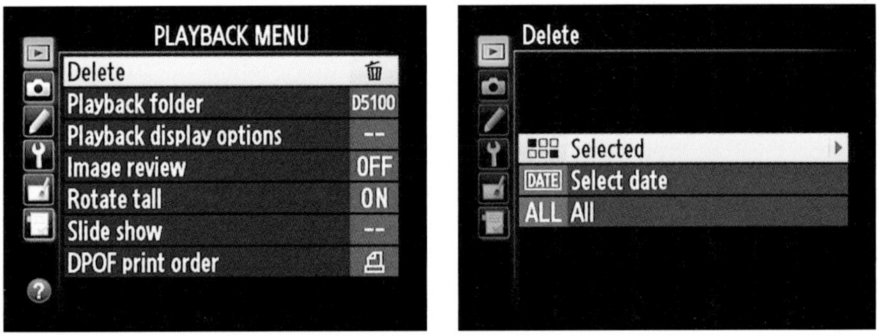

Figure 5-27: The Delete menu option also provides two ways to quickly delete selected pictures.

You then have two options for specifying which photos to erase:

✔ **Select individual photos.** Use this option if the pictures you want to delete weren't all taken on the same day. Highlight Selected, as shown on the right in Figure 5-27, and press the Multi Selector right to display a screen of thumbnails, as shown in Figure 5-28. Use the Multi Selector to place the yellow highlight box over the first photo you want to delete and then press the Zoom Out button, shown in the margin here. A little trash can icon, the universal symbol for delete, appears in the upper-right corner of the thumbnail, as shown in the figure. The picture is then tagged as no longer worthy of taking up space on your memory card.

If you change your mind, press the Zoom Out button again to remove the Delete tag from the image. To undo deletion for all selected photos, press the Playback button.

Delete symbol

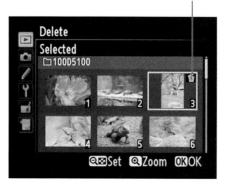

Figure 5-28: Use the Zoom Out button to tag pictures you want to delete.

For a closer look at the selected image, press and hold the Zoom In button. When you release the button, the display returns to normal thumbnails view.

✔ **Erase all photos taken on a specific date.** This time, choose Select Date from the main Delete screen, as shown on the left in Figure 5-29. Press the Multi Selector right to display a list of dates on which you took the pictures on the memory card, as shown on the right in the figure.

Next, highlight a date and press the Multi Selector right. A little check mark appears in the box next to the date, as shown on the right in Figure 5-29, tagging all images taken on that day for deletion. To remove the check mark and save the photos from the digital dumpster, press the Multi Selector right again.

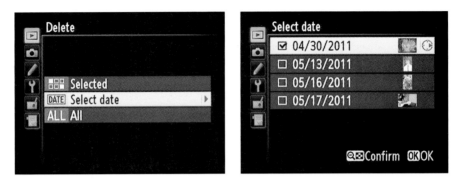

Figure 5-29: With the Select Date option, you can quickly erase all photos taken on a specific date.

Can't remember what photos are associated with the selected date? Try this:

- To display thumbnails of all images taken on the selected date, as shown in Figure 5-30, press the Zoom Out button.

- To temporarily view the selected thumbnail at full-size view, press the Zoom In button.

- To return to the date list, press the Zoom Out button again.

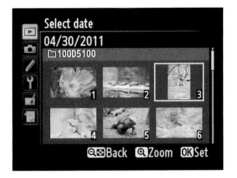

Figure 5-30: Press the Zoom Out button to display thumbnails of all photos taken on the selected date.

After tagging individual photos for deletion or specifying a shooting date to delete, press OK to start deleting. You see a confirmation screen asking permission to destroy the images; select Yes and press OK. The camera trashes the photos and returns you to the Playback menu.

You have one alternative way to quickly erase all images taken on a specific date: In the Calendar display mode, you can highlight the date in question and then press the Delete button instead of going through the Playback menu. You get the standard confirmation screen asking you whether you want to go forward. Press the Delete button again to dump the files. Visit the section "Displaying photos in Calendar view," earlier in this chapter, for the scoop on that display option.

Protecting Photos

You can protect pictures from accidental erasure by giving them *protected* status. After you take this step, the camera doesn't allow you to delete a picture from your memory card, whether you press the Delete button or use the Delete option on the Playback menu.

 I also use the Protect feature when I want to keep a handful of pictures on the card but delete the rest. Instead of using the options described in the preceding section to select all the pictures I want to trash, I protect the handful I want to preserve. Then I set the Delete menu option to All and dump the rest. The protected pictures are left intact.

 Formatting your memory card, however, *does* erase even protected pictures. In addition, when you protect a picture, it shows up as a read-only file when you transfer it to your computer. Files that have that read-only status can't be altered until you unlock them in your photo software. In Nikon ViewNX 2, you can do this by clicking the image thumbnail and then choosing File⇨ Protect Files⇨Unprotect.

Protecting a picture is easy:

1. **Display or select the picture you want to protect.**

     • *In single-image view,* just display the photo.

     • *In 4/9/72 Thumbnail mode,* use the Multi Selector as needed to place the yellow highlight box over the photo.

     • *In Calendar view,* highlight the image in the strip of thumbnails that appears on the right side of the screen. (Press the Zoom Out button to jump between the calendar dates and the thumbnails.)

 2. **Press the AE-L/AF-L button.**

    See the key symbol above the button? That's your reminder that you use the button to lock a picture. The same symbol appears on protected photos during playback, as shown in Figure 5-31.

To remove protection, display or select the image and then press the AE-L/AF-L button again.

Creating a Digital Slide Show

Many photo-editing and cataloging programs offer a tool for creating digital slide shows that can be viewed on a computer or, if copied to a DVD, on a DVD player. You can even add music, captions, graphics, special effects, and the like to jazz up your presentations.

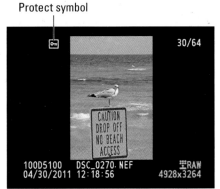

Protect symbol

Figure 5-31: Press the AE-L/AF-L button to give an image protected status.

But if you want to create a simple slide show — that is, one that simply displays the photos on the camera memory card one by one — you can create and run the show right on your camera by using the Slide Show function on the Playback menu. And by connecting your camera to a television, as outlined in the last section of this chapter, you can present your show to a whole roomful of people.

One important point to note about the Slide Show feature: The pictures displayed in the show depend on the current setting of the Playback Folder option on the Playback menu. If you haven't created any custom folders — a trick you can explore in Chapter 11 — you likely only have one folder on your card, so all pictures will be included in the show. If your memory card does contain multiple folders, see "Choosing which images to view," earlier in this chapter, for help with selecting the playback folder.

With that detail out of the way, follow these steps to present a slide show:

1. **Display the Playback menu and highlight Slide Show, as shown on the left in Figure 5-32.**

2. **Press OK to display the Slide Show screen shown on the right in Figure 5-32.**

3. **Highlight Frame Interval and press the Multi Selector right.**

   On the next screen, you can specify how long you want each image to be displayed. You can set the interval to two, three, five, or ten seconds.

4. **Highlight the frame interval you want to use and press OK.**

   You return to the Slide Show screen.

5. **To start the show, highlight Start and press OK.**

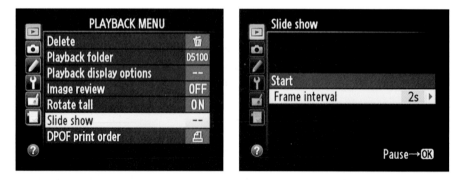

Figure 5-32: Choose Slide Show to set up automatic playback of all pictures on your memory card.

When the show ends, you see a screen offering three options: You can choose to restart the show, adjust the frame interval, or exit to the Playback menu. Highlight your choice and press OK.

During the show, you can control playback as follows:

✓ **Pause the show.** Press OK. Again, you see three options onscreen. To restart playback, select Restart and press OK. You also can adjust the frame interval or exit to the Playback menu.

✓ **Exit the show.** You have three options:

  • *To return to regular playback,* press the Playback button.

  • *To return to the Playback menu,* press the Menu button.

  • *To return to picture-taking mode,* press the shutter button halfway.

✓ **Skip to the next/previous image manually.** Press the Multi Selector right or left.

✓ **Change the information displayed with the image.** Press the Multi Selector up or down to cycle through the display modes. See the section "Viewing Picture Data" for help understanding the various modes.

Viewing Your Photos on a Television

Your camera is equipped with a feature that allows you to play your pictures and movies on a television screen. In fact, you have three playback options:

✓ **Regular (standard definition) video playback:** Haven't made the leap yet to HDTV? No worries: You can set the camera to send a regular standard-definition audio and video signal to the TV. The cable you need is even provided in the D5100 camera box. (Look for the cable that has a yellow plug and a white plug at one end.)

One hang-up to note about this option: For movies, the audio playback is monaural, even if you record sound using an external stereo microphone.

✔ **HDMI playback:** If you have a high-definition television, you need to purchase an HDMI cable to connect the camera and television. You need a Type C mini-pin HD cable; prices start at about $20. Nikon doesn't make its own cable, so just look for a quality third-party version.

By default, the camera decides the proper video resolution to send to the TV after you connect the two devices. But you have the option of setting a specific resolution as well. To do so, select HDMI from the Setup menu, press OK, and then choose Output Resolution, as shown in Figure 5-33. Press the Multi Selector right to access the available settings.

✔ **For HDMI CEC TV sets:** If your television is compatible with HDMI CEC, your D5100 enables you to use the buttons on the TV's remote control to perform the functions of the OK button and Multi Selector during full-frame picture playback and slide shows. To make this feature work, you must enable it via the Setup menu. Again, start with the HDMI option, but this time, select Device Control and set the option to On.

You need to make one final preflight check before connecting the camera and television: Verify the status of the Video Mode setting, located just above the HDMI option on the Setup menu. (Refer to the left screen in Figure 5-33.) You have just two options: NTSC and PAL. Select the video mode used by your part of the world. (In the United States, Canada, and Mexico, NTSC is the standard.) The mode should've been set at the factory to the right option for the country in which you bought your camera, but it never hurts to check.

SETUP MENU	
Format memory card	--
Monitor brightness	0
Info display format	info
Auto info display	ON
Clean image sensor	--
Lock mirror up for cleaning	--
Video mode	NTSC
HDMI	--

HDMI	
Output resolution	AUTO ▶
Device control	OFF

Figure 5-33: Select options for HD playback here.

After you select the necessary Setup menu options, grab your video cable, turn off the camera, and open the little rubber door on the left side of the camera. There you find two *ports* (connection slots): one for a standard audio/video (A/V) cable and one for the HDMI cable. Figure 5-34 labels the two ports.

The smaller plug on the A/V cable attaches to the camera. The yellow plug goes into your TV's video jack, and the white one goes into your TV's audio jack. For HDMI playback, a single plug goes to the TV.

At this point, I need to point you to your specific TV manual to find out exactly which jacks to use to connect your camera. You also need to consult your manual to find out which channel to select for playback of signals from auxiliary input devices. Then just turn on your camera to send the signal to the TV set. If you don't have the latest and greatest HDMI CEC capability (or lost your remote), control playback using the same techniques as you normally do to view pictures on your camera monitor. You can also run a slide show by following the steps outlined in the preceding section.

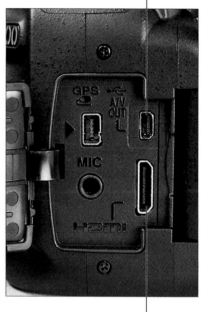

Standard A/V out

HD Out

Figure 5-34: The video-out ports are under the little rubber door on the side of the camera.

Deleting versus formatting: What's the diff?

Chapter 1 introduces the Format Memory Card command, which lives on the Setup menu and erases everything on your memory card. What's the difference between erasing photos by formatting and by choosing Delete from the Playback menu and then selecting the All option?

Well, if you happen to have stored other data on the card, such as, say, a music file or a picture taken on another type of camera, you need to format the card to erase those files. You can't use Delete to get rid of them.

Also keep in mind that the Delete function affects only the currently selected folder of camera images. The section "Choosing which images to view," earlier in this chapter, talks more about this issue; Chapter 11 explains how to create custom folders.

One final — and important — note: Although using the Protect feature (explained elsewhere in this chapter) prevents the Delete function from erasing a picture, formatting erases all pictures, protected or not.

6

Downloading, Printing, and Sharing Your Photos

In This Chapter

▶ Choosing photo software

▶ Transferring pictures to your computer using Nikon ViewNX 2

▶ Processing Raw (NEF) files

▶ Taking steps to ensure great print quality

▶ Preparing your photos for online sharing

For many novice digital photographers, the task of moving pictures to the computer is one of the more confusing aspects of the art form. Unfortunately, providing you with detailed downloading instructions is impossible because the steps vary widely depending on which computer software you use to do the job.

To give you as much help as I can, however, this chapter starts with a quick review of photo software, in case you aren't happy with your current solution. Following that, you can find information about downloading images, converting pictures that you shoot in the Raw format to a standard format, and preparing your pictures for print and online sharing.

Choosing the Right Photo Software

Programs for downloading, archiving, and editing digital photos abound, ranging from entry-level software designed for beginners to high-end options geared to professionals. The good news is that if you don't need serious photo-editing capabilities, you may find a free program that serves your needs — in fact, your camera ships with one free program, Nikon ViewNX 2.

The next section offers a look at Nikon ViewNX 2 along with two other free-bies; following that, I offer some advice on a few popular programs to consider when the free options don't meet your needs.

Three free photo programs

If you don't plan on doing a lot of retouching or other manipulation of your photos but simply want a tool for downloading and organizing your pictures, one of the following free programs may be a good solution:

- **Nikon ViewNX 2:** This program is on the CD that shipped in your camera box. As the name implies, the program provides a simple photo organizer and viewer, plus a few basic photo-editing features, including red-eye removal and exposure and color adjustment filters. You also can use the program to download pictures and to convert Raw files to a standard format. (See Chapter 2 for a primer on file formats.) I show you how to accomplish both tasks later in this chapter.

  Figure 6-1 offers a look at the ViewNX 2 window as it appears when you use the Thumbnail Grid view mode, one of three display options available from the View menu.

  After you download your photos, you can view camera *metadata* — the data that records the camera settings you used to take the picture — in ViewNX 2. Just display the Metadata panel, located on the right side of the program window, as shown in Figure 6-1. (If the panel is hidden, click the little triangle on the far right side of the window and then click the triangle at the top of the panel. I labeled both controls in the figure.) Many other photo programs also display metadata, but sometimes can't reveal data that's very camera specific, such as the Picture Control setting on the D5100. Every camera manufacturer records metadata differently, and the Raw data structure may vary even among cameras from the same manufacturer, so it's a little difficult for software companies to keep up with each new model.

  ViewNX 2 offers another cool feature that most other browsers don't: By clicking the Focus Point button, labeled in Figure 6-1, you can display a little red rectangle that indicates which focus point the camera used to establish focus for the shot, which can be helpful when you're trying to troubleshoot focus problems. You don't see the point if you used manual focusing when taking the shot, however, or if you used continuous auto-focusing and captured the shot before focus was completely set.

- **Apple iPhoto:** Most Mac users are very familiar with this photo browser, built into the Mac operating system. Apple provides some great tutorials on using iPhoto at its website (www.apple.com) to help you get started.

- **Windows Photo Gallery:** Some versions of Microsoft Windows also offer a free photo downloader and browser, Windows Photo Gallery (the name varies depending on your version of Windows).

Click to hide/display
focus point

Selected Focus Point

Click to hide/display
Metadata panel

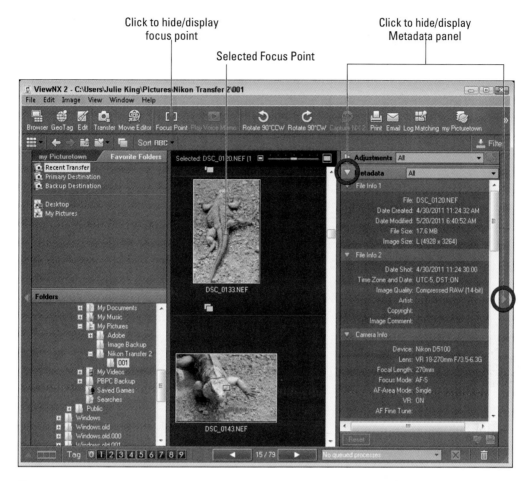

Figure 6-1: Nikon ViewNX 2 offers a basic photo viewer and some limited editing functions.

Advanced photo programs

Programs mentioned in the preceding section can handle simple photo downloading and organizing tasks. But if you're interested in serious photo retouching or digital-imaging artistry, you need to step up to a full-fledged photo-editing program.

As with software in the free category, you have many choices; the following list describes just the most widely known programs.

✔ **Adobe Photoshop Elements:** Elements has been the best-selling consumer-level photo-editing program for some time, and for good reason. With a full complement of retouching tools, onscreen guidance for beginners, and an assortment of templates for creating photo projects like scrapbooks, Elements offers all the features that most consumers need. Figure 6-2 shows the Elements editing window with some of the photo-creativity tools displayed to the right of the photo. The program includes a photo organizer as well, along with built-in tools to help you print your photos and upload them to photo-sharing sites. (www.adobe.com, about $100)

⌐ **Nikon Capture NX 2:** Shown in Figure 6-3, this Nikon program offers an image browser/organizer plus a wealth of photo-editing tools, including a sophisticated tool for processing Raw images. But as you can see from the figure, it's not exactly geared to casual photographers or novice photo editors, so expect a bit of a learning curve. Nor does this program offer the sort of photo-creativity tools you find in a program like Photoshop Elements (the same is true for the other advanced tools described in this list). (www.nikon.com, about $180)

⌐ **Apple Aperture:** Aperture is geared more to shooters who need to organize and process lots of images but typically do only light retouching work — wedding photographers and school-portrait photographers, for example. (www.apple.com, about $80, when purchased through Mac App store.)

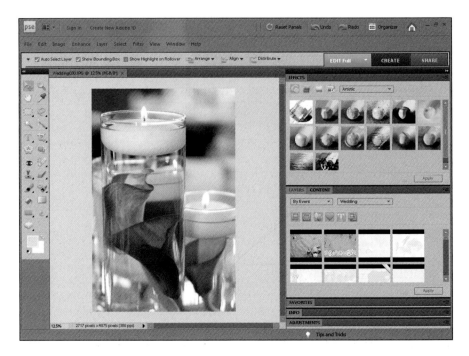

Figure 6-2: Adobe Photoshop Elements offers good retouching tools plus templates for creating scrapbooks, greeting cards, and other photo gifts.

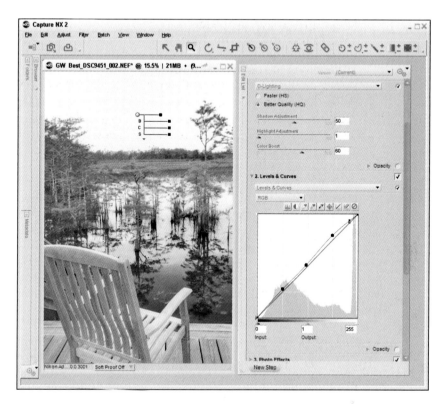

Figure 6-3: Nikon Capture NX 2 may appeal to photographers who need more robust image-editing tools than are found in ViewNX 2.

- **Adobe Photoshop Lightroom:** Lightroom is the Adobe counterpart to Aperture, although in its latest version, it offers some fairly powerful retouching tools as well. Many pro photographers rely on this program for all their work, in fact. (www.adobe.com, about $300)

- **Adobe Photoshop:** The granddaddy of photo editors, Photoshop offers the industry's most powerful, sophisticated retouching tools, including tools for producing HDR (high dynamic range) and 3D images. In fact, you probably won't use even a quarter of the tools in the Photoshop shed unless you're a digital imaging professional who uses the program on a daily basis — even then, some tools may never see the light of day. (www.adobe.com, about $700)

Not sure which tool you need, if any? Good news: You can download 30-day free trials of all these programs from the manufacturers' websites.

Sending Pictures to the Computer

Whatever photo software you choose, you can take the following approaches to downloading images to your computer:

- ✔ **Connect the camera to the computer via a USB cable.** The USB cable you need is supplied in the camera box.

- ✔ **Use a memory card reader.** With a card reader, you simply pop the memory card out of your camera and into the card reader instead of hooking the camera to the computer. Many computers and printers now have card readers, and you also can buy standalone readers for less than $30. *Note:* If you use the new SDHC (Secure Digital High Capacity) or SDXC (Secure Digital eXtended Capacity) cards, the reader must specifically support that type.

- ✔ **Invest in Eye-Fi memory cards and transfer images via a wireless network.** You can find out more about these special memory cards and how to set up the card to connect with your computer, at the manufacturer's website, www.eye.fi. Your computer must be connected to a wireless network for the transfer technology to work.

For most people, I recommend a card reader. Sending pictures directly from the camera, whether via cable or wirelessly, requires that the camera be turned on during the entire download process, wasting battery power. Additionally, not all devices can use Eye-Fi memory cards, meaning that you're spending money on cards that may have limited use beyond serving as storage on your camera. Card readers, on the other hand, can accept cards from any device that uses SD cards, which are fast becoming the standard storage medium for portable devices.

That said, I include information about cable transfer in the next section in case you don't have a card reader. To use a card reader, skip ahead to "Starting the transfer process," in this chapter.

Connecting the camera and computer for picture download

With the USB cable that shipped with your camera, you can connect the camera to your computer and then transfer images directly to the computer's hard drive.

The next section explains the actual transfer process; the steps here just walk you through the process of connecting the two devices. You need to follow a specific set of steps when connecting the camera to your computer. Otherwise, you can damage the camera or the memory card.

Also note that for your camera to communicate with the computer, Nikon suggests that your computer runs one of the following operating systems:

- ✓ Windows 7, Vista with Service Pack 2, or XP with Service Pack 3 (Home or Professional edition). The program runs as a 32-bit application in 64-bit installations of Windows 7 and Windows Vista.
- ✓ Mac OS X 10.4.11, 10.5.8, or 10.6.6

If you use another OS (operating system, for the nongeeks in the crowd), check the support pages on the Nikon website (www.nikon.com) for the latest news about any updates to system compatibility. You can always simply transfer images with a card reader, too.

With that preamble out of the way, here are the steps to link your computer and camera:

1. **Check the level of the camera battery.**

   If the battery is low, charge it before continuing. Running out of battery power during the transfer process can cause problems, including lost picture data. Alternatively, if you purchased the optional AC adapter, use that to power the camera during picture transfers.

2. **Turn on the computer and give it time to finish its normal startup routine.**

3. **Turn off the camera.**

4. **Insert the smaller of the two plugs on the USB cable into the USB port on the side of the camera.**

   Look under the top rubber door on the left side of the camera for this port, labeled in Figure 6-4.

5. **Plug the other end of the cable into the computer's USB port.**

   If possible, plug the cable into a port that's built in to the computer, as opposed to one that's on your keyboard or part of an external USB hub. Those accessory-type connections can sometimes foul up the transfer process.

6. **Turn on the camera.**

   What happens now depends on your computer operating system and what photo software you have installed on that

USB port

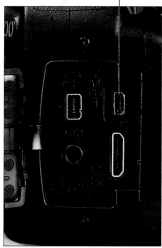

Figure 6-4: The USB slot is hidden under the top rubber door on the left side of the camera.

system. The next section explains the possibilities and how to proceed with the image transfer process.

7. **When the download is complete, turn off the camera and then disconnect it from the computer.**

I repeat: Turn off the camera before severing its ties with the computer. Otherwise, you can damage the camera.

Starting the transfer process

After you connect the camera to the computer or insert a memory card into your card reader, your next step depends, again, on the software installed on your computer and the computer operating system.

Here are the most common possibilities and how to move forward:

✔ **On a Windows-based computer, a Windows message box similar to the one in Figure 6-5 appears.** Again, the figure shows the dialog box as it appears on a computer running Windows 7. Whatever its design, the dialog box suggests different programs that you can use to download your picture files. Which programs appear depend on what you have installed on your system. If you installed Nikon ViewNX 2, for example, the list should contain a Nikon Transfer 2 entry, as shown in the figure. *Nikon Transfer 2* is the downloading utility built into ViewNX 2.

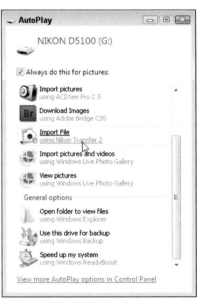

Figure 6-5: Windows may display this initial boxful of transfer options.

In Windows 7 and Vista, just click the transfer program that you want to use. In other versions of Windows, the dialog box may sport an OK button; if so, click that button to proceed.

If you want to use the same program for all your transfers, select the Always Do This for Pictures check box, as shown in the figure. (In other versions of Windows, the check box may have a slightly different name.) The next time you connect your camera or insert a memory card, Windows will automatically launch your program of choice instead of displaying the message box.

✒ **An installed photo program automatically displays a photo-download wizard.** For example, the Nikon Transfer 2 downloader or a downloader associated with Adobe Photoshop Elements, iPhoto, or some other photo software may leap to the forefront. Usually, the downloader that appears is associated with the software that you most recently installed. Each new program that you add to your system tries to wrestle control over your image downloads away from the previous program.

If you don't want a program's auto downloader to launch whenever you insert a memory card or connect your camera, you can turn off that feature. Check the software manual to find out how to disable the auto launch.

✒ **Nothing happens.** Don't panic; assuming that your card reader or camera is properly connected, all is probably well. Someone simply may have disabled all the automatic downloaders on your system. Just launch your photo software and then transfer your pictures using whatever command starts that process.

As another option, you can use Windows Explorer or the Mac Finder to drag and drop files from your memory card to your computer's hard drive. When you connect the card through a card reader, the computer sees the card as just another drive on the system. Windows Explorer also shows the camera as a storage device when you cable the camera directly to the computer. So the process of transferring files is exactly the same as when you move any other file from a CD, DVD, or other storage device onto your hard drive.

In the next section, I provide details on using Nikon Transfer 2 to download your files. If you use some other software, the concepts are the same, but check your program manual to get the small details. In most programs, you also can find lots of information by simply clicking open the Help menu.

Downloading photos with Nikon ViewNX 2

If you want to use the free Nikon software, Nikon ViewNX 2, to download, view, and organize your photos, dig out the program CD from your camera box and install the software on your system.

Also note that this book features Nikon ViewNX 2 version 2.1.2 for Windows and 2.1.1. for Mac. If you own an earlier version of the program, visit the Nikon website to install the updates. (To find out what version you have installed, open the program. Then, in Windows, choose Help➪About. On a Mac, choose the About command from the Nikon Transfer or Nikon ViewNX menu.) You also may be able to use the built-in software updater, depending on the age of your software. Open the program and choose Help➪Check for Updates to give it a go.

One final software-related point: You can use Nikon ViewNX 2 to download your photos and still use any photo-editing or image-management software you prefer. And to do your editing, you don't need to download photos a second time — after you transfer photos to your computer, you can access them from any program, just as you can any file that you put on your system. With some programs, however, you must first take the step of *importing* or *cataloging* the photo files, which enables the program to build thumbnails and, in some cases, working copies of your pictures.

With that preamble out of the way, the following steps walk you through the process of downloading via Nikon ViewNX 2:

1. **Attach your camera to the computer or insert a memory card into your card reader, as outlined in the first part of this chapter.**

   Depending on what software you have installed on your system, you may see a dialog box asking you how to download your photos. If the window that appears is the Nikon Transfer 2 window, shown in Figure 6-6, skip to Step 3. *Nikon Transfer 2* is the picture-downloading utility built into ViewNX 2.

   Similarly, if you see a Windows dialog box that contains the Nikon Transfer 2 option, as shown in Figure 6-5, click that option and skip to Step 3.

   If nothing happens, don't worry — just travel to Step 2, which shows you how to launch the Nikon Transfer 2 software if it didn't appear automatically.

2. **Launch Nikon Transfer 2, if it isn't already open.**

   To access the transfer tool, open Nikon ViewNX 2 and then choose File➪Launch Transfer or click the Transfer button at the top of the window. The window shown in Figure 6-6 appears. (If you use a Mac, the window decor is slightly different, but the main controls and features are the same.)

3. **Display the Source tab to view thumbnails of your pictures, as shown in the figure.**

   Don't see any tabs? Click the little Options triangle, located near the top-left corner of the window and labeled in Figure 6-6, to display them. Then click the Source tab. The icon representing your camera or memory card should be selected, as shown in the figure. If not, click the icon.

   Thumbnails of your images appear in the bottom half of the dialog box. If you don't see the thumbnails, click the arrow labeled in Figure 6-6 to open the thumbnails area.

4. **Select the images that you want to download.**

   A check mark in the little box under a thumbnail tells the program that you want to download the image. Click the box to toggle the check mark on and off.

Click to hide/display thumbnails

Click to hide/display options

Select All

Select Protected

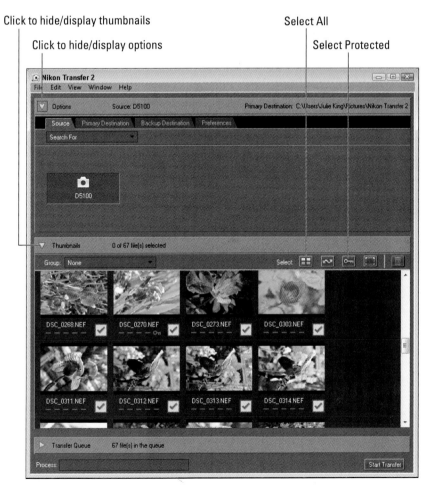

Figure 6-6: Select the check boxes of the images that you want to download.

If you used the in-camera function to protect pictures (see Chapter 5), you can select just those images by clicking the Select Protected icon, labeled in Figure 6-6. To select all images on the card, click the Select All icon instead.

5. **Click the Primary Destination tab at the top of the window.**

When you click the tab, the top of the transfer window offers options that enable you to specify where and how you want the images to be stored on your computer. Figure 6-7 offers a look.

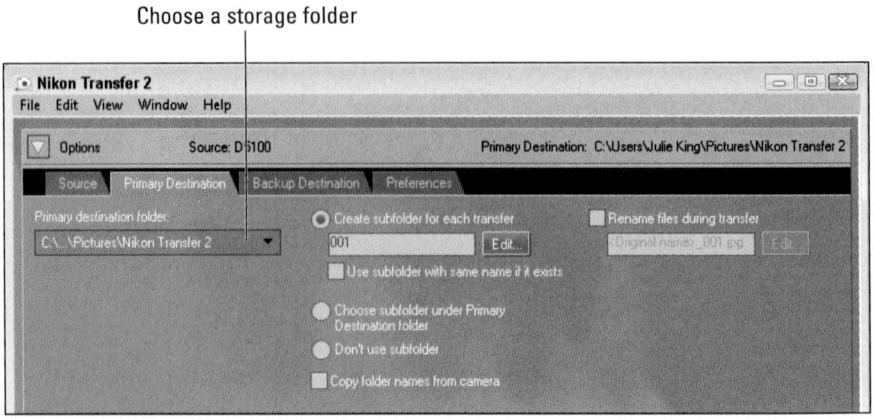

Choose a storage folder

Figure 6-7: Specify the folder where you want to put the downloaded images.

6. **Choose the folder where you want to store the images from the Primary Destination Folder drop-down list.**

The list is labeled in Figure 6-7. If the folder you want to use isn't in the list, open the drop-down list, choose Browse from the bottom of the list, and then track down the folder and select it.

By default, the program puts images in a Nikon Transfer folder, which is housed inside the My Pictures folder in Windows XP and Pictures in Windows 7, Windows Vista, and on a Mac. That My Pictures or Pictures folder is housed inside a folder that your system creates automatically for each registered user of the computer.

You don't have to stick with this default location — you can put your pictures anywhere you please. But because most photo programs automatically look for pictures in these standard folders, putting your pictures there simplifies things a little down the road. You can always move your pictures into other folders after you download them if needed, too.

7. **Specify whether you want the pictures to be placed inside a new subfolder.**

If you select the Create Subfolder for Each Transfer option, the program creates a new folder inside the storage folder you selected in Step 6. Then it puts all the pictures from the current download session into that new subfolder. You can either use the numerical subfolder name the program suggests or click the Edit button to set up your own naming system. You might find it helpful to go with a folder name that includes the date that the batch of photos was taken, for example. (You can reorganize your pictures into this type of setup after download, however.) If you created custom folders on the camera memory card, an option you can explore in Chapter 11, select the Copy Folder Names from Camera check box to use those folder names instead.

8. **Tell the program whether you want to rename the picture files during the download process.**

   If you do, select the Rename Files during Transfer check box. Then click the Edit button to display a dialog box where you can set up your new filenaming scheme. Click OK after you do so to close the dialog box.

9. **Click the Preferences tab to set the rest of the transfer options.**

   The tab shown in Figure 6-8 takes over the top of the program window. Here you find a number of options that enable you to control how the program operates, as follows:

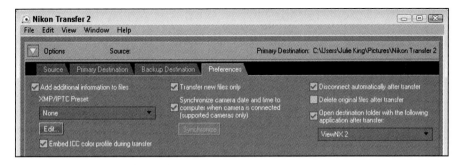

Figure 6-8: Control other aspects of the program's behavior via the Preferences tab.

- *Add Additional Information to Files:* Through this option, you can embed XMP/IPTC data in the file. *IPTC* refers to text data that press photographers are often required to tag onto their picture files, such as captions and copyright information. *XMP* refers to a data format developed by Adobe to enable that kind of data to be added to the file. IPTC stands for International Press Telecommunications Council; XMP stands for Extensible Metadata Platform.

  Click the Edit button beneath the option to create and store a preset that contains the data you want to add. On your next visit to the dialog box, you can choose the preset from the drop-down list above the Edit button.

  You also can tag a file with text comments in the camera, using the Image Comment feature that I cover in Chapter 11.

- *Embed ICC Color Profile during Transfer:* This option relates to the Color Space option on the Shooting menu. Nikon recommends that you enable this option if you capture images using the Adobe RGB color space instead of the default, sRGB space. Otherwise, some photo programs may simply assume that the files are in the sRGB space. Chapter 8 explains the Color Space setting.

- *Transfer New Files Only:* This option, when selected, ensures that you don't waste time downloading images that you've already transferred but are still on the memory card.

- *Synchronize Camera Date and Time . . . :* If you connect your camera to the computer via USB cable, selecting this option tells the camera to reset its internal clock to match the date and time of the computer.

- *Disconnect Automatically after Transfer:* Choose this option to tell the transfer tool to shut itself down automatically when the download is complete.

- *Delete Original Files after Transfer:* Turn off this option, as shown in Figure 6-8. Otherwise, your pictures are automatically erased from your memory card when the transfer is complete. Always make sure the pictures really made it to the computer before you delete them from your memory card. (See Chapter 5 to find out how to use the Delete function on your camera.)

- *Open Destination Folder with the Following Application after Transfer:* By default, Nikon ViewNX 2 starts automatically at the end of the download process if it isn't already open. If you want to use a program other than ViewNX 2 to view and edit your photos, open the drop-down list, choose Browse, and select the program from the dialog box that appears. Click OK after doing so.

Your choices remain in force for any subsequent download sessions, so you don't have to revisit this tab unless you want the program to behave differently.

10. **When you're ready to start the download, click the Start Transfer button.**

It's located in the lower-right corner of the program window. (Refer to Figure 6-6.) After you click the button, the Process bar in the lower-left corner indicates how the transfer is progressing. Again, what happens when the transfer completes depends on the choices you made in Step 9; by default, Nikon Transfer closes, and ViewNX 2 opens, automatically displaying the folder that contains your just-downloaded images.

Processing Raw (NEF) Files

Chapter 2 introduces you to the Raw file format. The advantage of capturing Raw files, or NEF files on Nikon cameras, is that you make the decisions about how to translate the original picture data into an actual photograph. You can specify attributes such as color intensity, image sharpening, contrast, and so on — which are all handled automatically by the camera if you use its other file format, JPEG. You take these steps by using a software tool known as a *Raw converter*.

The bad news: Until you convert your NEF files into a standard file format, you can't share them online or print them from most programs other than Nikon ViewNX 2. You also can't get prints from most retail outlets or open them in many photo-editing programs.

To process your D5100 NEF files, you have the following options:

- ✔ **Use the in-camera processing feature.** Through the Retouch menu, you can process your Raw images right in the camera. You can specify only limited image attributes, and you can save the processed files only in the JPEG format, but still, having this option is a nice feature.

- ✔ **Process and convert in ViewNX 2.** ViewNX 2 also offers a Raw processing feature. Again, the controls for setting picture characteristics are a little limited, but you can save the adjusted files in either the JPEG or TIFF format. See the next section for an explanation of TIFF.

- ✔ **Use Nikon Capture NX 2 or a third-party Raw conversion tool.** For the most control over your Raw images, you need to open your wallet and invest in a program that offers a truly capable converter. See the first part of this chapter for a review of Capture NX 2 as well as some other programs with good Raw converters.

The next two sections show you how to convert Raw files using your camera and ViewNX 2. If you opt for a third-party conversion tool, check the program's Help system for details on how to use the various controls, which vary from program to program.

Processing Raw images in the camera

Through the NEF (RAW) Processing option on the Retouch menu, you can convert Raw files right in the camera — no computer or other software required. I want to share two reservations about this option, however:

- ✔ You can save your processed files only in the JPEG format. As discussed in Chapter 2, that format results in some quality loss because of the file compression that JPEG applies. You can choose the level of JPEG compression you want to apply during Raw processing; you can create a JPEG Fine, Normal, or Basic file. Each of those settings produces the same quality that you get when you shoot new photos in the JPEG format and select Fine, Normal, or Basic from the Image Quality menu.

- Chapter 2 details the JPEG options, but, long story short, choose Fine for the best JPEG quality. And if you want to produce the absolute best quality from your Raw images, use a software solution and save your processed file in the TIFF format instead. *TIFF* is a *lossless* format, which means that all original image quality is retained. TIFF is the publishing industry standard format, so almost every photo program can open TIFF files.

✔ You can make adjustments to exposure, color, and a few other options as part of the in-camera Raw conversion process. Evaluating the effects of your adjustments on the camera monitor can be difficult because of the size of the display compared to your computer monitor. So for really tricky images, you may want to forgo in-camera conversion and do the job on your computer, where you can get a better — and bigger — view of things. If you do go the in-camera route, make sure that the monitor brightness is set to its default position so that you aren't misled by the display. (The Monitor Brightness adjustment option is found on the Setup menu.)

That said, in-camera Raw processing offers a quick and convenient solution when you need JPEG copies of your Raw images for immediate online sharing — JPEG is the standard format for online use — or to share with someone who doesn't have photo software that can handle Raw images. And you can always process the image once on the camera and then create a second version after downloading files to your computer — the original NEF image is always maintained, so you can create as many processed variations as you like.

Follow these steps to get the job done:

1. **Press the Playback button to switch to playback mode.**

2. **Display the picture you want to process in the single-image (full-frame) view.**

   If necessary, you can shift from thumbnails view to single-image view by just pressing OK. Chapter 5 has more playback details.

3. **Press OK.**

   The Retouch menu then appears atop your photo, as shown in Figure 6-9.

4. **Use the Multi Selector to scroll to the NEF (RAW) Processing option, as shown in Figure 6-9.**

5. **Press OK to display your processing options, as shown in Figure 6-10.**

   This screen is command central for specifying what settings you want the camera to use when creating the JPEG version of your Raw image.

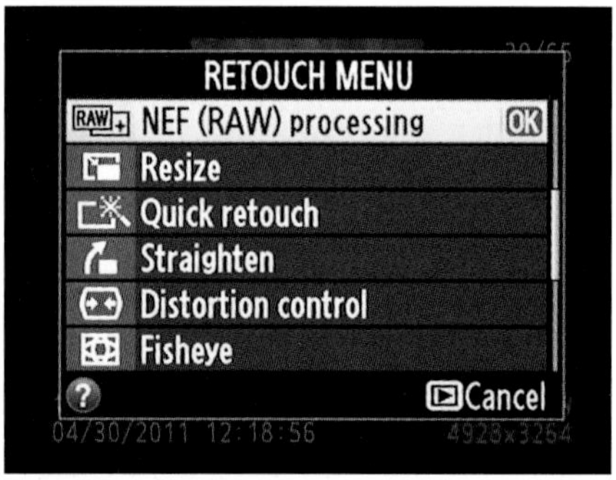

Figure 6-9: In single-image playback mode, press OK to display the Retouch menu over your photo.

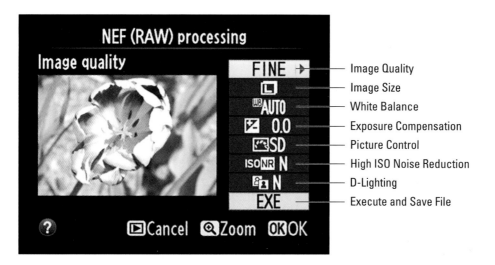

Figure 6-10: Specify Raw conversion settings here.

6. Set the conversion options.

Along the right side of the screen, you see a vertical column offering the conversion options labeled in Figure 6-10. To establish the setting for an option, highlight it and then press the Multi Selector right. You then see the available settings for the option. For example, if you choose the White Balance option, you see the screen shown in Figure 6-11. Highlight the setting you want to use and press OK to return to the main Raw conversion screen. Or, if a triangle appears to the right of the options name, you can press the Multi Selector right

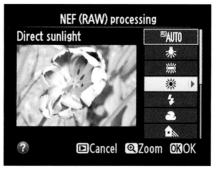

Figure 6-11: After selecting a White Balance setting, press the Multi Selector right to reveal a screen where you can fine-tune the setting.

to uncover additional options. For example, pressing the Multi Selector right after choosing one of the White Balance settings takes you to a screen where you can fine-tune the setting, just as you can when adjusting White Balance during shooting. (Chapter 8 explains that feature.)

Rather than detailing all the options here, the following list points you to the chapter where you can explore the settings available for each:

- *Image Quality:* See the Chapter 2 section related to the JPEG quality settings for details on this option. Choose Fine to retain maximum picture quality.

- *Image Size:* Chapter 2 explains this one, too. Choose Large to retain all the original image pixels.

- *White Balance:* Check out Chapter 8 for details about White Balance options, which affect picture colors.

- *Exposure Compensation:* With this option, you can adjust image brightness by applying Exposure Compensation, a feature that I cover in Chapter 7.

- *Picture Control:* This option enables you to adjust color, contrast, and image sharpness. For a review of the available settings, see the last part of Chapter 8.

- *High ISO Noise Reduction:* See Chapter 7 for an explanation of this feature, which is designed to reduce the amount of noise in pictures shot using a high ISO Sensitivity setting.

- *D-Lighting:* This feature does the same thing as Active D-Lighting, covered in Chapter 7: It helps brighten too-dark areas of a picture without blowing out highlights at the same time. You can specify the level of correction (High, Normal, Low, or none).

7. **When you finish setting all the conversion options, highlight EXE on the main conversion screen (refer to Figure 6-10) and then press OK.**

The camera records a JPEG copy of your Raw file and displays the copy in the monitor. To remind you that the image was created with the help of the Retouch menu, the top-left corner of the display sports the little Retouch icon, as shown in Figure 6-12. In addition, filenames of pictures created with the Retouch menu begin with the three-letter prefix CSC instead of the usual DSC (or _CSC, if you captured the original in the Adobe RGB color space, as explained in Chapter 8). The camera assigns the next available file number to the image, so the number of the original and the number of the processed JPEG don't match.

Retouch icon

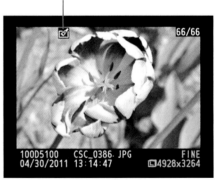

Figure 6-12: The Retouch icon indicates that you created the picture file by using an option on the Retouch menu.

Processing Raw files in ViewNX 2

In ViewNX 2, you can convert your Raw files to the JPEG format or, for top picture quality, to the TIFF format. Although the ViewNX 2 converter isn't as full-featured as the ones in Nikon Capture NX 2 and some other photo-editing programs, it does enable you to make some adjustments to your Raw images. Follow these steps to try it out:

1. **Open ViewNX 2 and click the thumbnail of the image that you want to process.**

   You may want to set the program to Image Viewer mode, as shown in Figure 6-13, so that you can see a larger preview of your image. Just choose View➪Image Viewer to switch to this display mode. To give the photo even more room, also hide the Browser panel, which normally occupies the left third of the window, and the Filmstrip panel that usually runs across the bottom of the window. Choose Window➪Browser and Window➪Filmstrip to toggle those window elements on and off.

Click to hide/display Adjustments panel

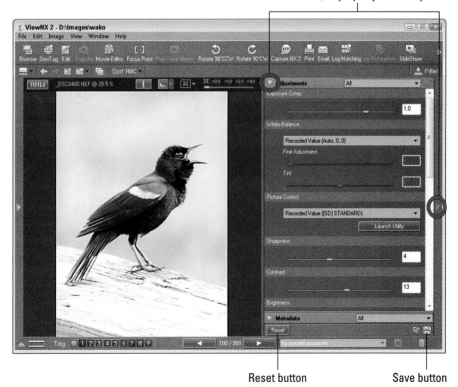

Reset button   Save button

Figure 6-13: Display the Adjustments panel to tweak Raw images before conversion.

2. **Display the Adjustments panel on the right side of the program window.**

   I labeled the panel in Figure 6-13. You show and hide this panel and the Metadata panel by choosing Window➪Edit or by clicking the triangle on the far right side of the window. You can then display and collapse the individual panels by clicking the triangles to the left of their names. (I labeled the triangles in the figure.) To allow the maximum space for the Raw conversion adjustments, collapse the Metadata panel, as shown in the figure. If necessary, drag the vertical bar between the image window and the Adjustments panel to adjust the width of the panel.

3. **To display all available image settings, choose All from the Adjustments drop-down list at the top of the panel, as shown in the figure.**

   Unless you use a large monitor, you may need to use the scroll bar on the right side of the panel to scroll the display to see all the options.

4. **Use the panel controls to adjust your image.**

   The preview you see in the image window reflects the default conversion settings chosen by Nikon. But you can play with any of the settings as you see fit. If you need help understanding any of the options, open the built-in help system (via the Help menu), where you can find descriptions of how each adjustment affects your image.

   To return to the original image settings, click the Reset button at the bottom of the panel, labeled in Figure 6-13.

5. **Click the Save button at the bottom of the panel (refer to Figure 6-13).**

   This step stores your conversion settings as part of the image file but doesn't actually create your JPEG or TIFF copy of the photo. Don't worry — your original Raw data remains intact; all that's saved with the file is a "recipe" for processing the image, which you can change at any time.

6. **To save the processed file, choose File➪Convert Files.**

   Or just click the Convert Files button on the toolbar at the top of the program window. Either way, you see the Convert Files dialog box, as shown in Figure 6-14.

7. **Choose TIFF(8 Bit) from the File Format drop-down list.**

   A *bit* is a unit of computer data; the more bits you have, the more colors your image can contain. Although you can create 16-bit TIFF files in the converter, many photo-editing programs either can't open them or limit you to a few editing tools, so I suggest you stick with the standard, 8-bit image option. Your image will contain more than enough colors, and you'll avoid potential conflicts caused by so-called *high-bit* images.

   Don't choose JPEG; the JPEG format applies *lossy compression,* thereby sacrificing some image quality. If you need a JPEG copy of your processed Raw image for online sharing, you can easily create one from your TIFF version by following the steps laid out near the end of this chapter.

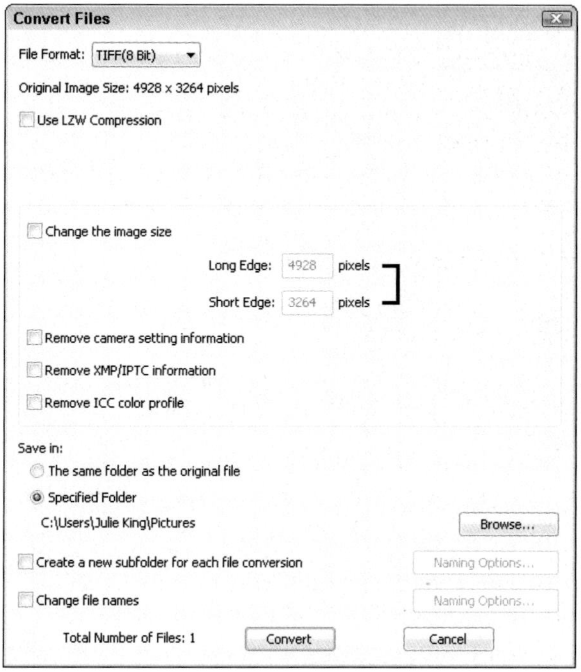

Figure 6-14: To retain the best image quality, save processed Raw files in the TIFF format.

8. Deselect the Use LZW Compression option, as shown in the figure.

Although LZW compression reduces the file size somewhat and does not cause any quality loss, some programs can't open files that were saved with this option enabled. So turn it off.

9. Deselect the Change the Image Size check box.

This step ensures that you retain all the original pixels in your image, which gives you the most flexibility in terms of generating quality prints at large sizes. For details on this issue, check out Chapter 2.

10. Deselect each of the three Remove check boxes.

If you select the check boxes, you strip image *metadata* — the extra text data that's stored by the camera — from the file. Unless you have some specific reason to do so, clear all three check boxes so that you can continue to access the metadata when you view your processed image in programs that know how to display metadata.

The first check box relates to data that you can view on the Metadata panel in ViewNX; the first section of the chapter gives you the lowdown. The second box refers to the XMP/IPTC data that you can embed during file transfer; see the section "Downloading photos with Nikon ViewNX 2" for a discussion of that issue. The ICC profile item refers to the image *color space,* which is either sRGB or Adobe RGB on your D5100. Chapter 8 explains the difference.

11. **Select a storage location for the processed TIFF file.**

    You do this in the Save In area of the dialog box. Select the top option to save your processed file in the same folder as the original Raw file. Or, to put the file in a different folder, click the Specified Folder button. The name of the currently selected alternative folder appears below the button, as shown in Figure 6-14. You can change the storage destination by clicking the Browse button and then selecting the drive and folder where you want to put the file.

    By selecting the Create a New Subfolder for Each File Conversion check box, you can put your TIFF file into a separate folder within the destination folder. If you select the box, click the Naming Options button and then specify how you want to name the subfolder.

12. **Specify whether you want to give the processed TIFF a different filename from the original Raw image.**

    To do so, select the Change File Names check box, click the Naming Options button, and enter the name you want to use.

    If you don't change the filename, the program gives the file the same name as the original Raw file. But you don't overwrite that Raw file because you're storing the copy in a different file format (TIFF). In Windows, the filename of the processed TIFF image has the three-letter extension TIF.

13. **Click the Convert button.**

    A window appears to show you the progress of the conversion process. When the window disappears, your TIFF image appears in the storage location you selected in Step 11.

One neat thing about working with Raw images is that you can easily create as many variations of your photo as you want. For example, you might choose one set of options when processing your Raw file the first time and then use an entirely different set to create another version of the photo. Just be sure to give each processed file a unique name so that you don't overwrite the first TIFF file you create with your second version.

Planning for Perfect Prints

Images from your D5100 can produce dynamic prints, and getting those prints made is easy and economical, thanks to an abundance of digital printing services in stores and online. For home printing, today's printers are better and less expensive than ever, too. That said, getting the best prints from your picture files requires a little bit of knowledge and prep work on your part, whether you decide to do the job yourself or use a retail lab. To that end, the next three sections offer tips to help you avoid the most common causes of printing problems.

Check the pixel count before you print

Resolution — the number of pixels in your digital image — plays a huge role in how large you can print your photos and still maintain good picture quality. You can get the complete story on resolution in Chapter 2, but here's a quick recap as it relates to printing:

✏ **Choose the right resolution before you shoot:** Set resolution via the Image Size option, found on the Shooting menu, or via the Quick Settings screen.

You must select the size *before* you capture an image, which means that you need some idea of the ultimate print size before you shoot. When you do the resolution math, remember to take any cropping you plan to do into account.

✏ **Aim for a minimum of 200 pixels per inch (ppi):** You'll get a wide range of recommendations on this issue, even among professionals. But in general, if you aim for a resolution in the neighborhood of 200 ppi, you should be pleased with your results. If you want a 4-x-6-inch print, for example, you need at least 800 x 1200 pixels.

Depending on your printer, you may get even better results at a slightly lower resolution. On the other hand, some printers do their best work when fed 300 ppi, and a few request 360 ppi as the optimum resolution. However, using a resolution higher than that typically doesn't produce any better prints.

Unfortunately, because most printer manuals don't bother to tell you what image resolution produces the best results, finding the right pixel level is a matter of experimentation. (Don't confuse *ppi* with the manual's statements related to the printer's dpi. *Dots per inch (dpi)* refers to the number of dots of color the printer can lay down per inch; many printers use multiple dots to reproduce one image pixel.)

If you're printing photos at a retail kiosk or at an online site, the software you use to order prints should determine the resolution of your files and then suggest appropriate print sizes. If you're printing on a home printer, though, you need to be the resolution cop.

What do you do if you don't have enough pixels for the print size you have in mind? You have the following two choices, neither of which provides a good outcome:

✏ **Keep the existing pixel count and accept lowered photo quality.** In this case, the pixels simply get bigger to fill the requested print size. When pixels grow too large, they produce a defect known as *pixelation:* The picture starts to appear jagged, or stairstepped, along curved or oblique lines. Or, at worst, your eye can make out the individual pixels, and your photo begins to look more like a mosaic than, well, like a photograph.

✏ **Add more pixels and accept lowered photo quality.** In some photo programs, you can add pixels to an image (the technical term for this process is *upsampling*). Some other photo programs even upsample the photo automatically for you, depending on the print settings you choose.

Although adding pixels might sound like a good option, it actually doesn't help in the long run. You're asking the software to make up photo information out of thin air, and the resulting image usually looks worse than the original. You don't see pixelation, but details turn muddy, giving the image a blurry, poorly rendered appearance.

Just to hammer home the point and remind you again of the impact of resolution picture quality, Figures 6-15 through 6-17 show you the same image as it appears at 300 ppi (the resolution required by the publisher of this book), at 50 ppi, and then resampled from 50 ppi to 300 ppi. As you can see, there's just no way around the rule: If you want the best-quality prints, you need the right pixel count from the get-go.

300 ppi

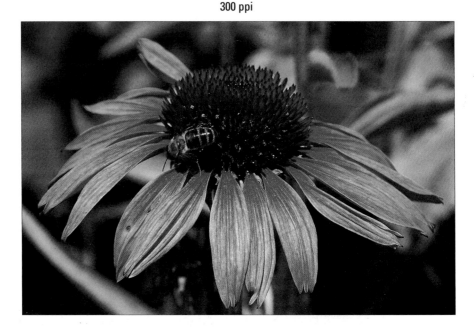

Figure 6-15: A high-quality print depends on a high-resolution original.

50 ppi

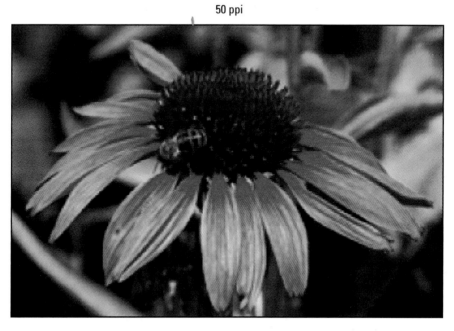

Figure 6-16: At 50 ppi, the image has a jagged, pixelated look.

50 ppi resampled to 300 ppi

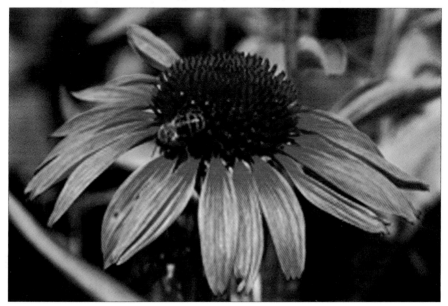

Figure 6-17: Adding pixels in a photo editor doesn't rescue a low-resolution original.

Allow for different print proportions

The D5100 produces images that have a 3:2 aspect ratio, which matches the proportions of a 4-x-6-inch print. To print your photo at other traditional sizes — 5 x 7, 8 x 10, and so on — you need to crop the photo to match those proportions. Alternatively, you can reduce the photo size slightly and leave an empty margin along the edges of the print as needed.

As a point of reference, both images in Figure 6-18 are original, 3:2 images. The red outlines indicate how much of the original can fit within a 5-x-7-inch frame and an 8-x-10-inch frame, respectively.

Chapter 10 shows you how to crop your image using the Trim option on the Retouch menu. You also can usually crop your photo using the software provided at online printing sites and at retail print kiosks. If you plan to simply drop off your memory card for printing at a lab, be sure to find out whether the printer automatically crops the image without your input. If so, use your photo software to crop the photo, save the cropped image to your memory card, and deliver that version of the file to the printer.

5 x 7   8 x 10

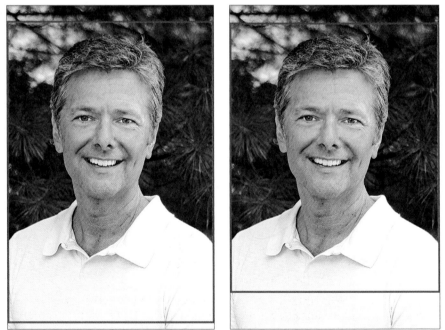

Figure 6-18: Composing your shots with a little head room enables you to crop to different frame sizes.

To allow yourself some printing flexibility, leave at least a little margin of background around your subject when you shoot (refer to Figure 6-18). That way, you don't clip off the edges of the subject, no matter what print size you choose. (Some people refer to this margin padding as *head room,* especially when describing portrait composition.)

Get print and monitor colors in sync

Ah, your photo colors look perfect on your computer monitor. But when you print the picture, the image is too red or too green or has another nasty color tint. This problem, which is probably the most prevalent printing issue, can occur because of any or all the following factors:

✔ **Your monitor needs to be calibrated.** When print colors don't match the ones you see on your monitor, the most likely culprit is the monitor, not the printer. If the monitor isn't accurately calibrated, the colors it displays aren't a true reflection of your image colors. The same caveat applies to monitor brightness: You can't accurately gauge the exposure of a photo if the brightness of the monitor is cranked way up or down. It's worth noting that many of today's new monitors are very bright, providing ideal conditions for web browsing and watching movies but not necessarily for photo editing. So you may need to turn the brightness way, way down to get to a true indication of image exposure.

To ensure that your monitor displays photos on a neutral canvas, you can start with a software-based *calibration utility,* which is just a small program that guides you through the process of adjusting your monitor. The program displays various color swatches and other graphics, and then asks you to provide feedback about the colors you see onscreen.

If you use a Mac, its operating system (OS) offers a built-in calibration utility, the Display Calibrator Assistant; Windows 7 offers a similar tool: Display Color Calibration. You also can find free calibration software for both Mac and Windows systems online; just enter the term *free monitor calibration software* into your favorite search engine.

Software-based tools, though, depend on your eyes to make decisions during the calibration process. For a more reliable calibration, you may want to invest in a hardware solution, such as the huey PRO (about $100, www.pantone.com) or the Spyder3Express (about $90, www.data color.com). These products use a device known as a *colorimeter* to accurately measure display colors.

Whichever route you take, the calibration process produces a monitor *profile,* which is simply a data file that tells your computer how to adjust the display to compensate for any monitor color casts or brightness and contrast issues. Your Windows or Mac operating system loads this file automatically when you start your computer. Your only responsibility is to perform the calibration every month or so because monitor colors drift over time.

✔ **One of your printer cartridges is empty or clogged.** If your prints look great one day but are way off the next, the number-one suspect is an empty ink cartridge or a clogged print nozzle or head. Check your manual to find out how to perform the necessary maintenance to keep the nozzles or print heads in good shape.

If black-and-white prints have a color tint, a logical assumption is that your black ink cartridge is to blame, if your printer has one. But the truth is that images from a printer that doesn't use multiple black or gray cartridges typically have a slight color tint even when all ink cartridges are fine. Why? Because to create gray, the printer instead has to mix yellow, magenta, and cyan in perfectly equal amounts, and that's a difficult feat for the typical inkjet printer to pull off. If your black-and-white prints have a strong color tint, however, a color cartridge might be empty, and replacing it may help somewhat. Long story short: Unless your printer is marketed for producing good black-and-white prints, you'll probably save yourself some grief by simply having your black-and-whites printed at a retail lab.

When you buy replacement ink, by the way, keep in mind that third-party brands (though perhaps cheaper) may not deliver the same performance as cartridges from your printer manufacturer. A lot of science goes into getting ink formulas to mesh with the printer's ink-delivery system, and the printer manufacturer obviously knows most about that delivery system.

✔ **You chose the wrong paper setting in your printer software.** When you set up a print job, be sure to select the right setting from the paper type option — glossy or matte, for example. This setting affects the way the printer lays down ink on the paper.

✔ **Your photo paper is low quality.** Sad but true: Cheap, store-brand photo papers usually don't render colors as well as the higher-priced, name-brand papers. For best results, try papers from your printer manufacturer; again, those papers are engineered to provide top performance with the printer's specific inks and ink-delivery system.

Some paper manufacturers, especially those that sell fine-art papers, offer downloadable *printer profiles,* which are simply little bits of software that tell your printer how to manage color for the paper. Refer to the manufacturer's website for information on how to install and use the profiles. And note that a profile mismatch can also cause incorrect colors in your prints, including the color tint in black-and-white prints alluded to earlier.

✔ **Your printer and photo software fight over color management duties.** Some photo programs offer *color management* tools, which enable you to control how colors are handled as an image passes from camera to monitor to printer. Most printer software also offers color management features. The problem is, if you enable color management controls in both your photo software and printer software, you can create conflicts that lead to wacky colors. Check your photo software and printer manuals for color management options and ways to turn them on and off.

DPOF, PictBridge, and computerless printing

The D5100 offers two features that enable you to print directly from your camera or a memory card, assuming that your printer offers the required options.

One of the direct-printing features is *Digital Print Order Format,* or *DPOF.* With this option, accessed via the DPOF Print Order option on the Playback menu, you select pictures from your memory card to print and then specify how many copies you want of each image. Then, if your photo printer has a Secure Digital (SD) memory card slot (or SDHC/SDXC slots, if you use these new, high-capacity cards) and supports DPOF, you just pop the memory card into that slot. The printer reads your "print order" and outputs just the requested copies of your selected images. (You use the printer's own controls to set paper size, print orientation, and other print settings.)

A second direct-printing feature, *PictBridge,* works a little differently. If you have a PictBridge-enabled photo printer, you can connect the camera to the printer by using a USB cable. (You use the same cable as for picture downloads.) A PictBridge interface appears on the camera monitor, and you use the camera controls to select the pictures you want to print. With PictBridge, you specify additional print options from the camera, such as page size and whether to print a border around the photo.

Both DPOF and PictBridge are especially useful when you need fast printing. For example, if you shoot pictures at a party and want to deliver prints to guests before they go home, DPOF and PictBridge offer quicker options than firing up your computer, downloading pictures, and so on. And, if you invest in one of the tiny portable photo printers on the market today, you can easily make prints away from your home or office. You can take both your portable printer and camera along to your regional sales meeting, for example.

If you're interested in exploring either printing feature, look for details in the electronic version of your camera manual, provided on one of the two CDs that shipped with the camera.

Even if all the aforementioned issues are resolved, however, don't expect perfect color matching between printer and monitor. Printers simply can't reproduce the entire spectrum of colors that a monitor can display. In addition, monitor colors always appear brighter because they are, after all, generated with light.

Finally, be sure to evaluate print colors and monitor colors in the same ambient light — daylight, office light, whatever — because that light source has its own influence on the colors you see. Also allow your prints to dry for 15 minutes or so before you make any final judgments.

Preparing Pictures for E-Mail and Online Sharing

How many times have you received an e-mail message that looks like the one in Figure 6-19? Some well-meaning friend or relative sent you a digital photo that's so large you can't view the whole thing on your monitor.

The problem is that computer monitors can display only a limited number of pixels. The exact number depends on the monitor's resolution setting and the capabilities of the computer's video card, but suffice it to say that the average photo from one of today's digital cameras has a pixel count in excess of what the monitor can handle.

In general, a good rule is to limit a photo to no more than 640 pixels at its longest dimension. That ensures that people can view your entire picture without scrolling, as in Figure 6-20. This image measures 640 x 424 pixels.

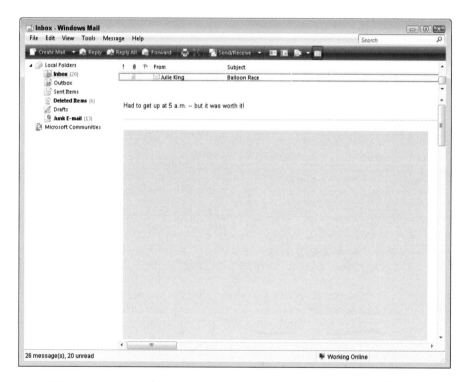

Figure 6-19: The attached image has too many pixels to be viewed without scrolling.

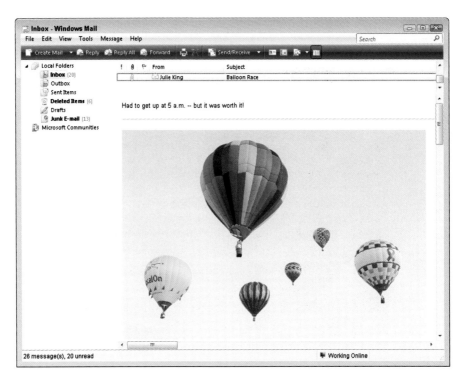

Figure 6-20: Keep e-mail pictures to no larger than 640 pixels wide or tall.

This size recommendation means that even if you shoot at your D5100's lowest Image Size setting (2464 x 1632), you wind up with lots more pixels than you need for onscreen viewing. Some new e-mail programs have a photo-upload feature that creates a temporary low-res version for you, but if not, creating your own copy is easy. (Details later.) If you're posting to an online photo-sharing site, you may be able to upload all your original pixels, but many sites have resolution limits.

In addition to resizing high-resolution images, check their file types; if the photos are in the Raw (NEF) or TIFF format, you need to create a JPEG copy for online use. Web browsers and e-mail programs can't display Raw or TIFF files.

You can tackle both bits of photo prep in ViewNX 2 or by using the Resize option in your camera. The next two sections explain both methods.

Resizing photos in ViewNX 2

To resize pictures that you already downloaded to the computer, ViewNX 2 offers a quick solution. Click the image thumbnail and then choose the Convert Files command, found on the File menu. When the Convert Files dialog box appears, set up things as follows:

✔ **Select JPEG as the file format.** Make your choice from the File Format drop-down list, as shown in Figure 6-21.

✔ **Set the picture quality level.** Use the Quality slider, labeled in the figure, to set the picture quality, which is controlled by how much JPEG compression is applied when the file is saved. For best quality, drag the slider all the way to the right, but remember the tradeoff: As you raise the quality, less compression occurs, which results in a larger file size. (See Chapter 2 for more information about JPEG compression.)

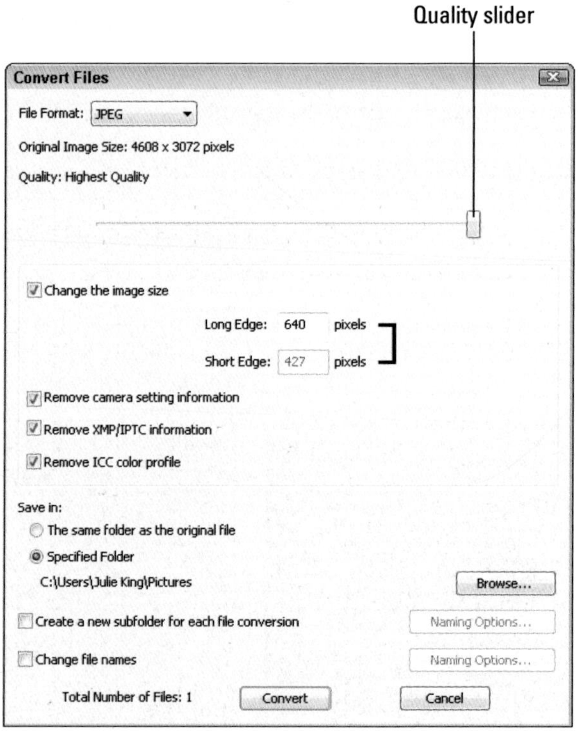

Quality slider

Figure 6-21: In ViewNX 2, select the Convert Files option to create a JPEG version of a Raw or TIFF photo.

✔ **Set the image size (number of pixels).** To resize the photo, select the Change the Image Size check box and then enter a value (in pixels) for the longest dimension of the photo. The program automatically fills in the other value.

For pictures that you want to share online, also select all three of the Remove check boxes, as shown in the figure, to eliminate adding to file sizes unnecessarily.

The rest of the options work just as they do during Raw conversion; see the "Processing Raw files in ViewNX 2," earlier in this chapter, for details. If you're resizing a JPEG original, be sure to give the small version a new name to avoid overwriting that original.

Resizing pictures from the Retouch menu

The in-camera resizing tool, found on the Retouch menu, works on both JPEG and Raw images. If you apply it directly to a Raw image, though, you lose the chance to adjust the resized image through the camera's Raw conversion tool. So you may prefer to do the conversion first, which creates a JPEG copy at the original size, and then create a small copy of that JPEG image.

Either way, to create a small copy of one or more images, take these steps:

1. **Press the Menu button and then display the Retouch menu.**

2. **Select the Resize option, as shown on the left in Figure 6-22, and press OK.**

   You see the screen shown on the right in Figure 6-22.

RETOUCH MENU	
Resize	
Quick retouch	
Straighten	
Distortion control	
Fisheye	
Color outline	
Color sketch	
Perspective control	

Resize	
Select image	
Choose size	2.5M ▶

Figure 6-22: Use the Resize option to create a low-resolution version of a picture on your memory card.

3. **Select Choose Size and press the Multi Selector right.**

   You see the screen shown in Figure 6-23, listing the possible sizes for your small copy. For each option, you see two values: the size in mega-pixels (M, in the menu screens) and the pixel dimensions (number of pixels across by pixels down).

4. **Highlight the size you want to use for your copy and press OK.**

   You're returned to the main Resize menu.

5. **Choose Select Image and press the Multi Selector right to display thumbnails of your pictures, as shown in Figure 6-24.**

6. **Move the yellow highlight box over a thumbnail and press the Zoom Out button to "tag" the photo for copying.**

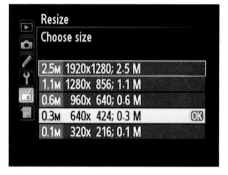

Figure 6-23: Set the size for your small copies here.

   You see a little icon in the top-right corner of the thumbnail, as shown in Figure 6-24. Press the Zoom Out button again to remove the tag if you change your mind.

7. **After selecting all your pictures, press OK.**

   A screen appears asking you for permission to make small copies of the selected photos.

8. **Highlight Yes and press OK.**

   The camera duplicates the selected images and *downsamples* (eliminates pixels from) the copies to achieve the size you specified. Your original picture files remain untouched.

Resize icon

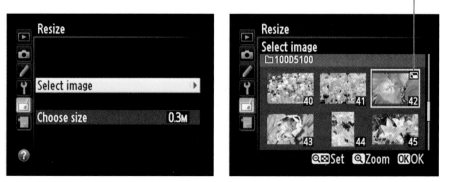

Figure 6-24: Press the ISO button to tag a picture for resizing.

Safeguarding your digital photo files

To make sure that your digital photos enjoy a long, healthy life, follow these storage guidelines:

✐ Don't rely on your computer's hard drive for long-term, archival storage. Hard drives occasionally fail, wiping out all files in the process. This warning applies to both internal and external hard drives. At the very least, having a dual-drive backup is in order — you might keep one copy of your photos on your computer's internal drive and another on an external drive. If one breaks, you still have all your goodies on the other one.

✐ Camera memory cards, flash memory keys, and other portable storage devices, such as one of those wallet-sized media players, are similarly risky. All are easily damaged if dropped or otherwise mishandled. And being of diminutive stature, these portable storage options also are easily lost.

✐ The best way to store important files is to copy them to nonrewritable CDs. (The label should say CD-R, not CD-RW.) Look for quality, brand-name CDs that have a gold coating, which offer a higher level of security than other coatings and boast a longer life than your garden-variety CDs.

✐ Recordable DVDs offer the advantage of holding lots more data than a CD. However, be aware that the DVDs you create on one computer may not be playable on another because multiple recording formats and disc types exist: DVD minus, DVD plus, dual-layer DVD, and so on. If you do opt for DVD, look for the archival, gold-coated variety, just as for CDs.

✐ For a double backup, you may want to check into online storage services, such as Mozy (www.mozy.com) and IDrive (www.idrive.com). You pay a monthly subscription fee to back up your important files to the site's servers.

Note, though, the critical phrase here: *double backup.* Online storage sites have a troubling history of closing down suddenly, taking all their customers' data with them. (One extremely alarming case was the closure of a photography-oriented storage site called Digital Railroad, which gave clients a mere 24-hours' notice before destroying their files.) So anything you store online should be also stored on DVD or CD and kept in your home or office. Also note that photo-sharing sites such as Shutterfly, Kodak Gallery, and the like *aren't* designed to be long-term storage tanks for your images. Usually, you get access to only a small amount of file storage space, and the site may require you to purchase prints or other photo products periodically to maintain your account.

If you want to resize just one photo, you can save some time by following this alternative path: Put the camera into playback mode, display the picture in single-image view, and press OK. The Retouch menu appears over your photo. Highlight the Resize option and press OK. You then see the screen offering the list of possible new sizes; select your choice and press OK to go to the confirmation screen. Highlight Yes and press OK to finish.

Either way, when you view your small-size copies on the camera monitor, they appear with a Retouch icon at the top of the screen and a Resize icon at the bottom, as shown in Figure 6-25. The filename of the resized image begins with SSC_ (or _SSC, if the original was captured using the Adobe RGB Color Space). You can't zoom in to magnify the view of copies that you created by using the two smallest sizes. (See Chapter 5 for details on magnifying images during playback.)

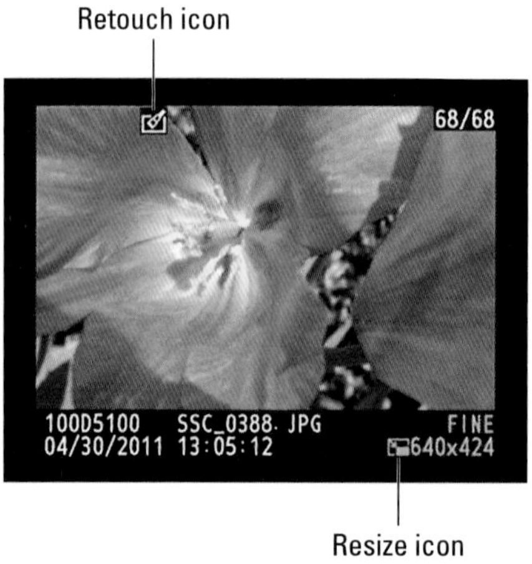

Retouch icon

Resize icon

Figure 6-25: The Resize icon indicates a small-size copy.

Part III
Taking Creative Control

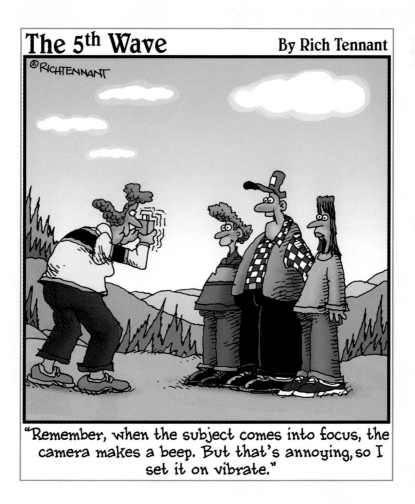

The 5th Wave   By Rich Tennant

©RICHTENNANT

"Remember, when the subject comes into focus, the camera makes a beep. But that's annoying, so I set it on vibrate."

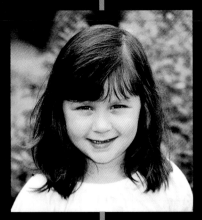

In this part . . .

As nice as it is to be able to set your D5100 to automatic mode and let the camera handle most of the photographic decisions, I encourage you to take creative control and explore the advanced exposure modes (P, S, A, and M). In these modes, you can make your own decisions about the exposure, focus, and color characteristics of your photo, which are key to capturing a compelling image as you see it in your mind's eye. And don't think that you have to be a genius or spend years to be successful — adding just a few simple techniques to your photographic repertoire can make a huge difference in the quality of the pictures you take.

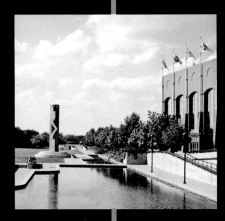

The first two chapters in this part explain everything you need to know to do just that, providing both some necessary photography fundamentals as well as details about using the advanced exposure modes. Following that, Chapter 9 helps you draw together all the information presented earlier in the book, summarizing the best camera settings and other tactics to use when capturing portraits, action shots, landscapes, and close-up shots. In short, this part helps you get the most out of your camera, which results in you becoming a better photographer.

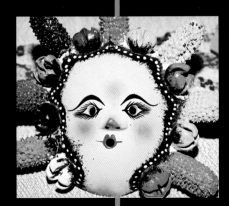

7

Getting Creative with Exposure and Lighting

*U*nderstanding exposure is one of the most intimidating challenges for the new photographer. Discussions of the topic are loaded with technical terms — *aperture, metering, shutter speed, ISO,* and the like. Add the fact that your D5100 offers many exposure controls, all sporting equally foreign names, and it's no wonder that most people throw up their hands and decide that their best option is to simply stick with the Auto exposure mode and let the camera take care of all exposure decisions.

You can, of course, turn out good shots in Auto mode. And I fully relate to the exposure confusion you may be feeling — I've been there. But I can also promise that when you take things nice and slow, digesting just a piece of the exposure pie at a time, the topic is not nearly as complicated as it seems on the surface. And I guarantee that the payoff will be well worth your time and brain energy. You'll not only gain the power to resolve just about any exposure problem, but also discover ways to use exposure to put your own creative stamp on a scene.

To that end, this chapter provides everything you need to know to really exploit your D5100's exposure options, from a primer in exposure science (it's not as bad as it sounds) to explanations of all the camera's exposure controls. In addition, because some controls aren't accessible in the fully automatic exposure modes, this chapter also provides more details about the four advanced modes, P, S, A, and M, first introduced in Chapter 2.

Introducing the Exposure Trio: Aperture, Shutter Speed, and ISO

Any photograph, whether taken with a film or digital camera, is created by focusing light through a lens onto a light-sensitive recording medium. In a film camera, the film negative serves as that medium; in a digital camera, it's the *image sensor,* which is an array of light-responsive computer chips.

Between the lens and the sensor are two barriers, known as the *aperture* and *shutter,* which together control how much light makes its way to the sensor. The actual design and arrangement of the aperture, shutter, and sensor vary depending on the camera, but Figure 7-1 offers an illustration of the basic concept.

The aperture and shutter, along with a third feature known as *ISO,* determine *exposure* — what most would describe as the picture's overall brightness and contrast. This three-part exposure formula works as follows:

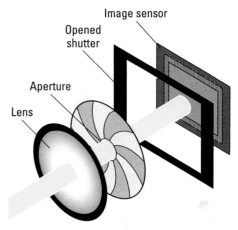

Figure 7-1: The aperture size and shutter speed determine how much light strikes the image sensor.

✏ **Aperture (controls amount of light):** The *aperture* is an adjustable hole in a diaphragm set just behind the lens. By changing the size of the aperture, you control the size of the light beam that can enter the camera. Aperture settings are stated as *f-stop numbers,* or simply *f-stops,* and are expressed with the letter *f* followed by a number: f/2, f/5.6, f/16, and so on. The lower the f-stop number, the larger the aperture, and the more light is permitted into the camera, as illustrated by Figure 7-2.

The range of possible f-stops depends on your lens and, if you use a zoom lens, on the zoom position (focal length) of the lens. When you use the 18–55mm lens that Nikon bundles in the D5100 kit, you can select apertures from f/3.5–f/22 when zoomed all the way out to the shortest focal length, 18mm. When you zoom in to the maximum focal length, 55mm, the aperture range is f/5.6–f/36. (See Chapter 8 for a discussion of focal lengths.)

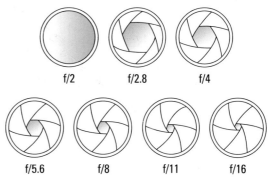

Figure 7-2: A lower f-stop number means a larger aperture, allowing more light into the camera.

✔ **Shutter speed (controls duration of light):** Set behind the aperture, the shutter works something like, er, the shutters on a window. When you aren't taking pictures, the camera's shutter stays closed, preventing light from striking the image sensor, just as closed window shutters prevent sunlight from entering a room. When you press the shutter button, the shutter opens briefly to allow light that passes through the aperture to hit the image sensor. The exception to this scenario is when you compose in Live View mode — when you enable Live View, the shutter opens and remains open so that your image can form on the sensor and be displayed on the camera's LCD. When you press the shutter button, the shutter first closes and then reopens for the actual exposure.

The length of time that the shutter is open to expose the image is called the *shutter speed* and is measured in seconds: 1/60 second, 1/250 second, 2 seconds, and so on. Shutter speeds on the D5100 range from 30 seconds to 1/4000 second when you shoot without flash. If you use flash, the range is more limited. See the sidebar "In sync: Flash timing and shutter speed," later in this chapter, for information.

Should you want a shutter speed longer than 30 seconds, manual (M) exposure mode also provides a feature called *bulb* exposure. At this setting, the shutter stays open indefinitely as long as you press the shutter button.

✔ **ISO (controls light sensitivity):** ISO, which is a digital function rather than a mechanical structure on the camera, enables you to adjust how responsive the image sensor is to light. The term ISO is a holdover from film days, when an international standards organization rated each film stock according to light sensitivity: ISO 200, ISO 400, ISO 800, and so on.

On a digital camera, the sensor itself doesn't actually get more or less sensitive when you change the ISO — rather, the light "signal" that hits the sensor is either amplified or dampened through electronics wizardry, sort of like how raising the volume on a radio boosts the audio signal. But the upshot is the same as changing to a more light-reactive film stock: A higher ISO means that less light is needed to produce the image, enabling you to use a smaller aperture, faster shutter speed, or both. (In other words, from now on, don't worry about the technicalities and just remember that ISO equals light sensitivity.)

The normal ISO settings on the D5100 range from ISO 100 to 6400. But if you really need to push things, you can extend that range all the way to ISO 25600. (This uber-high setting goes by the name Hi 2.) High ISO settings have a downside that you can explore in the upcoming section "ISO affects image noise."

Distilled to its essence, the image-exposure formula is just this simple:

✐ Aperture and shutter speed together determine the quantity of light that strikes the image sensor.

✐ ISO determines how much the sensor reacts to that light and, therefore, how much light you need to expose the picture.

The tricky part of the equation is that aperture, shutter speed, and ISO settings affect your pictures in ways that go *beyond* exposure. You need to be aware of these side effects, explained in the next section, to determine which combination of the three exposure settings will work best for your picture.

Understanding exposure-setting side effects

You can create the same exposure with many combinations of aperture, shutter speed, and ISO. You're limited only by the aperture range allowed by the lens and the shutter speeds and ISO range offered by the camera.

But the settings you select impact your image beyond mere exposure, as follows:

✐ Aperture affects *depth of field,* or the zone of sharp focus.

✐ Shutter speed determines whether moving objects appear blurry or sharply focused.

✐ ISO affects the amount of image *noise,* which is a defect that looks like tiny specks of sand.

As you can imagine, understanding how aperture, shutter speed, and ISO affect your image enables you to have much more creative control over your photographs — and, in the case of ISO, to ensure the quality of your images. (Chapter 2 discusses other factors that affect image quality.)

The next three sections explore the details of each exposure side effect.

Aperture affects depth of field

The aperture setting, or f-stop, affects *depth of field,* which is the range of sharp focus in your image. I introduce this concept in Chapter 3, but here's a quick recap: With a shallow depth of field, your subject appears more sharply focused than faraway objects; with a large depth of field, the sharp-focus zone spreads over a greater distance.

As you reduce the aperture size — or *stop down the aperture,* in photo lingo — by choosing a higher f-stop number, you increase depth of field. As an example, take a look at the two images in Figure 7-3. For both shots, I established focus on the female statue atop the fountain. Notice that the background in the first image, taken at an aperture setting of f/14, is slightly softer than in the right example, taken at f/29. Aperture is just one contributor to depth of field, however; the focal length of your lens and the distance between that lens and your subject also affect how much of the scene stays in focus. See Chapter 8 for the complete story, including more examples of how changing the f-stop affects depth of field.

f/14, 1/80 second, ISO 100   f/29, 1/20 second, ISO 100

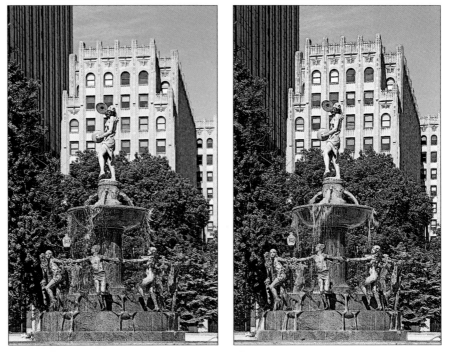

Figure 7-3: Stopping down the aperture (by choosing a higher f-stop number) increases depth of field, or the zone of sharp focus.

One way to remember the relationship between f-stop and depth of field is to think of the *f* as standing for *focus*. A higher f-stop number produces a larger depth of field, so if you want to extend the zone of sharp focus to cover a greater distance from your subject, you set the aperture to a higher f-stop. Higher *f*-stop number, greater zone of sharp focus. (Please *don't* share this tip with photography elites, who will roll their eyes and inform you that the *f* in *f-stop* most certainly does *not* stand for focus but for the ratio between the aperture size and lens focal length — as if *that's* helpful to know if you're not an optical engineer. Again, Chapter 8 explains focal length, which *is* helpful to know.)

Shutter speed affects motion blur

At a slow shutter speed, moving objects appear blurry, whereas a fast shutter speed captures motion cleanly. This phenomenon has nothing to do with the actual focus point of the camera but rather on the movement occurring — and being recorded by the camera — during the time that the shutter is open.

Compare the photos in Figure 7-3, for example. The static elements are perfectly focused in both images, although the background in the right photo appears slightly sharper because I shot that image using a higher f-stop, increasing the zone of sharp focus. But the way the camera rendered the moving portion of the scene — the fountain water — was determined by the shutter speed. At a shutter speed of 1/20 second (right photo), the water blurs, giving it a misty look. At 1/80 second (left photo), the droplets appear more sharply focused. How high a shutter speed you need to freeze action depends on the speed of your subject.

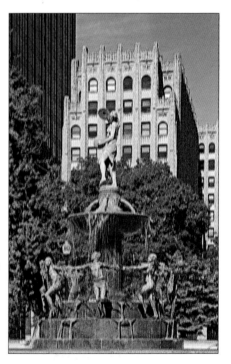

If your picture suffers from overall blur, where even stationary objects appear out of focus, the camera itself moved during the exposure, which is always a danger when you handhold the camera. The slower the shutter speed, the longer the exposure time and the longer you have to hold the camera still to avoid the blur that's caused by camera shake. For example, I was able to successfully handhold the 1/80 second exposure you see on the left in Figure 7-3, but at 1/20 second, there was enough camera movement to result in the blurry shot shown in Figure 7-4. I mounted the camera on the tripod to get the shake-free version shown on the right in Figure 7-3.

Figure 7-4: If both stationary and moving objects are blurry, camera shake is the usual cause.

Keep in mind that freezing action isn't the only way to use shutter speed to creative effect. When shooting waterfalls, for example, most photographers use a very slow shutter speed to give the water even more of a flowing, romantic look than you see in my fountain example. With colorful moving subjects, a slow shutter can produce some cool abstract effects and create a heightened sense of motion. Chapter 9 offers examples of both effects.

ISO affects image noise

As ISO increases, making the image sensor more reactive to light, you increase the risk of producing noise. *Noise* is a defect that looks like sprinkles of sand and is similar in appearance to film *grain,* a defect that often mars pictures taken with high ISO film. Figure 7-5 offers an example.

Ideally, then, you should always use the lowest ISO setting on your camera to ensure top image quality. But sometimes, the lighting conditions simply don't permit you to do so and still use the aperture and shutter speeds you need. Take my rose image as an example. When I shot these pictures, I didn't have a tripod, so I needed a shutter speed fast enough to allow a sharp handheld image. I opened the aperture to f/6.3, which was the maximum on the lens I was using, to allow as much light as possible into the camera. At ISO 100, I needed a shutter speed of 1/40 second to expose the picture, and that shutter speed wasn't fast for a successful handheld shot. By raising the ISO to 200, I was able to use a shutter speed of 1/80 second, which enabled me to capture the flower cleanly, as shown in Figure 7-6.

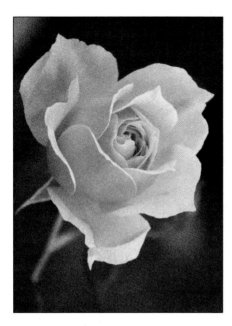
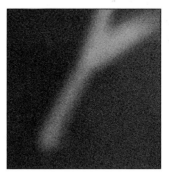

Figure 7-5: Caused by a very high ISO or long exposure time, noise becomes more visible as you enlarge the image.

ISO 100, f/6.3, 1/40 second ISO 200, f/6.3, 1/80 second

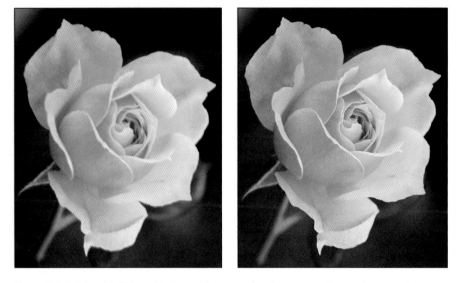

Figure 7-6: Raising the ISO enabled me to bump up the shutter speed enough to permit a blur-free handheld shot.

Fortunately, you don't encounter serious noise on the D5100 until you really crank up the ISO. In fact, you may even be able to get away with a fairly high ISO if you keep your print or display size small. Some people probably wouldn't even notice the noise in the left image in Figure 7-5 unless they were looking for it, for example. But as with other image defects, noise becomes more apparent as you enlarge the photo, as shown on the right in that same figure. Noise is also easier to spot in shadow areas of your picture and in large areas of solid color.

How much noise is acceptable, and, therefore, how high an ISO is safe, is a personal choice. Even a little noise isn't acceptable for pictures that require the highest quality, such as images for a product catalog or a travel shot that you want to blow up to poster size.

It's also important to know that a high ISO isn't the only cause of noise: A long exposure time (slow shutter speed) can also produce the defect. So how high you can raise the ISO before the image gets ugly varies depending on shutter speed. I can pretty much guarantee, though, that your pictures will exhibit visible noise at the camera's highest ISO settings, which produce ISO sensitivity ranging from ISO 8000 to 25600. In fact, that's why Nikon gave these settings their special labels, Hi 0.3, Hi 0.7, Hi 1, and Hi 2 — it's a way to let you know that you should use these settings only if the light is so bad that you have no other way to get the shot.

Handholding the camera: How low can you go?

My students often ask how slow they can set the shutter speed and still handhold the camera instead of using a tripod. Unfortunately, there's no one-size-fits-all answer to this question.

The slow-shutter safety limit varies depending on a couple factors, including your physical capabilities and your lens — the heavier the lens, the harder it is to hold steady. For reasons that are too technical to get into, camera shake also affects your picture more when you shoot with a lens that has a long focal length. So you may be able to use a much slower shutter speed when you shoot with a lens that has a maximum focal length of 55mm, like the kit lens, than if you switch to a 200mm telephoto lens. (Chapter 8 explains focal length, if the term is new to you.)

A standard photography rule is to use the inverse of the lens focal length as the minimum handheld shutter speed. For example, with a 50mm lens, use a shutter speed no slower than 1/50 second. But that rule was developed before the advent of today's modern lenses, which tend to be significantly lighter and smaller than older lenses, as do cameras themselves. I have a very light, super-zoom lens that I can handhold at speeds as low as 1/80 second even when I zoom to focal lengths way beyond 80mm, for example.

So the best idea is to do your own tests to see where your handholding limit lies. Start with a slow shutter speed — say, in the 1/40 second neighborhood, and then click off multiple shots, increasing the shutter speed for each picture. If you have a zoom lens, run the test first at the minimum focal length (widest angle) and then zoom to the maximum focal length for another series of shots. Then it's simply a matter of comparing the images in your photo-editing program. (You may not be able to accurately judge the amount of blur on the camera monitor.) See Chapter 6 to find out how to see the shutter speed you used for each picture when you view your images. That information, along with other camera settings, appears in the file *metadata,* which you can display in Nikon ViewNX 2 and many other programs.

Remember, too, that if your lens offers Vibration Reduction (as does the D5100 kit lens), enabling that feature can compensate for small amounts of camera shake, enabling you to capture sharp images at slightly slower shutter speeds than normal when handholding the camera. Again, your mileage may vary, but most people can expect to go at least two or three notches down the shutter-speed ramp. See Chapter 1 for more information about this feature.

Doing the exposure balancing act

REMEMBER

As you change any of the three exposure settings — aperture, shutter speed, and ISO — one or both of the others must also shift in order to maintain the same image brightness. Say that you're shooting a soccer game, for example, and you notice that although the overall exposure looks great, the players appear slightly blurry at your current shutter speed. If you raise the shutter speed, you have to compensate with either a larger aperture, to allow in more light during the shorter exposure, or a higher ISO setting, to make the camera more sensitive to the light — or both.

As the previous sections explain, changing these settings impacts your image in ways beyond exposure. As a quick reminder:

✔ Aperture affects depth of field, with a higher f-stop number producing a greater zone of sharp focus.

✔ Shutter speed affects whether motion of the subject or camera results in a blurry photo. A faster shutter "freezes" action and also helps safeguard against allover blur that can result from camera shake when you're handholding the camera.

✔ ISO affects the camera's sensitivity to light. A higher ISO makes the camera more responsive to light but also increases the chance of image noise.

So when you boost that shutter speed to capture your soccer subjects, you have to decide whether you prefer the shorter depth of field that comes with a larger aperture or the increased risk of noise that accompanies a higher ISO.

Everyone has their own approach to finding the right combination of aperture, shutter speed, and ISO, and you'll no doubt develop your own system as you become more practiced at using the advanced exposure modes. In the meantime, here's how I handle things:

✔ I always use the lowest possible ISO setting unless the lighting conditions are so poor that I can't use the aperture and shutter speed I want without raising the ISO.

✔ If my subject is moving (or might move, as with a squiggly toddler or antsy pet), I give shutter speed the next highest priority in my exposure decision. I might choose a fast shutter speed to ensure a blur-free photo or, on the flip side, select a slow shutter to intentionally blur that moving object, an effect that can create a heightened sense of motion.

✔ For images of non-moving subjects, I make aperture a priority over shutter speed, setting the aperture according to the depth of field I have in mind. For portraits, for example, I use the largest aperture (the lowest f-stop number, known as shooting *wide open,* in photographer speak) so that I get a short depth of field, creating a nice, soft background for my subject. For landscapes, I usually go the opposite direction, stopping down the aperture as much as possible to capture the subject at the greatest depth of field.

I know that keeping all this straight is a little overwhelming at first, but the more you work with your camera, the more the whole exposure equation will make sense to you. You can find tips for choosing exposure settings for specific types of pictures in Chapter 9; keep moving through this chapter for details on how to actually monitor and adjust aperture, shutter speed, and ISO settings on the D5100.

Exploring the Advanced Exposure Modes

In the automatic modes described in Chapter 3, you have very little control over exposure. You may be able to choose from one or two Flash modes, and you can adjust ISO in the Scene modes. But to gain full control over exposure, set the Mode dial to one of the advanced modes highlighted in Figure 7-7: P, S, A, or M. You also need to shoot in these modes to use certain other features, such as manual white balancing, a color control that you can explore in Chapter 8.

The major difference among the four advanced modes is the level of control over aperture and shutter speed, as follows:

Advanced exposure modes

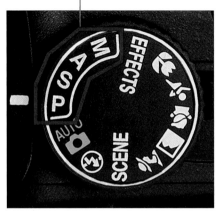

Figure 7-7: You can control exposure and certain other picture properties fully only in P, S, A, or M mode.

- ✏ **P (programmed autoexposure):** In this mode, the camera selects both aperture and shutter speed. But you can choose from different combinations of the two for creative flexibility.

- ✏ **S (shutter-priority autoexposure):** In this mode, you select a shutter speed, and the camera chooses the aperture setting that produces a good exposure at your selected ISO setting.

- ✏ **A (aperture-priority autoexposure):** The opposite of shutter-priority autoexposure, this mode asks you to select the aperture setting. The camera then selects the appropriate shutter speed to properly expose the picture.

- ✏ **M (manual exposure):** In this mode, you specify both shutter speed and aperture.

To sum up, the first three modes are semi-automatic exposure modes that are designed to help you get a good exposure while still providing you with some photographic flexibility. You can even modify the autoexposure results by using features such as Exposure Compensation, explained later in this chapter. But it's important to note that in extreme lighting conditions, the camera may not be able to select settings that will produce a good exposure, and it doesn't stop you from taking a poorly exposed photo.

Manual mode puts all exposure control in your hands. If you're a longtime photographer who comes from the days when manual exposure was the only game in town, you may prefer to stick with this mode. If it ain't broke, don't fix it, as they say. And in some ways, manual mode is simpler than the semi-auto modes because if you're not happy with the exposure, you just change the aperture, shutter speed, or ISO setting and shoot again. You don't have to fiddle with features that enable you to modify your autoexposure results — although again, the lighting conditions determine whether a good exposure is possible at any combination of settings.

My own personal choice is to use aperture-priority autoexposure when I'm shooting still subjects and want to control depth of field — aperture is my *priority* — and to switch to shutter-priority autoexposure when I'm shooting a moving subject and so I'm most concerned with controlling shutter speed. Frankly, my brain is taxed enough by all the other issues involved in taking pictures — what my White Balance setting is, what resolution I need, where I'm going for lunch as soon as I make this shot work — that I just appreciate having the camera do some of the exposure lifting.

However, when I know exactly what aperture and shutter speed I want to use, or I'm after an out-of-the-ordinary exposure, I use manual exposure. For example, sometimes when I'm doing a still life in my studio, I want to create a certain mood by underexposing a subject or even shooting it in silhouette. The camera is always going to fight you on that result in the P, S, and A modes because it so dearly wants to provide a good exposure. Rather than dialing in all the autoexposure tweaks that could eventually force the result I want, I simply set the mode to M, adjust the shutter speed and aperture directly, and give the autoexposure system the afternoon off.

But even in manual mode, you're never really flying without a net — the camera assists you by displaying the exposure meter, explained next.

Reading (And Adjusting) the Meter

To help you determine whether your exposure settings are on cue in M (manual) exposure mode, the camera displays an *exposure meter* in the viewfinder and Shooting Information display. The meter is the little linear graphic highlighted in Figure 7-8. You can see a close-up look at how the meter looks in the viewfinder in Figure 7-9. To activate the meter displays, just press the shutter button halfway and then release it.

The minus-sign end of the meter represents underexposure; the plus sign, overexposure. So if the little notches on the meter fall to the right of 0, as shown in the first example in Figure 7-9, the image will be underexposed. If the indicator moves to the left of 0, as shown in the second example, the image will be overexposed. The farther the indicator moves toward the plus or minus sign, the greater the potential problem. If the meter blinks, the amount of over- or underexposure has exceeded the range of the meter. When the meter shows a balanced exposure, as in the third example, you're good to go.

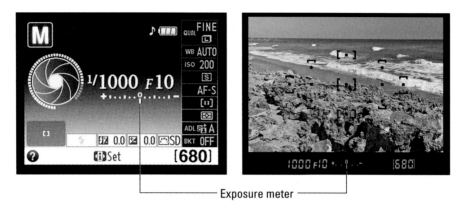

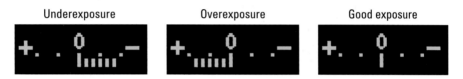

Exposure meter

Figure 7-8: In M exposure mode, the exposure meter appears in the Shooting Information display and viewfinder.

Underexposure   Overexposure   Good exposure

Figure 7-9: The meter indicates whether your exposure settings are on target.

In the other exposure modes, the meter flashes in the viewfinder and Shooting Info screen if the camera anticipates an exposure problem — your cue to adjust exposure settings until the meter disappears. In dim lighting, you may also see a blinking flash symbol. It's a not-so-subtle suggestion to add some light to the scene. A blinking question mark tells you that you can press the Zoom Out button to display a Help screen with more information.

Keep in mind, too, that the meter's suggestion on exposure may not always be the one you want to follow. For example, you may want to shoot a back-lit subject in silhouette, in which case you *want* that subject to be under-exposed. In other words, the meter is a guide, not a dictator. In addition, remember that the exposure information the meter reports is based on the *exposure metering mode,* which determines which part of the frame the camera considers when calculating exposure. At the default setting, exposure is based on the entire frame, but you can select two other metering modes. See the upcoming section "Choosing an Exposure Metering Mode" for details.

If you're so inclined, you can customize the meter in the following ways:

✔ **Adjust the meter shutoff timing.** The meter turns on anytime you press the shutter button halfway. But then it turns off automatically if you don't press the button again for a period of time — eight seconds, by default. You can adjust the shut-off timing through the Auto Off Timers option, found on the Timers/AE Lock submenu of the Custom Setting menu. After selecting the option and pressing OK, you see the screen shown on the left in Figure 7-10. Select Custom and press OK to access the options shown on the right in the figure. Then select Auto Meter-Off and press OK to get to the meter timing options, which range from 4 seconds to 30 minutes. Remember that the metering system uses battery power, so keeping it active for long periods of time on a regular basis isn't a good move. After selecting your choice, press OK; then highlight Done and press OK once more.

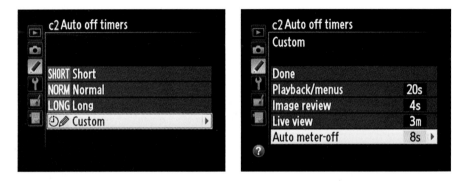

Figure 7-10: You can adjust the automatic shutdown timing of the exposure meter.

As an alternative, you can control meter shutdown timing by choosing the Short, Normal (the default setting), or Long option when you get to the left screen in Figure 7-10, but doing so also affects the timing of the playback/ menu display, image review period, and Live View display. For details, check out Chapter 1.

✔ **Reverse the meter orientation.** For photographers used to a camera that orients the meter with the positive (overexposure) side appearing on the right and the neg- ative (underexposure) side on the left, the D5100 offers the option to flip the meter to that design. This option also lies on the Custom Setting menu, but on the Controls submenu. Look for the Reverse Indicators option, as shown in Figure 7-11. The setting shown in the figure is the default.

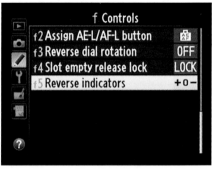

Figure 7-11: The Reverse Indicators option enables you to reverse the orientation of the exposure meter.

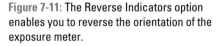

Exposure stops: How many do you want to see?

In photography, the term *stop* refers to an increment of exposure. To increase exposure by one stop means to adjust the aperture or shutter speed to allow twice as much light into the camera as the current settings permit. To reduce exposure a stop, you use settings that allow half as much light. Doubling or halving the ISO value also adjusts exposure by one stop.

By default, all the major exposure-related settings on the D5100 are based on one-third stop adjustments. For example, when you adjust the Exposure Compensation value, a feature that enables you to request a brighter or darker picture than the camera's autoexposure system thinks is correct, you can choose settings of EV 0.0 (no adjustment), +0.3, +0.7, and +1.0 (a full stop of adjustment).

If you prefer, you can tell the camera to present exposure adjustments in half-stop increments so that you don't have to cycle through as many settings each time you want to make a change. Make your preferences known through the EV Steps for Exposure Cntrl (Control) option, found in the Exposure section of the Custom Setting menu and shown here. (The option name uses the word *steps* instead of *stops,* but the meaning is the same.) Your choice affects the increments used for shutter speed, aperture, Exposure Compensation, Flash Compensation, and exposure bracketing settings. In addition, the setting determines the increments of exposure in the meter.

Obviously, the default setting, 1/3 step, provides the greatest degree of exposure fine-tuning, so I stick with that option. In this book, all instructions also assume that you're using the defaults.

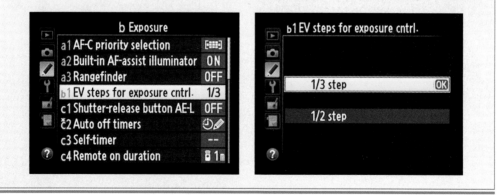

Setting Aperture, Shutter Speed, and ISO

The next sections detail how to view and adjust these three critical exposure settings. Remember, you can adjust ISO in any exposure mode except Auto, Auto Flash Off and Night Vision Effects mode. (Chapter 10 explains Effects modes.). But to control aperture (f-stop) or shutter speed, you must switch to one of the four advanced exposure modes (P, S, A, or M).

Adjusting aperture and shutter speed

You can view the current aperture (f-stop) and shutter speed in the Shooting Info display and viewfinder, as shown in Figure 7-12. If you stick with the default setting for the Info Display Format option on the Setup menu (Graphic), an aperture symbol appears just to the left of the shutter speed to remind you of the impact of changing the f-stop. As you raise the f-stop value, the yellow center of the graphic shrinks, representing the narrowing of the aperture. (See Chapter 11 to find out how to switch to a different display format.)

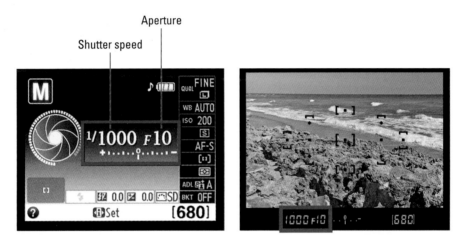

Figure 7-12: Look for the current f-stop and shutter speed here.

In the viewfinder, shutter speeds are presented as whole numbers, even if the shutter speed is set to a fraction of a second. For example, the number 1000 indicates a shutter speed of 1/1000 second. When the shutter speed slows to one second or more, quote marks appear after the number — 1" indicates a shutter speed of one second, 4" means four seconds, and so on.

To select aperture and shutter speed, start by pressing the shutter button halfway to kick the exposure system into gear. You can then release the button if you want. The next step depends on the exposure mode, as follows:

  ✓ **P (programmed autoexposure):** In this mode, the camera shows you its recommended f-stop and shutter speed when you press the shutter button halfway. But you can rotate the Command dial to select a different combination of settings. The number of possible combinations depends upon the aperture settings the camera can select, which depends on your lens.

An asterisk (*) appears next to the P exposure mode symbol in the upper-left corner of the Shooting Information display if you rotate the Command dial to adjust the aperture/shutter speed settings. You see a tiny P* symbol at the left end of the viewfinder display as well. To get back to the initial combo of shutter speed and aperture, rotate the Command dial until the asterisk disappears from the Shooting Info display and the P* symbol turns off in the viewfinder.

✐ **S (shutter-priority autoexposure):** In this mode, you select the shutter speed. Just rotate the Command dial to get the job done. The camera automatically adjusts the aperture as needed to maintain proper exposure. Remember that as the aperture shifts, so does depth of field — so even though you're working in shutter-priority mode, keep an eye on the f-stop, too, if depth of field is important to your photo. Also note that in extreme lighting conditions, the camera may not be able to adjust the aperture enough to produce a good exposure at your current shutter speed — again, possible aperture settings depend on your lens. So you may need to compromise on shutter speed or ISO.

✐ **A (aperture-priority autoexposure):** In this mode, you control aperture, and the camera adjusts shutter speed automatically. To set the aperture (f-stop), rotate the Command dial.

When you raise the f-stop value, be careful that the shutter speed doesn't drop so low that you risk camera shake if you handhold the camera. And if your scene contains moving objects, make sure that the shutter speed that the camera selects is fast enough to stop action (or slow enough to blur it, if that's your creative goal). These same warnings apply when you use P mode.

✐ **M (manual exposure):** In this mode, you select both aperture and shutter speed, like so:

- *To adjust shutter speed:* Rotate the Command dial. Rotate the dial one notch past the slowest speed (30 seconds) to access the Bulb setting, which keeps the shutter open as long as the shutter button is pressed. If you attach the optional ML-L3 wired remote, you also see a Time setting. At this setting, you press the remote's shutter button once to begin the exposure and a second time to end it; maximum exposure time is 30 minutes.

- *To adjust aperture:* Press the Exposure Compensation button while rotating the Command dial. Notice the little aperture-like symbol that lies next to the button, on the top of the camera? That's your reminder of the button's role in setting the f-stop in manual mode.

Keep in mind that when you use P, S, or A mode, the settings that the camera selects are based on what it thinks is the proper exposure. If you don't agree with the camera, you can switch to manual exposure mode and dial in the aperture and shutter speed that deliver the exposure you want, or if you want to stay in P, S, or A mode, you can tweak exposure using the features explained in the section "Sorting through Your Camera's Exposure-Correction Tools," later in this chapter.

When you view the f-stop and shutter speed in the Shooting Info display, by the way, remember that the camera continues to meter and adjust exposure up to the time you take the shot. (The exception is when you use the autoexposure lock feature, explained later in this chapter.) So if you frame the shot and then move the camera to better see the display, the exposure settings no longer reflect the ones the camera chose for your subject — instead, they show the settings for whatever is now in front of the lens. And if you (like most people) hold the camera with the lens pointing down to view the monitor, the camera begins calculating the correct settings to use to photograph the ground.

The best practice is to use the Shooting Info display to select your initial shutter speed, or aperture, or both, if necessary. Then frame the shot in the viewfinder, press the shutter button halfway to meter the scene in front of the lens, and then, if the viewfinder exposure meter indicates a problem, adjust the exposure settings as necessary without taking your eye away from the viewfinder. (After you get familiar with the operation of the camera, this technique won't be as hard as it first seems, I promise.)

Controlling ISO

The ISO setting, introduced at the start of this chapter, adjusts the camera's sensitivity to light. At a higher ISO, you can use a faster shutter speed or a smaller aperture (higher f-stop number) because less light is needed to expose the image. But remember that a higher ISO also increases the possibility of noise, as illustrated in Figure 7-5. (Be sure to check out the upcoming sidebar "Dampening noise" for features that may help calm noise somewhat.)

On the D5100, you can choose ISO values ranging from 100 to 6400, plus four Hi settings, 0.3, 0.7, 1, and 2, which stretch the ISO range from roughly 8000 (Hi 0.3) to 25600 (Hi 2). You also have the option of choosing Auto ISO; at this setting, the camera selects the ISO needed to expose the picture at the current shutter speed and aperture.

The number of settings available between the top and bottom of the ISO range depend on the ISO Sensitivity Step Value option, covered in the sidebar "Exposure stops: How many do you want to see?" earlier in this chapter. By default, ISO settings are presented in one-third stop increments.

You can't adjust ISO in Auto and Auto Flash Off exposure modes or in Night Vision Effects mode. In any other exposure mode, adjust ISO as follows:

✔ **Quick Settings screen:** Press the Info Edit button to shift from the Shooting Info display to the Quick Settings display. Highlight the ISO setting, as shown on the left in Figure 7-13 and press OK to display the options shown on the right. Choose the desired ISO setting and press OK.

✔ **Shooting menu:** You also can adjust the ISO Sensitivity Settings on the Shooting menu, shown in Figure 7-14. Note that the second screen in the figure shows options available in the P, S, A, and M modes; you can access only the top option in the other exposure modes.

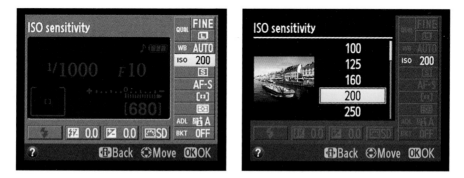

Figure 7-13: You can adjust ISO easily through the Quick Settings screen.

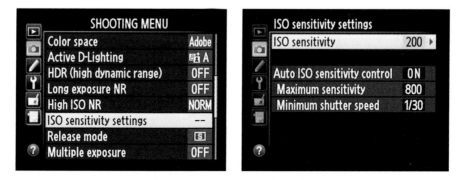

Figure 7-14: You can access additional ISO options through the Shooting menu.

✔ **Fn (Function) button:** By default, pressing the Fn button on the side of the camera changes the Release mode to the Self-Timer setting for your next shot. But if you prefer, you can change the function of the button to provide one-button access to the ISO setting. If you take that step — Chapter 11 provides specifics — press and hold the button to display the screen shown in Figure 7-15. Keep holding the button while rotating the Command dial to change the ISO setting.

TIP

Dampening noise

High ISO settings can result in *noise*, the digital defect that gives your pictures a speckled look. (Refer to Figure 7-5.) Long exposure times (slow shutter speeds) also create a noise potential. To help solve these problems, the D5100 offers two noise-removal filters: *High ISO Noise Reduction*, designed to reduce the appearance of ISO-related noise; and *Long Exposure Noise Reduction*, which dampens the type of noise that occurs during long exposures. You can enable both filters through the Shooting menu, as shown in the figure below.

If you turn on Long Exposure Noise Reduction, the camera applies the filter to pictures taken at shutter speeds of longer than one second. For High ISO Noise Reduction, you can choose from four settings. The High, Normal, and Low settings apply the filter at ISO 800 or higher; the setting you choose determines the strength of the filter. At the fourth setting, Off, the camera actually still applies a tiny amount of noise removal, but only at ISO 1600 or higher.

Before you enable noise reduction, be aware that doing so has a few disadvantages. First, the filters are applied after you take the picture, as the camera processes the image data. While the Long Exposure Noise Reduction filter is being applied, the message "Job Nr" appears

in the viewfinder, in the area normally reserved for the shutter speed and aperture. The time needed to apply this filter can significantly slow down your shooting speed — in fact, it can double the time the camera needs to record the file to the memory card.

Second, although filters that go after long-exposure noise work fairly well, those that attack high ISO noise work primarily by applying a slight blur to the image. Don't expect this process to totally eliminate noise, and do expect some resulting image softness. You may be able to get better results by using the blur tools or noise-removal filters found in many photo editors because you can blur just the parts of the image where noise is most noticeable — usually in areas of flat color or little detail, such as skies.

SHOOTING MENU	
Color space	Adobe
Active D-Lighting	A
HDR (high dynamic range)	OFF
Long exposure NR	OFF
High ISO NR	NORM
ISO sensitivity settings	---
Release mode	S
Multiple exposure	OFF

Keep these additional ISO points in mind:

✔ **Auto ISO in the fully automatic exposure modes and Effects modes:** In Auto, Auto Flash Off, and Night Vision Effects modes, the camera uses the Auto ISO setting and selects the ISO setting for you. In the Scene modes, you can stick with Auto ISO (the default setting) or select a specific ISO value.

✔ **Auto ISO in P, S, A, and M modes:** Auto ISO doesn't appear on the ISO settings list, but you still can enable Auto ISO as sort of a safety net. Here's how it works: You dial in a specific ISO setting — say, ISO 100. If the camera decides that it can't properly expose the image at that ISO given your current aperture and shutter speed, it automatically adjusts ISO as necessary.

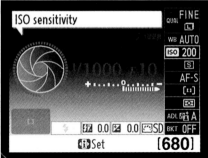

To get to this option, select ISO Sensitivity Settings on the Shooting menu, as shown on the left in Figure 7-14, and press OK. On the next screen, turn the Auto ISO Sensitivity Control option to On, as shown on the right in the figure. The camera will now override your ISO choice when it thinks a proper exposure is not possible with the settings you've specified.

Figure 7-15: You can configure the Fn button to display this screen; press the button while rotating the Command dial to adjust the ISO setting.

Next, use the two options under the Auto ISO Sensitivity Control setting to tell the camera exactly when it should step in and offer ISO assistance:

- *Maximum Sensitivity:* This option lets you set the highest ISO value that the camera can use when it overrides your selected ISO setting — a great feature because it enables you to decide how much noise potential you're willing to accept in order to get a good exposure. For example, the value in Figure 7-14 is set to ISO 800. So even if the picture can't be properly exposed at ISO 800, the camera won't go any higher than that limit.

- *Minimum Shutter Speed:* Set the minimum shutter speed at which the ISO override engages when you use the P and A exposure modes. For example, you can specify that you want the camera to amp up ISO if needed to prevent the shutter speed from dropping below 1/30 second, as shown in the figure.

If the camera is about to override your ISO setting, it alerts you by blinking the ISO Auto label in the viewfinder. The message "ISO-A" blinks at the top of the Shooting Info screen as well. And in playback mode, the ISO value appears in red if you view your photos in a display mode that includes the ISO value. (Chapter 5 has details.)

To disable Auto ISO override, just reset the Auto ISO Sensitivity Control option to Off.

✔ **ISO value display:** Although the Shooting Info screen always displays the current ISO setting, the viewfinder reports the ISO value only when the option is set to Auto. Otherwise, the ISO area of the viewfinder is empty.

If you don't like this setup, you can modify things through the ISO Display option, found in the Shooting/Display section of the Custom Setting menu. At the default setting, Off, things work as just described. Choose On to replace the shots remaining value in the viewfinder with the ISO value at all times. You can still see the shots remaining value in the Shooting Information display.

Choosing an Exposure Metering Mode

To fully interpret what your exposure meter tells you, you need to know which *metering mode* is active. The metering mode determines which part of the frame the camera analyzes to calculate the proper exposure. The metering mode affects the exposure-meter reading as well as the exposure settings that the camera chooses in the fully automatic shooting modes (Auto, Auto Flash Off, and the Scene modes) as well as in the semi-auto modes (P, S, and A).

Your D5100 offers three metering modes, described in the following list and represented on the Shooting Information display by the icons you see in the margins:

✔ **Matrix:** The camera analyzes the entire frame and then selects an exposure that's designed to produce a balanced exposure.

Your camera manual refers to this mode as 3D Color Matrix II, which is the label that Nikon created to describe the specific technology used in this mode.

✔ **Center-weighted:** The camera bases exposure on the entire frame but puts extra emphasis — or *weight* — on the center of the frame.

✔ **Spot:** In this mode, the camera bases exposure entirely on a circular area that's about 3.5mm in diameter, or about 2.5 percent of the frame. The exact location used for this pin-point metering depends on an autofocusing option called the AF-Area mode. Detailed in Chapter 8, this option determines which of the camera's 11 focus points the autofocusing system uses to establish focus. Here's how the setting affects exposure:

- *If you choose the Auto Area mode,* in which the camera chooses the focus point for you, exposure is based on the center focus point.

- *If you use any of the other AF-Area modes,* which enable you to select a specific focus point, the camera bases exposure on that point.

Because of this autofocus/autoexposure relationship, it's best to switch to one of the AF-Area modes that allow focus-point selection when you want to use spot metering. In the Auto Area mode, exposure may be incorrect if you compose your shot so that the subject isn't at the center of the frame.

As an example of how metering mode affects exposure, Figure 7-16 shows the same image captured at each mode. In the matrix example, the bright background caused the camera to select an exposure that left the statue quite dark. Switching to center-weighted metering helped somewhat, but didn't quite bring the statue out of the shadows. Spot metering produced the best result as far as the statue goes, although the resulting increase in exposure left the sky a little washed out.

Matrix metering is the default setting, and you can change the metering mode only in the P, S, A, and M exposure modes. Make your selection via the Quick Settings display, as shown in Figure 7-17. (Press the Info Edit button once to bring up the Shooting Information display and a second time to shift to the Quick Settings screen.)

Matrix metering   Center-weighted metering   Spot metering

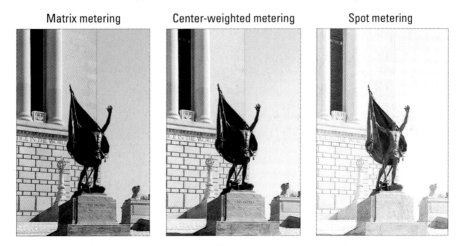

Figure 7-16: The metering mode determines which area of the frame the camera considers when calculating exposure.

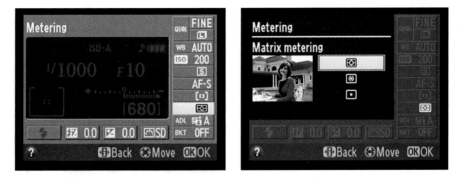

Figure 7-17: The only way to adjust the metering mode is to use the Quick Settings display.

In theory, the best practice is to check the metering mode before you shoot and choose the one that best matches your exposure goals. But in practice, that's a bit of a pain, not just in terms of having to adjust yet one more capture setting but in terms of having to *remember* to adjust one more capture setting. So here's my advice: Until you're really comfortable with all the other controls on your camera, just stick with the default setting, which is matrix metering. That mode produces good results in most situations, and after all, you can see in the monitor whether you disagree with how the camera metered or exposed the image and simply reshoot after adjusting the exposure settings to your liking. This option, in my mind, makes the whole metering mode issue a lot less critical than it is when you shoot with film.

The one exception to this advice might be when you're shooting a series of images in which a significant contrast in lighting exists between subject and background, as in Figure 7-16. Then, switching to center-weighted metering or spot metering may save you the time of having to adjust the exposure for each image.

Sorting Through Your Camera's Exposure-Correction Tools

In addition to the normal controls over aperture, shutter speed, and ISO, your D5100 offers a collection of tools that enable you to solve tricky exposure problems. The next several sections give you the lowdown on these features.

Applying Exposure Compensation

When you set your camera to the P, S, or A modes, you can enjoy autoexposure support but still retain some control over the final exposure. If you think that the image the camera produced is too dark or too light, you can use *Exposure Compensation*. This feature enables you to tell the camera to produce a darker or lighter exposure than what its autoexposure mechanism thinks is appropriate. You also can use Exposure Compensation in the Night Vision Effects mode, explained in Chapter 10.

Here's what you need to know to take advantage of it:

✔ Exposure Compensation settings are stated in terms of EV numbers, as in EV +2.0. Possible values range from EV +5.0 to EV –5.0. (*EV* stands for *exposure value.*)

Each full number on the EV scale represents an exposure shift of one *stop*. If you're new to this terminology, see the sidebar "Exposure stops: How many do you want to see?" earlier in this chapter. That sidebar also explains how you can tweak the increments of EV adjustment the camera offers.

✔ A setting of EV 0.0 results in no exposure adjustment.

✔ For a brighter image, raise the Exposure Compensation value. The higher you go, the brighter the image becomes.

✔ For a darker image, lower the EV.

As an example, take a look at the first image in Figure 7-18. The initial exposure selected by the camera left the balloon a tad too dark for my taste. So I just amped the Exposure Compensation setting to EV +1.0, which produced the brighter exposure on the right.

EV 0.0   EV +1.0

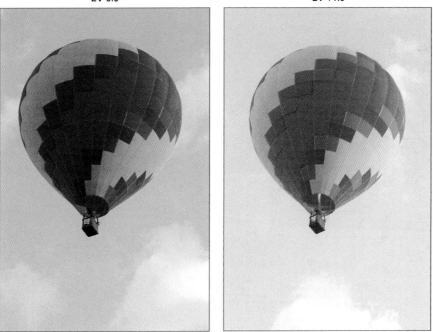

Figure 7-18: For a brighter exposure, raise the Exposure Compensation value.

To change the setting, you have two options:

✔ **Press the Exposure Compensation button while rotating the Command dial.** As soon as you press the button, the Shooting Info display changes to appear as shown in Figure 7-19. If you're looking through the viewfinder, the shots remaining value is temporarily replaced by the Exposure Compensation value when you press the Exposure Compensation button.

While holding the Exposure Compensation button, rotate the Command dial to adjust the EV. As you change the setting, the exposure meter in the viewfinder and Shooting Information display updates to show you the degree of adjustment you're making. Each bar that appears under the meter equals an adjustment of 1/3 stop (EV +/–0.3).

After you release the button, the Shooting Info screen goes back to normal, and the shots remaining value returns to the viewfinder.

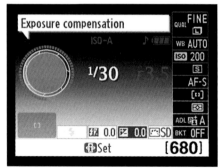

✓ **Use the Quick Settings display:** You also can adjust the Exposure Compensation setting via the Quick Settings display, as shown in Figure 7-20. Remember, you

Figure 7-19: Press the Exposure Compensation button and rotate the Command dial to quickly adjust the setting.

can shift from the Shooting Info screen to the Quick Settings display by pressing the Info Edit button.

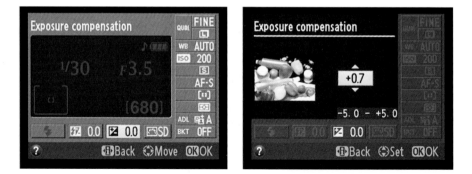

Figure 7-20: You also can raise or lower Exposure Compensation through the Quick Settings screen.

In either case, the 0 on the meter in the viewfinder and Shooting Information display blinks to remind you that Exposure Compensation is active. You also see a little plus/minus symbol (the same one that decorates the Exposure Compensation button) in the viewfinder display, and the meter readout indicates the amount of compensation you applied.

In P, S, and A exposure modes, your Exposure Compensation setting remains in force until you change it, even if you power off the camera. So you may want to make a habit of checking the setting before each shoot or always setting the value back to EV 0.0 after taking the last shot for which you want to apply compensation.

In Night Vision mode, the value is automatically reset to 0 as soon as you change to a different exposure mode.

Just a few other tips:

- How the camera arrives at the brighter or darker image you request through your Exposure Compensation setting depends on the exposure mode:

  - *In A (aperture-priority autoexposure) mode,* the camera adjusts the shutter speed but leaves your selected f-stop in force. Be sure to check the resulting shutter speed to make sure that it isn't so slow that camera shake or blur from moving objects is problematic.

  - *In S (shutter-priority autoexposure) mode,* the camera opens or stops down the aperture.

  - *In P (programmed autoexposure) mode,* the camera decides whether to adjust aperture, shutter speed, or both.

  - *In all three modes,* the camera may also adjust ISO if you have Auto ISO enabled.

  - *In Night Vision mode,* the camera may adjust ISO, shutter speed, or aperture.

  Keep in mind that the camera can adjust f-stop only so much, according to the aperture range of your lens. And the range of shutter speeds, too, is limited by the camera itself. So if you reach the ends of those ranges, you either have to compromise on shutter speed or aperture or adjust ISO.

- When you use flash, the Exposure Compensation setting affects both background brightness and flash power. But you can further modify the flash power through a related option, Flash Compensation. You can find out more about that feature later in this chapter.

- Finally, if you don't want to fiddle with Exposure Compensation, just switch to manual exposure mode — M, on the Mode dial — and select whatever aperture and shutter speed settings produce the exposure you're after.

Although the camera doesn't change your selected exposure settings in manual mode even if Exposure Compensation is enabled, the exposure meter *is* affected by the current setting, which can lead to some confusion. The meter indicates whether your shot will be properly exposed based on the Exposure Compensation setting. So if you don't realize that Exposure Compensation is enabled, you may mistakenly adjust your exposure settings when they're actually on target for your subject. This is yet another reason why it's best to always reset the Exposure Compensation setting back to EV 0.0 after you're done using that feature.

Using autoexposure lock

To help ensure a proper exposure, your camera continually meters the light until the moment you depress the shutter button fully. In autoexposure modes, it also keeps adjusting exposure settings as needed to maintain a good exposure.

For most situations, this approach works great, resulting in the right settings for the light that's striking your subject at the moment you capture the image. But on occasion, you may want to lock in a certain combination of exposure settings. For example, perhaps you want your subject to appear at the far edge of the frame. If you were to use the normal shooting technique, you'd place the subject under a focus point, press the shutter button halfway to lock focus and set the initial exposure, and then reframe to your desired composition to take the shot. The problem is that exposure is then recalculated based on the new framing, which can leave your subject under- or overexposed.

The easiest way to lock in exposure settings is to switch to M (manual) exposure mode and use the f-stop, shutter speed, and ISO settings that work best for your subject. But if you prefer to stay with an autoexposure mode, you can press the AE-L/AF-L button to lock exposure before you reframe. This feature is known as *autoexposure lock,* or AE Lock for short.

You can take advantage of AE Lock in any autoexposure mode except Auto or Auto Flash Off. Here's the technique I recommend:

1. **Set the metering mode to spot metering.**

   Select the option via the Quick Settings screen. The icon representing spot metering looks like the one shown in Figure 7-21.

2. **If autofocusing, set the Focus mode to AF-S and the AF-Area mode to Single Point.**

   Use the Quick Settings screen to select both settings; again, Figure 7-21 shows you how the icons that represent each setting appear in the Shooting Information display.

3. **Frame the subject so that it falls under one of the focus points, and then use the Multi Selector to select that point.**

   You sometimes need to press the shutter button halfway and release it to activate the exposure meters before you can do so. As you press the Multi Selector to cycle through the focus points, the currently selected point flashes red.

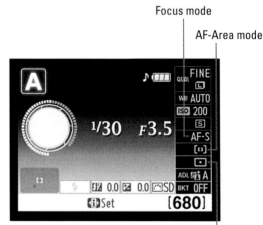

Figure 7-21: Use these metering and autofocus settings for best results when applying autoexposure lock.

In spot metering mode, the focus point determines the area used to calculate exposure, so this step is critical whether you use autofocusing or manual focusing.

4. Press the shutter button halfway.

The camera sets the initial exposure settings. If you're using autofocusing, focus is also set at this point. For manual focusing, twist the focusing ring on the lens to bring the subject into focus.

5. Press and hold the AE-L/AF-L button.

This button's just to the left of the Command dial.

While the button is pressed, the letters AE-L appear at the left end of the viewfinder to remind you that exposure lock is applied.

By default, focus is locked at the same time if you're using autofocusing. You can change this behavior by customizing the AE-L/AF-L button function, as outlined in Chapter 11.

6. Reframe the shot if desired and take the photo.

Be sure to keep holding the AE-L/AF-L button until you release the shutter button! And if you want to use the same focus and exposure settings for your next shot, just keep the AE-L/AF-L button pressed.

Expanding tonal range

A scene like the one in Figure 7-22 presents the classic photographer's challenge: Choosing exposure settings that capture the darkest parts of the subject appropriately causes the brightest areas to be overexposed. And if you instead *expose for the highlights* — that is, set the exposure settings to capture the brightest regions properly — the darker areas are underexposed.

In the past, you had to choose between favoring the highlights or the shadows. But with the D5100, you can expand the possible *tonal range* — that's photo speak for the range of brightness values in an image — through two features: Active D-Lighting and HDR (high dynamic range). The next two sections explain both options.

Applying Active D-Lighting

One way to cope with a high-contrast scene like the one in Figure 7-22 is to turn on Active D-Lighting. This feature is designed to give you a better chance of keeping your highlights intact while better exposing the darkest areas.

The *D* in Active D-Lighting is a reference to the term *dynamic range,* which is used to describe the range of brightness values that an imaging device can capture. By turning on this feature, you enable to camera to produce an image with a slightly greater dynamic range than usual.

Active D-Lighting Off   Active D-Lighting On

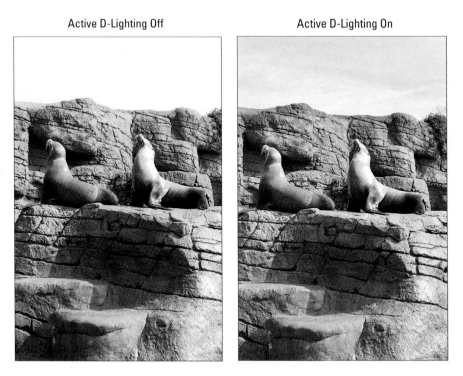

Figure 7-22: Active D-Lighting captured the shadows without blowing out the highlights.

In my seal scene, turning on Active D-Lighting produced a brighter rendition of the darkest parts of the rocks and the seals, for example, and yet the color in the sky didn't get blown out as it did when I captured the image with Active D-Lighting turned off. The highlights in the seal and in the rocks on the lower-right corner of the image also are toned down a tad in the Active D-Lighting version.

Active D-Lighting actually does its thing in two stages. First, it selects exposure settings that result in a slightly darker exposure than normal. This half of the equation guarantees that you retain details in your highlights. After you snap the photo, the camera brightens the darkest areas of the image. This adjustment rescues shadow detail.

In Auto, Auto Flash Off, Scene, and Effects exposure modes, the camera decides how much Active D-Lighting adjustment is needed. In the P, S, A, and M modes, you can control the adjustment as follows:

✔ **Quick Settings display:** After displaying the Shooting Information screen, press the Information Edit button to shift to Quick Settings mode. Then highlight the Active D-Lighting option, as shown on the left in Figure 7-23, and press OK to get to the screen shown on the right in

the figure. You can choose from Auto (the camera sets the adjustment amount), H* (extra high), H (high), N (normal), L (low), and Off. Select the setting you want to use and press OK.

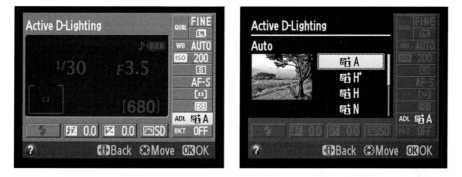

Figure 7-23: You can change the Active D-Lighting setting easily via the Quick Settings screen.

✔ **Shooting menu:** If you prefer menus to the Quick Settings display, you can enable and disable the Active D-Lighting adjustment from the Shooting menu, as shown in Figure 7-24.

✔ **Fn button plus Command dial:** You also can set the Fn (Function button) to immediately call up the Active D-Lighting setting instead of performing its default role, which is to offer quick access to the Self-Timer Release mode. Chapter 11 shows you how. If you make the change, rotate the Command dial while pressing the Fn button to cycle through the available Active D-Lighting settings.

Figure 7-24: Or enable the adjustment through the Shooting menu.

A couple of pointers:

✔ You get the best Active D-Lighting results in matrix metering mode.

✔ Active D-Lighting doesn't work when the ISO is set to Hi 0.3 or above.

✔ In the M exposure mode, the camera doesn't change your shutter speed or f-stop to achieve the darker exposure it needs for Active D-Lighting to work; instead, the meter readout guides you to select the right settings unless you have automatic ISO override enabled. In that case, the camera may instead adjust ISO to manipulate the exposure.

✓ When you shoot in the M exposure mode or set the metering mode to spot or center-weighted, the Auto Active D-Lighting setting produces the amount of adjustment that is applied by the Normal setting.

✓ If you're not sure how much adjustment to apply, try Active D-Lighting bracketing, which automatically records the scene using different adjustment levels. See the last section in this chapter for details.

If you opt out of Active D-Lighting, remember that the camera's Retouch menu offers a D-Lighting filter that applies a similar adjustment to existing pictures. (See Chapter 10 for help.) Some photo-editing programs, including Nikon ViewNX 2, also have good shadow and highlight recovery filters. (In ViewNX 2, investigate the D-Lighting HS, Shadow Protection, and Highlight Protection filters; the program's Help system explains how to use them.) In any case, when you shoot with Active D-Lighting disabled, you're better off setting the initial exposure settings to record the highlights as you want them. It's very difficult to bring back lost highlight detail after the fact, but you typically can unearth at least a little bit of detail from the darkest areas of the image.

Exploring high dynamic range (HDR) photography

In the past few years, many photographers have been experimenting with a technology called HDR photography. HDR stands for *high dynamic range* — again, dynamic range refers to the spectrum of brightness values that a camera or other imaging device can record.

The idea behind HDR is to capture the same shot multiple times, using different exposure settings for each image. You then use special imaging software, called *tone mapping software,* to combine the exposures in a way that uses specific brightness values from each shot. By using this process, you get a shot that contains a much higher dynamic range than the camera can capture in a single image.

The HDR option on the D5100 Shooting menu is designed to let you enjoy HDR photography without having to mess with any special software. When you enable the feature, the camera automatically records two images, each at different exposure settings, and then does the tone-mapping manipulation for you to produce a single HDR image.

So how is HDR different from Active D-Lighting — other than the fact that it records two photos instead of manipulating a single capture? Well, with the HDR feature, you can request an exposure shift of up to three stops between the two photos. That enables you to create an image that has a broader dynamic range than you can get with Active D-Lighting.

Figure 7-25 shows an example of the type of results you can expect. In this scene, half of the area is in bright sunshine, and the other is in shadow. For the top-left photo in the figure, I exposed for the highlights, which left the right side of the scene too dark. For the top-right image, I set exposure for the shaded area, which blew out the highlights in the sunny areas. With the HDR feature set to a three-stop adjustment between the two frames, I was able to produce the bottom image in the figure. The shadows aren't completely eliminated and some parts of the rose bush on the left side of the shot are a little brighter than I want, but on the whole, the camera balanced out the exposure fairly well.

Before you get too excited about the HDR feature, however, note a couple important points:

- ✓ Because the camera is actually recording and merging two photos, the feature works well only on stationary subjects. If the subject is moving, it will appear as two translucent forms in different areas in the merged frame.

- ✓ Similarly, it's important for you to use a tripod to make sure that you don't move the camera between shots.

- ✓ You can't use the HDR feature if you set the Image Quality option to Raw (NEF). It works only for photos that you capture in the JPEG format.

- ✓ Flash isn't compatible with the HDR option.

Exposed for highlights

Exposed for shadows

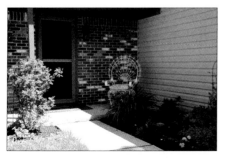
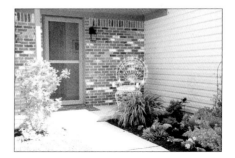

HDR, 3-stop adjustment

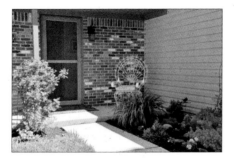

Figure 7-25: HDR enables you to produce an image with an even greater tonal range than Active D-Lighting.

> ✔ Finally, the feature disables itself automatically after your first two frames are captured and merged. That makes experimenting cumbersome because you have to continuously return to the Shooting menu and enable the feature each time you want to try different exposure settings. Annoying, to say the least.

More critically, if you want to do "real" HDR imagery — and by that, I mean the type you see in photography and art magazines — you need to go beyond the two-frame, three-stop limitations of the in-camera HDR feature. Just to give you a point of comparison, Figure 7-26 shows an example that I created by blending five frames with a variation of five stops between frames. The first two images show you the brightest and darkest exposures; the bottom image shows the HDR composite.

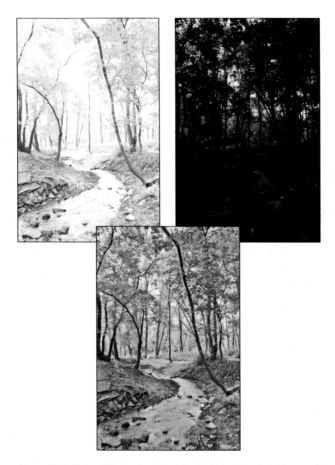

Figure 7-26: Using HDR software tools, I merged the brightest and darkest exposures (top) along with several intermediate exposures, to produce the composite image (bottom).

On the other hand, the effect created by the camera's HDR tool looks more realistic than mine because the tonal range isn't stretched to such an extent. When applied to its extreme limits, HDR produces images that have something of a graphic-novel look. My example is pretty tame; some people might not even realize that any digital trickery has been involved. To me, it has the look of a hand-tinted photo.

And of course, even though the in-camera HDR tool may not be enough to produce the surreal HDR look that's all the rage these days, you can still use your D5100 for HDR work — you just have to adjust the exposure settings yourself between shots and then merge the frames using your own HDR software. You should also shoot the images in the Raw format because HDR tone-mapping tools work best on Raw images, which contain more bits of picture data than JPEG files.

To try out the tamer, point-and-shoot version of HDR on the D5100, take these steps:

1. **Open the Shooting menu and select HDR (high dynamic range), as shown on the left in Figure 7-27.**

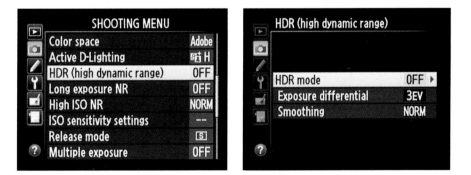

Figure 7-27: Enable HDR from the Shooting menu.

2. **Press the Multi Selector right to display the screen shown on the right in Figure 7-27.**

3. **Select your HDR settings, as follows:**

   • *HDR Mode:* Set this option to On to enable HDR for your next shot.

   • *Exposure Differential:* This setting controls the amount of exposure shift between your two frames. You can choose from a one, two, or three stop adjustment — listed on the menu as 1 EV, 2 EV, and 3 EV (EV for *exposure value*). Or you can select Auto, in which case the camera decides how much adjustment to apply. I set the option to 3 EV for the example in Figure 7-25.

- *Smoothing:* This feature affects the way the camera smoothes out the boundaries between dark and light areas when merging the two images. For the most realistic results, stick with Low smoothing. At high levels of smoothing, you may see shadows around bright objects and halos around dark objects. Some HDR aficionados like that look, so go with whatever suits your eye, however.

4. **After setting the menu options, press the shutter button halfway and release it to return to shooting mode.**

   The letters HDR appear in the Shooting Information display, as shown in Figure 7-28, and in the shots remaining area of the viewfinder to remind you what you did a few seconds ago.

5. **Select the exposure settings and other picture settings as usual.**

6. **Frame, focus, and shoot.**

   Frame your subject a little loosely; the camera may need to trim the edges of the frame away in order to perfectly align the two shots in the HDR image.

   The camera records two frames in quick succession and then creates the merged HDR image.

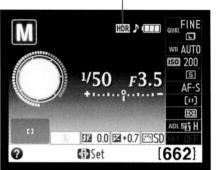

HDR enabled

Figure 7-28: The Shooting Information display reminds you that HDR is enabled.

If you enjoy the HDR feature, you may want to visit Chapter 11 to find out about setting the Fn (Function) button to toggle the HDR Mode setting on and off instead of using the Shooting menu. You still have to visit the menu to adjust the Exposure Differential and Smoothing settings.

Investigating Advanced Flash Options

Sometimes, no amount of fiddling with aperture, shutter speed, and ISO produces a bright-enough exposure — in which case, you simply have to add more light. The built-in flash on your D5100 offers the most convenient solution, but you can also attach an external flash to the camera's *hot shoe,* labeled in Figure 7-29. When you first take the camera out of the box, the contacts on the shoe are protected by a little cover; remove the cover to reveal the contacts and attach a flash.

How much flash control you have depends on your exposure mode:

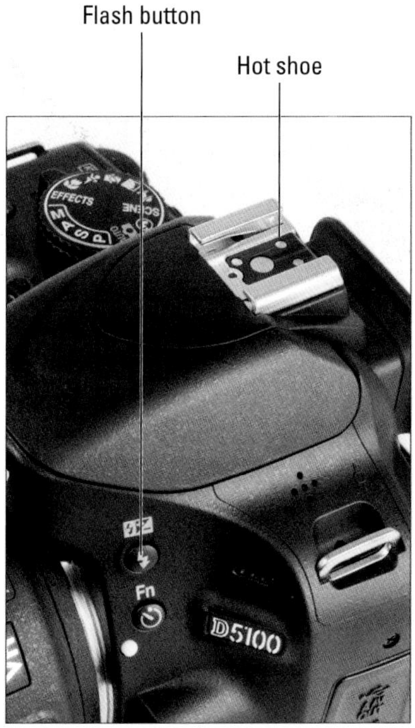

Figure 7-29: Press the Flash button to pop up the built-in flash in the P, S, A, M, and Food exposure modes.

 ✏ **Auto, Scene, and Effects modes:** With one exception, the Food Scene mode, these modes all feature automatic flash, meaning that in dim lighting, the camera automatically raises and fires the built-in flash (assuming that an external flash isn't attached, in which case popping up the built-in flash would deliver a nasty punch in the nose). You may be able to choose from a couple Flash modes, but other flash controls are roped off. And certain Scene and Effects modes disable flash altogether.

 ✏ **P, S, A, and M modes and the Food Scene mode:** In these modes, you take total control over flash. If you want to use the built-in flash, press the Flash button, also labeled in Figure 7-29. To go flashfree, just press the top of the flash unit gently down to close it.

Chapter 3 offers assistance with using the flash in the Auto and Scene modes; Chapter 10 discussers Effects modes. The rest of this chapter digs into features available in the advanced exposure modes. Like everything else on the D5100, those features range from fairly simple to fairly not. Unfortunately, to keep this book from being exorbitantly large (and expensive), I can cover only the basics here. So I point you toward a couple of my favorite resources for delving more deeply into flash photography:

 ✏ Nikon's United States website (www.nikonusa.com) offers some great tutorials on flash photography (as well as other subjects). Start in the Learn & Explore section of the site.

 ✏ A website completely dedicated to flash photography, www.strobist. com, enables you to learn from and share with other photographers.

 ✏ You can find several good books detailing the entire Nikon flash system, which it calls the *Creative Lighting System* (*CLS,* for short).

 ✏ Chapter 9 of this book offers additional flash and lighting tips related to portraits and other specific types of photographs.

Before moving on, though, here's one preliminary tip: Pay careful attention to your results when you use the built-in flash with a telephoto lens that's very long. You may find that the flash casts an unwanted shadow when its light strikes the lens. For best results, try switching to an external flash head.

Choosing the right Flash mode

Chapter 3 details the art of setting the Flash mode, but here's a quick recap. You can view the current mode in the Shooting Info display, in the area labeled in Figure 7-30. (The viewfinder doesn't display any mode information; you simply see the little lightning-bolt icon to tell you that flash is enabled.)

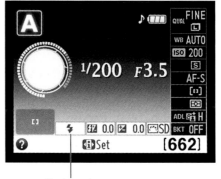

To change the Flash mode, use either of these two techniques:

- **Press the Flash button as you rotate the Command dial.** As soon as you press the button, the Shooting Info screen changes to display the Flash mode flag, as shown in Figure 7-31. Keep the button pressed while rotating the dial to cycle through the available Flash modes.

Figure 7-30: The current Flash mode appears in the Shooting Info display.

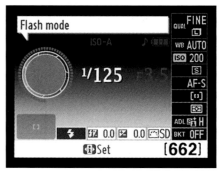

- **Use the Quick Settings display.** Alternatively, you can set the Flash mode through the Quick Settings screen, as shown in Figure 7-32.

Your Flash mode choices break down into three basic categories, described in the next sections: Fill Flash; Red-Eye Reduction; and the sync modes, Slow-Sync and Rear-Sync, which are special-purpose flash options. Note that the list of available Flash modes doesn't include three options available in some of the fully automatic exposure modes: Auto, in which the camera makes the decisions about when to fire the flash; its companion, Auto with Red-Eye Reduction; and Off. Instead, if you don't want the flash to fire, simply keep the flash unit closed.

Figure 7-31: After raising the flash, press the Flash button while rotating the Command dial to change the Flash mode.

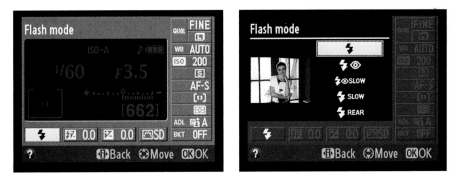

Figure 7-32: You also can adjust the Flash mode through the Quick Settings display.

The camera does give you a little auto-flash input though: You see a blinking question mark, flash symbol, or both in the viewfinder in the P, S, and A modes if the camera thinks you need flash, and the Shooting Info display also tells you that the scene is too dark. Press the Zoom Out button (the one with the question mark above it), and a message appears recommending that you use flash.

Fill Flash

 The Fill Flash setting is represented by the plain-old lightning-bolt symbol you see in the margin here. You can think of this setting as "normal flash" — at least in the way that most think of using a flash. You may also hear this mode called *force* flash because the flash fires no matter what the available light, unlike in the Auto Flash mode provided for the fully automatic exposure modes, in which the camera decides when flash is needed. In Fill Flash mode, the flash fires even in the brightest daylight — which, by the way, is often an excellent idea.

Yep, you read me correctly: Adding a flash can really improve outdoor photos, even when the sun is at its sunniest. After all, your main light source — the sun — is overhead, so although the top of the subject may be adequately lit, the front typically needs some additional illumination. As an example, Figure 7-33 shows a floral image taken both with and without a flash. The small pop of light provided by the built-in flash is also extremely beneficial when shooting subjects that happen to be slightly shaded, such as the carousel horses featured in the "Adjusting flash output" section. For outdoor portraits, a flash is even more important; the section on shooting still portraits in Chapter 9 discusses that subject and offers a look at the difference a flash can make.

No Flash   Fill Flash

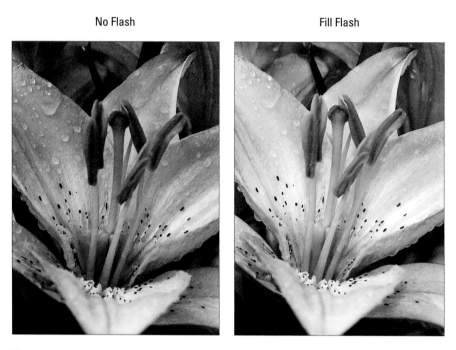

Figure 7-33: Adding flash resulted in better illumination and a slight warming effect.

You do need to beware of a couple complications with using flash in bright light, however:

- **Colors may need tweaking when you mix light sources.** When you combine multiple light sources, such as flash with daylight, colors may appear warmer or cooler than neutral. In Figure 7-33, colors became warmer with the addition of flash. For outdoor portraits, the warming effect is usually flattering, and I usually like the result with nature shots as well. But if you prefer a neutral color rendition, see the Chapter 8 section related to the White Balance control to find out how to address this issue. You can adjust white balance only in P, S, A, and M exposure modes.

- **Keep an eye on shutter speed.** Because of the way the camera needs to synchronize the firing of the flash with the opening of the shutter, the fastest shutter speed you can use with the built-in flash is 1/200 second. In bright sun, you may need to stop down the aperture significantly or lower ISO, if possible, to avoid overexposing the image even at 1/200 second. As another option, you can place a neutral density filter over your lens; this accessory reduces the light that comes through the lens without affecting colors. Of course, if possible, you can simply move your subject into the shade.

On the flip side, the camera may select a shutter speed as slow as 1/60 second in the P and A modes, depending on the lighting conditions. So if your subject is moving, it's a good idea to work in the S or M modes so that you control shutter speed.

✓ **For close-ups, you may need to reduce flash power to avoid overexposing the subject.** I find that at the default flash power, the built-in flash is almost always too strong. No worries — you can dial down the flash output, as explained later in this chapter.

Red-Eye Reduction flash

Red-eye is caused when flash light bounces off a subject's retinas and is reflected back to the camera lens. Red-eye is a human phenomenon, though; with animals, the reflected light usually glows yellow, white, or green, producing an image that looks like your pet is possessed by some demon.

Man or beast, this issue isn't nearly the problem with the type of pop-up flash found on your D5100 as it is on non-SLR cameras. The D5100's flash is positioned in such a way that the flash light usually doesn't hit a subject's eyes straight on, which lessens the chances of red-eye. However, red-eye may still be an issue when you use a lens with a long focal length (a telephoto lens) or you shoot subjects from a distance. Even then, the problem usually crops up only in dark settings — in outdoor shots and other brightly lit scenes, the pupils constrict in reaction to the light, lessening the chance of red-eye. And because of the bright light, the flash power needed to expose the picture is lessened, also helping eliminate red-eye.

If you do notice red-eye, you can try the Red-Eye Reduction mode, represented by the icon shown in the margin here. In this mode, the AF-assist lamp on the front of the camera lights up briefly before the flash fires. The subject's pupils constrict in response to the light, allowing less flash light to enter the eye and cause that glowing red reflection. Be sure to warn your subjects to wait for the flash, or they may step out of the frame or stop posing after they see the light from the AF-assist lamp.

For an even better solution, try the flash-free portrait tips covered in Chapter 9. If you do a lot of portrait work that requires flash, you may also want to consider an external flash unit, which enables you to aim the flash light in ways that virtually eliminate red-eye.

If all else fails, check out Chapter 10, which shows you how to use the built-in red-eye removal tool on your camera's Retouch menu. Sadly, though, this feature removes only red-eye, not the yellow/green/white eye that you get with animal portraits.

Slow-Sync and Rear-Sync flash

In Fill Flash and Red-Eye Reduction Flash modes, the flash and shutter are synchronized so that the flash fires at the exact moment the shutter opens.

Technical types refer to this flash arrangement as *front-curtain sync,* which refers to how the flash is synchronized with the opening of the shutter. Here's the deal: The D5100 uses a type of shutter that involves two curtains moving across the frame each time you press and release the shutter button. When you press the shutter button, the first curtain opens, allowing light through to the sensor. At the end of the exposure, the second curtain draws across the frame to once again shield the sensor from light. With front-curtain sync, the flash fires at the moment the front curtain opens.

Your D5100 also offers four special sync modes, which work as follows:

⚡ SLOW

- **Slow-Sync:** This mode, available only in the P and A exposure modes, also uses front-curtain sync but allows a shutter speed slower than the 1/60 second minimum that's in force when you use Fill Flash and Red-Eye Reduction flash.

  The benefit of this longer exposure is that the camera has time to absorb more ambient light, which in turn has two effects: Background areas that are beyond the reach of the flash appear brighter; and less flash power is needed, resulting in softer lighting.

  The downside of the slow shutter speed is, well, the slow shutter speed. As discussed earlier in this chapter, the longer the exposure time, the more you have to worry about blur caused by movement of your subject or your camera. A tripod is essential to a good outcome, as are subjects that can hold very, very still. I find that the best practical use for this mode is shooting nighttime still-life subjects like the one you see in Figure 7-34. However, if you're shooting a nighttime portrait and you have a subject that *can* maintain a motionless pose, slow-sync flash can produce softer, more flattering light. Again, the portrait section of Chapter 9 offers an example.

  Some photographers, on the other hand, turn the downside of slow-sync flash to an upside, using it to purposely blur their subjects. The idea is to use the blur to emphasize motion.

  Note that even though the official Slow-Sync mode appears only in the P and A exposure modes, you can get the same result in the M and S modes by simply using a slow shutter speed and the normal, Fill Flash mode. You can use a shutter speed as slow as 30 seconds when using flash in those modes. In fact, I prefer those modes when I want the slow-sync look because I can directly control shutter speed.

Normal flash   Slow-sync flash

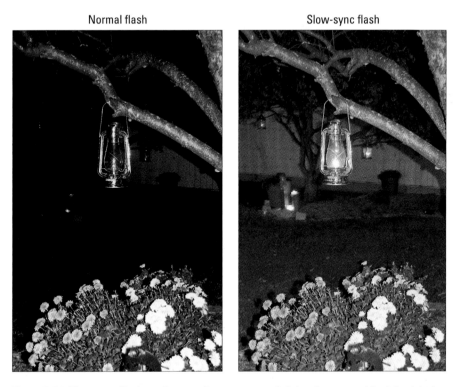

Figure 7-34: Slow-sync flash produces softer, more even lighting than nighttime pictures.

⚡ REAR

↳ **Rear-Curtain Sync:** In this mode, available only in shutter-priority (S) and manual (M) exposure modes, the flash fires at the very end of the exposure, just before the shutter closes. The classic use of this mode is to combine the flash with a slow shutter speed to create trailing-light effects like the one you see in Figure 7-35. With Rear-Curtain Sync, the light trails extend behind the moving object (my hand, and the match, in this case), which makes visual sense. If instead you use slow-sync flash, the light trails appear in front of the moving object.

You can set the shutter speed as low as 30 seconds and as high as 1/200 second in this Flash mode.

↳ **Slow-Sync with Rear-Curtain Sync:** Hey, not confusing enough for you yet? This mode enables you to produce the same motion trail effects as with Rear-Curtain Sync, but in the P and A exposure modes. The camera automatically chooses a slower shutter speed than normal after you set the f-stop, just as with regular Slow-Sync mode.

Note that as you scroll through the available Flash modes, the symbol for this mode initially shows just the flash symbol and the word Rear; after you finish selecting the setting, the label changes to Slow Rear.

✓ **Slow-Sync with Red-Eye Reduction:** In P and A exposure modes, you can also combine a slow-sync flash with the red-eye reduction feature. Given the potential for blur that comes with a slow shutter, plus the potential for subjects to mistake the pre-light from the AF-assist lamp for the real flash and walk out of the frame before the image is actually recorded, I vote this Flash mode as the most difficult to pull off successfully.

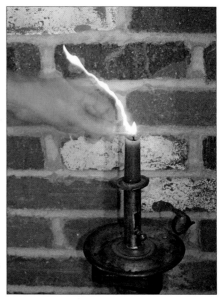

Figure 7-35: I used rear-curtain sync flash to create this candle-lighting image.

All these modes are somewhat tricky to use successfully, however. So have fun playing around, but at the same time, don't feel too badly if you don't have time right now to master these modes plus all the other exposure options presented to you in this chapter. In the meantime, search the web for slow-sync and rear-sync image examples if you want to get a better idea of the special effects that other photographers create with these Flash modes.

Adjusting flash output

When you shoot with your built-in flash, the camera attempts to adjust the flash output as needed to produce a good exposure. But if you shoot in the P, S, A, or M exposure modes and you want a little more or less flash light than the camera thinks is appropriate, you can adjust the flash output by using *Flash Compensation.*

This feature works just like Exposure Compensation, discussed earlier in the chapter, except that it enables you to override the camera's flash-power decision instead of its autoexposure decision. As with Exposure Compensation, the Flash Compensation settings are stated in terms of EV *(exposure value)* numbers. A setting of 0.0 indicates no flash adjustment; you can increase the flash power to EV +1.0 or decrease it to EV –3.0.

REMEMBER

In sync: Flash timing and shutter speed

To properly expose flash pictures, the camera has to synchronize the timing of the flash output with the opening and closing of the shutter. For this reason, the range of shutter speeds available to you is more limited when you use flash than when you go flash-free.

When you use flash, the maximum shutter speed is 1/200 second. The minimum shutter speed varies depending on your exposure mode, as follows:

✔ **Close-Up, Food:** 1/125 second

✔ **Nighttime Portrait:** 1 second

✔ **Auto, Color Sketch (Effects mode), and all other Scene modes:** 1/60 second

✔ **P, A:** 1/60 second (unless you use one of the Slow-Sync Flash modes, which permit a slower shutter speed)

✔ **S:** 30 seconds

✔ **M:** 30 seconds (can exceed that limit if the shutter speed is set to bulb)

These same shutter-speed requirements apply to both the built-in flash and an external flash head.

As an example of the benefit of this feature, look at the carousel images in Figure 7-36. The first image shows you a flash-free shot. Clearly, I needed a flash to compensate for the fact that the horses were shadowed by the roof of the carousel. But at normal flash power, as shown in the middle image, the flash was too strong, creating glare in some spots and blowing out the highlights in the white mane. By dialing the flash power down to EV –0.7, I got a softer flash that straddled the line perfectly between no flash and too much flash.

As for boosting the flash output, well, you may find it necessary on some occasions, but don't expect the built-in flash to work miracles even at a Flash Compensation of +1.0. Any built-in flash has a limited range, and you simply can't expect the flash light to reach faraway objects. In other words, don't even try taking flash pictures of a darkened recital hall from your seat in the balcony — all you'll wind up doing is annoying everyone.

The current Flash Compensation setting appears in the Shooting Info display, in the area highlighted in Figure 7-37. Don't confuse the setting with the neighboring Exposure Compensation setting, also labeled in the figure. (The flash symbol in the Flash Compensation icon is the key reminder to which setting does what.)

No flash   Flash EV 0.0

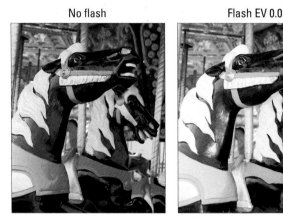

Flash EV –0.7

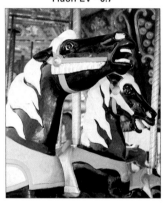

Figure 7-36: When normal flash output is too strong, dial in a lower Flash Compensation etting.

To adjust the amount of Flash Compensation, you have two options:

✓ **Use the two-button plus Command dial maneuver.** First, press the Flash button to pop up the built-in flash. Then press and hold the Flash button and the Exposure Compensation button simultaneously. When you press the buttons, you see the screen shown in Figure 7-38. In the viewfinder, the current setting takes the place of the usual frames remaining value. While keeping both the buttons pressed, rotate the Command dial to adjust the setting. I find that any technique that involves coordinating this many fingers a little complex, but you may find it easier than I do.

✔ **Use the Quick Settings screen.**
Just bring up the Shooting Info display, press the Info Edit button to shift to Quick Settings mode, and highlight the Flash Compensation setting, as shown on the left in Figure 7-39. Press OK to display a screen where you can set the flash power, as shown in the second screen of the figure. Press the Multi Selector up or down to change the setting and then press OK.

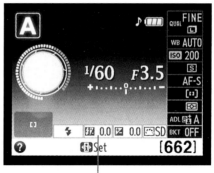

Flash Compensation

Figure 7-37: The Flash Compensation setting lives just next door to the Exposure Compensation setting.

As with Exposure Compensation, any flash-power adjustment you make remains in force, even if you turn off the camera, until you reset the control. So be sure to check the setting before you next use your flash.

Controlling flash output manually

If you're experienced in the way of the flash, you can manually set the flash output instead of letting the camera dictate the right amount of flash light. Just open the Custom Setting menu, choose Bracketing/Flash, press OK, and then choose Flash Cntrl for Built-In Flash, as shown on the left in Figure 7-40. Press OK, select Manual, as shown on the right, and press OK again to display the available settings. Your options are from Full power to 1/32 power.

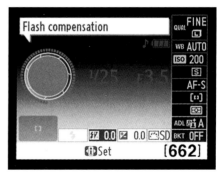

Figure 7-38: Rotate the Command dial while pressing the Flash and Exposure Compensation buttons to adjust flash power.

The TTL setting is the default flash setting, in which the camera sets the proper flash power for you. *TTL* stands for *through the lens*.

While manual flash control is enabled, an icon that looks like the Shooting Info screen's Flash Compensation icon (a lightning bolt with a plus-minus sign) blinks in the viewfinder. If you want to get really tricky, you can employ Flash Compensation even with manual flash control.

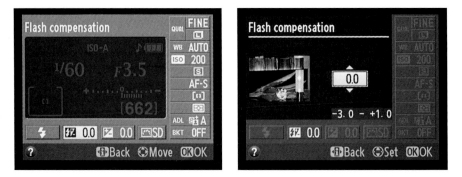

Figure 7-39: For a less cumbersome way to adjust flash power, use the Quick Settings screen.

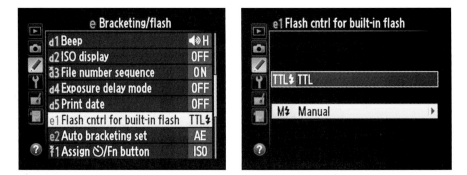

Figure 7-40: Through this option, you can control the flash output manually.

Bracketing Exposures

Many photographers use *exposure bracketing* to ensure that at least one shot of a subject is properly exposed. *Bracketing* simply means to shoot the same subject multiple times, slightly varying the exposure settings for each image.

In the P, S, A, and M exposure modes, your camera offers *automatic bracketing*. When you enable this feature, your only job is to press the shutter button to record the shots; the camera automatically adjusts the exposure settings between each image. This feature is especially helpful for situations where you don't have time to review images and adjust exposure settings between shots. The D5100, however, takes things one step further than most cameras that offer automatic bracketing, enabling you to bracket not just basic exposure, but also Active D-Lighting or white balance.

With the D5100, you record a three-shot series of bracketed images when you use the autoexposure and white-balance bracketing options. For Active D-Lighting, you can take only two shots in the series, one with the feature turned off and one at the setting currently in force for the Active D-Lighting option. (See "Applying Active D-Lighting," earlier in this chapter, for details on changing that setting.)

Chapter 8 explains how to use the white-balance bracketing option; to try your hand at exposure or Active D-Lighting bracketing, follow these steps:

1. **Set your camera to the P, S, A, or M exposure mode.**

   You can't take advantage of the feature in any other modes.

2. **Display the Custom Setting menu, highlight Bracketing/Flash, and press OK.**

3. **Highlight the Auto Bracketing Set option from the menu shown on the left in Figure 7-41 and press OK.**

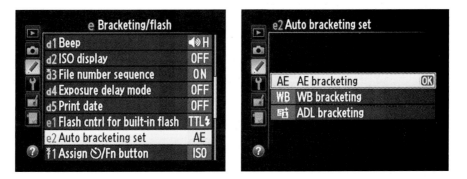

Figure 7-41: Before enabling auto bracketing, select the feature you want the camera to adjust between shots.

You see the options shown on the right in the figure. This screen is where you tell the camera whether you want to bracket exposure (AE), white balance (WB), or Active D-Lighting (ADL). Note that even though the first option is called AE (for autoexposure), it enables you to bracket exposure in M (manual exposure) mode just the same.

4. **Select the desired bracketing option and press OK.**

5. **Use the Quick Settings screen to specify the bracketing increment.**

   After shifting to Quick Settings mode, highlight the Bracketing Increment setting in the lower-right corner of the screen, as shown on the left in

Figure 7-42. Press OK to display the second screen in the figure. The available settings depend on the feature you're bracketing (exposure or Active D-Lighting), as follows:

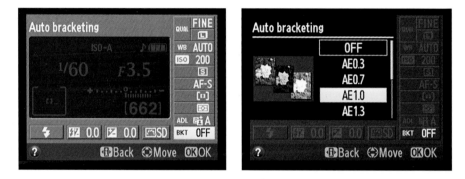

Figure 7-42: Set the bracketing amount through the Quick Settings screen.

- *For exposure bracketing,* the settings control the amount of exposure shift between frames. The settings are based on Exposure Compensation values. For example, if you choose 0.7 for an auto-exposure bracketing set, the camera makes three exposures, one with exposure values as metered by the camera, one exposure with EV +0.7, and one exposure with EV –0.7 Your choices are from 0.3 EV to 2.0 EV. Choosing Off disables bracketing.

- *For Active D-Lighting bracketing,* you get only two options: ADL and Off. Select ADL. (This option is a little weird — if you select Off, you just disable bracketing.)

6. **After selecting the bracketing increment, press OK to return to the Shooting Information display.**

7. **Shoot your first bracketed series.**

Remember, for autoexposure bracketing, a series consists of three shots. For Active D-Lighting, the camera records only two shots per series.

When bracketing is enabled, the exposure meter in the Shooting Information display offers a *bracketing progress indicator* as shown in Figure 7-43. That's a pretty technical way of saying, "Little bars appear under the meter, each one representing one shot in your bracketed series." The indicator updates after each picture to show you how many more shots are left in the series. For example, the middle bar represents your first shot; after you take your first picture, it disappears. You then see one or two bars — and thus, one or two shots left to shoot — depending on whether you're bracketing exposure or Active D-Lighting. A little label to the left of the meter reminds you which feature you're bracketing — AE (autoexposure) bracketing, in the figure.

You can speed up things when bracketing exposures if you specify Continuous for the Release mode. When you press the shutter, the camera takes three exposures using the setting you specify in Step 5. See Chapter 2 for help with changing the Release mode setting.

8. **To disable bracketing, repeat Step 5 and select Off from the second screen shown in Figure 7-42.**

Don't be put off by the length of these steps, by the way. Although describing the feature takes quite a few words, using bracketing really isn't all that complicated. Bracketing is a wonderful way to hedge your bet, especially when you're taking pictures of a place you may never visit again, or experiencing a once-in-a-lifetime photo opportunity such as your son's first birthday party.

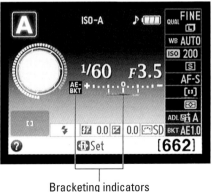

Bracketing indicators

Figure 7-43: The bars under the meter tell you which frame of the bracketed series you're about to shoot.

8

Manipulating Focus and Color

In This Chapter

- Adjusting the camera's autofocusing performance
- Perfecting your manual focusing technique
- Understanding focal lengths, depth of field, and other focus factors
- Exploring white balance and its effect on color
- Investigating other color options
- Taking a quick tour of Picture Controls

To many people, the word *focus* has just one interpretation when applied to a photograph: Either the subject is in focus or it's blurry. And although it's true that this characteristic of your photographs is an important one, an artful photographer knows that there's more to focus than simply getting a sharp image of a subject. You also need to consider *depth of field,* or the distance over which objects remain sharply focused.

This chapter explains all the ways to control depth of field and also explains how to use your D5100's advanced focusing options. Note, however, that the autofocusing features covered here relate only to regular, through-the-viewfinder photography; Chapter 4 focuses (yuk yuk) on Live View and movie autofocusing, which involves a different set of features and techniques.

Additionally, this chapter dives into the topic of color, explaining your camera's White Balance control, which compensates for the varying color casts created by different light sources. You also can get my take on the other advanced color options on your D5100, including the Color Space option and Picture Controls, in this chapter.

Mastering the Autofocus System

The D5100 offers a fast and trustworthy autofocusing system — you can rely on it for tack-sharp images 99 percent of the time, in my experience. But to get the best autofocusing performance, you need to understand which autofocus settings work best for different types of subjects. The default settings usually work fine for portraits, for example, but for sports photography, adjusting the settings typically produces more reliable results.

You have two major avenues of control over the autofocusing system:

- **AF-Area mode:** This setting determines which focus points are used to establish focus. You can tell the camera to consider all 11 autofocus points or to base focus on a single point that you select.

- **Focus mode:** You can set the camera to lock focus when you press the shutter button halfway or adjust focus continually up to the moment you depress the button fully to take the picture.

The next several sections provide the background you need to master these options and other aspects of the autofocus system.

Reviewing autofocus basics

The Chapter 3 section on taking your first pictures in the Auto and Auto Flash Off exposure modes provides an introduction to the process of autofocusing with the D5100. But in case you haven't dug into that chapter, the following steps get you up to speed.

These steps apply to any exposure mode, not just Auto or Auto Flash Off. However, they *don't* apply to Live View photography or movie recording; again, check Chapter 4 for information on autofocusing in those modes.

1. **Set the focusing switch on the lens to A (autofocus), as shown in Figure 8-1.**

   These directions are specific to the kit lens sold with the D5100. Other lenses may have a different sort of switch or no switch at all, so check the lens instruction manual. And note that not all lenses provide autofocusing when paired with the D5100; the camera manual provides information on compatible lenses.

2. **Frame the picture so that your subject falls under one of the 11 focus points.**

   The focus points are represented by the little black markings in the viewfinder.

   For most exposure modes, all 11 focus points are active by default, which means that the camera considers all points when deciding where to set focus. Typically, the camera picks the closest object as the focusing target.

   The exceptions are the Close Up, Sports, Pet Portrait, Food, and Candlelight Scene modes. In these modes, focus is set on the center point, so be sure to frame your subject under that point. To find out how to modify this autofocus behavior, see the next section.

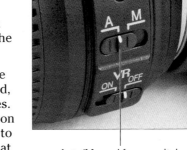

Auto/Manual focus switch

Figure 8-1: Set the lens switch to the A position to use autofocusing.

3. **Press and hold the shutter button halfway down to indicate focusing.**

   Depending on the lighting conditions, the AF-assist lamp on the front of the camera may emit a beam to help the autofocus system find its target. (Chapter 1 explains how to disable the light if you're shooting in a setting where it's problematic.)

   A second or two after you press the button halfway, one or more of the focus points flashes red, as shown in Figure 8-2, to let you know which points the camera used to establish focus.

Selected focus points

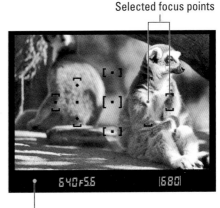

Focus indicator light

Figure 8-2: The red dots indicate selected focus points.

The camera offers these additional cues that it set focus successfully:

- *For stationary subjects:* The green focus indicator dot lights in the lower-left corner of the viewfinder, as shown in Figure 8-2, and the camera emits a tiny beep. (See Chapter 1 to find out how to disable the beep if you want it to keep quiet.) Focus is now locked as long as you keep the shutter button depressed halfway. That means that you can reframe the picture if desired and still retain focus on the subject.

- *For moving subjects:* If the camera detects movement, it sets the initial focus point and then adjusts focus if the subject moves out of the selected point. You need to reframe the picture as needed to keep the subject within the area covered by the 11 focus points, however. The green focus indicator may flicker on and off as the camera continues to track focus. But if the light blinks continuously, the camera isn't having any luck focusing on your subject. The beep may or may not sound.

To find out how to adjust this aspect of autofocus behavior, check out the upcoming discussion related to the Focus mode.

Your half-press of the shutter button also kicks the exposure metering system into gear. And the shots remaining value in the viewfinder changes to show the number of frames that will fit in the camera's buffer. For more on exposure, travel to Chapter 7; information about the buffer awaits in Chapter 2.

4. Press the button the rest of the way to take the picture.

Now that you understand how things work at the default AF-Area mode and Focus mode settings, the next several sections explain how to modify the settings to best suit your subject.

Understanding the AF-Area mode setting

The AF-Area mode option determines which of the 11 focusing points the camera uses to establish focus. (*AF* stands for *autofocus.*) You can view the current setting in the Shooting Info display. In fact, the display contains two icons representing the setting, as shown in Figure 8-3. The one in the lower-left corner is designed to give you a bit more information than the simplified version on the right side of the screen. More about what you can glean from that detailed icon momentarily.

WARNING!

Shutter speed and blurry photos

A poorly focused photo isn't always related to the issues discussed in this chapter. Any movement of the camera or subject can also cause blur. Both of these problems are related to shutter speed, an exposure control that I cover in Chapter 7. Be sure to also visit Chapter 9, which provides some additional tips for capturing moving objects without blur.

You can choose from four settings, which work as described in the following list and are represented in the lower-left corner of the Shooting Info display by the margin icons shown here. (Flip ahead to Figure 8-4 to see the simplified icons that appear on the right side of the Shooting Info display.)

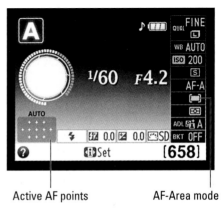

Active AF points   AF-Area mode

Figure 8-3: These symbols show the current AF-Area mode setting and which focus points are active.

- **Single Point:** This mode is designed for shooting still subjects. You use the Multi Selector to choose one of the 11 focus points (details to come), and the camera sets focus on the object that falls within that point. The camera uses this mode by default when you shoot in the Close Up, Food, and Candlelight Scene modes.

  In the lower-left corner of the Shooting Info display, the position of the brackets in the AF-Area mode icon show you which point is selected. For example, an icon like the one you see in the margin here tells you that the center point is selected.

- **Dynamic Area:** In this mode, designed for shooting moving subjects, you select an initial focus point, just as in Single Point mode. But if the subject within that focus point moves after you press the shutter button halfway to set focus, the camera looks for focus information from the other focus points. The idea is that the subject is likely to wind up within one of the 11 focus areas. Dynamic Area is the default setting when you shoot in the Sports and Pet Portrait Scene modes.

However — and this is a biggie — for the automatic focus adjustment to occur, you also must set the Focus mode (explained in the next section) to either AF-A, the default setting, or AF-C. In fact, Dynamic Area doesn't even appear as an AF-Area mode option when the Focus mode is set to AF-S.

In the lower-left corner of the Shooting Info display, the icon for the Dynamic Area mode looks similar to the one in the margin here. Your selected focus point is surrounded by brackets, but you also see little plus signs marking the other points to indicate that they're ready to take over if your subject moves. Note that the brackets surrounding your selected focus point don't move if the camera shifts to a different point to focus, but the focus shift is happening just the same.

✔ **Auto Area:** The camera analyzes the objects under all 11 autofocus points and selects the one it deems most appropriate. This mode is the default setting for all exposure modes except the five Scene modes previously mentioned.

✔ **3D Tracking:** This one is a variation of Dynamic Area autofocusing. As with the Dynamic Area mode, you have to set the Focus mode to AF-A or AF-C to access the 3D Tracking option. And as with Dynamic Area mode, you start by selecting a single focus point and then press the shutter button halfway to set focus. But the goal of this mode is to maintain focus on your subject if you recompose the shot after you press the shutter button halfway to lock focus.

The 3D Tracking icon appears in the lower-left corner of the Shooting Info display as shown in the margin here; the brackets indicate your selected focus point.

The only problem with 3D Tracking is that the way the camera detects your subject is by analyzing the colors of the object under your selected focus point. So if not much difference exists between the subject and other objects in the frame, the camera can get fooled. And if your subject moves out of the frame, you must release the shutter button and reset focus by pressing it halfway again.

To keep my life simple, I stick with Single Point for still subjects and Dynamic Area for moving subjects. Auto Area can work well in most cases, but if it makes the wrong focus assumptions, there's no way to select a different focus point. And I prefer Dynamic Area to 3D Tracking for the reasons I just mentioned — it doesn't work for all action subjects, and by the time you figure out whether your subject is compatible with the mode, you can easily miss the shot. Still, I urge you to practice with that mode, too, in case you regularly shoot the types of subjects that it's designed to handle.

Whatever your conclusions on the subject, you can adjust the AF-Area mode and select a specific focus point as follows:

- ✔ **Setting the AF-Area mode:** The only way to change the setting is via the Quick Settings display. If the Shooting Info screen is visible, tap the Info Edit button to shift to Quick Settings mode. Otherwise, press the button twice. Then highlight the AF-Area mode icon, as shown on the left in Figure 8-4, and press OK to access the second screen in the figure, where you see the simplified versions of the icons representing the different mode options. From top to bottom, the settings are Single Point, Dynamic Area, 3D Tracking, and Auto Area.

  Don't see the 3D Tracking or Dynamic Area options? That happens if the Focus mode is set to AF-S. So if you want to use either of those AF-Area modes, set the Focus mode to AF-C or AF-A — the setting is located directly above the AF-Area mode option in the Quick Settings display. Refer to the next section for more information.

- ✔ **Selecting a single focus point:** To choose a focus point in the Single Area, Dynamic Area, or 3D Tracking modes, press the shutter button halfway and release it to engage the exposure meters. The currently selected point flashes red. For example, in Figure 8-5, the point directly over the top of the clock tower is selected. Use the Multi Selector to cycle through all 11 points until the one you want to use flashes red.

  To quickly select the center focus point, press OK. No need to cycle your way through all the other focus points to get to the center.

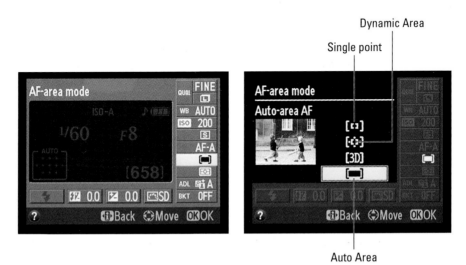

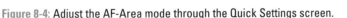

Figure 8-4: Adjust the AF-Area mode through the Quick Settings screen.

Changing the Focus mode setting

Throughout this book, I sometimes use the term *auto/manual focusing mode* generically to refer to the lens switch that shifts your camera from autofocusing to manual focusing — at least, on the kit lens sold with the D5100. But there is also an official Focus mode setting, which offers three settings for tweaking autofocusing behavior and one option that tells the camera that you prefer to focus manually.

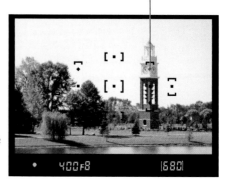

Selected focus point

Figure 8-5: Use the Multi Selector to select the focus point that's over your subject.

As with the AF-Area mode setting, you choose the Focus mode via the Quick Settings screen. The option lives directly upstairs from the AF-Area mode setting, as shown in Figure 8-6.

Figure 8-6: You can access all four Focus mode settings only in the P, S, A, and M exposure modes.

When you shoot in the P, S, A, or M exposure mode, you can choose from the four options shown in the figure, which work as follows:

- **AF-S (single-servo autofocus):** With this option, the camera locks focus when you depress the shutter button halfway. It's designed for shooting stationary subjects.

Use this mode if you want to frame your subject so that it doesn't fall under an autofocus point: Compose the scene initially to put the subject under a focus point, press the shutter button halfway to lock focus, and then reframe to the composition you have in mind. As long as you keep the button pressed halfway, focus remains set on your subject. Remember, though, that exposure is adjusted up to the time you take the picture. See Chapter 7 to find out how to use the AE-L/AF-L button to lock exposure at the same time you lock focus.

One other critical point about AF-S mode: When this mode is selected, the camera won't release the shutter to take a picture until focus is achieved. If you can't get the camera to lock onto your focusing target, switching to manual focusing is the easiest solution. Also be sure that you're not too close to your subject; if you exceed the minimum focusing distance of the lens, you can't focus manually, either.

✔ **AF-C (continuous-servo autofocus):** In this mode, which is designed for moving subjects, the camera focuses continuously for the entire time you hold the shutter button halfway down.

Remember these keys to continuous autofocusing:

- By default, AF-C mode prevents you from taking a picture until focus is achieved, just like AF-S mode. But you can tell the camera to capture the shot at the instant you fully depress the shutter button, regardless of whether focus is set. Make the call via the AF-C Priority Selection option, found in the Autofocus section of the Custom Setting menu and shown in Figure 8-7. Focus is the default setting; choose Release to allow shutter release before focus is set.

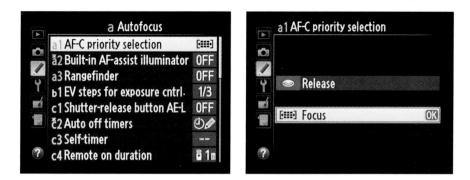

Figure 8-7: This setting controls whether you can take a picture before focus is achieved in the AF-C Focus mode.

For the most part, I stick with Focus. Yes, I may miss a few shots waiting for the focus to occur, but if they're going to be out of focus, who cares? But when my subject is moving at a really rapid pace, I do unlock the shutter release for AF-C mode. Although I may wind up with lots of wasted shots, I also increase the odds that I'll capture that split-second "highlight reel" moment. If the subject is slightly out of focus, I can probably retouch it enough to make it passable, especially if the picture content is truly special. And by using camera settings that produce a large *depth of field* (zone of sharp focus), the subject may appear in focus even if the actual focusing point the camera used wasn't dead on. Later sections in this chapter discuss depth of field.

- To lock focus at a certain distance while using AF-C mode, use the technique described in the section, "Using autofocus lock," later in this chapter.

✓ **AF-A (auto-servo autofocus):** This mode is the default setting. The camera analyzes the scene and, if it detects motion, automatically selects continuous-servo mode (AF-C). If the camera instead believes you're shooting a stationary object, it selects single-servo mode (AF-S). Shutter release is prevented if the camera can't focus successfully.

This mode works pretty well, but it can get confused sometimes. For example, if your subject is motionless but other people are moving in the background, the camera may mistakenly switch to continuous autofocus. By the same token, if the subject is moving only slightly, the camera may not make the switch. So my best advice is to choose either AF-S or AF-C instead.

✓ **MF (manual focus):** Choose this setting if you want to focus manually, by twisting the focusing ring on the lens, instead of using autofocus.

On the kit lens featured in this book, simply setting the switch on the lens to M automatically sets the Focus mode to MF. However, the opposite isn't true: Choosing the MF setting for the Focus mode does not free the focusing ring so that you can set focus manually; you must set the lens switch to the M position. For other lenses, check the lens instruction manual for manual-focusing details.

In exposure modes other than P, S, A, and M, you can choose from AF-A and MF only. If you're not ready to step up to those modes and you can't get the camera to autofocus on your subject in AF-A Focus mode, don't waste time trying over and over again — you're not likely to get different results. Instead, just focus manually. You can get help with that approach a few sections later in this chapter.

Choosing the right autofocus combo

You get the best autofocus results if you pair your chosen Focus mode with the most appropriate AF-Area mode because the two settings work in tandem. Here are the combinations that I suggest for the maximum autofocus control:

✔ **For still subjects, use Single Point as the AF-Area mode and AF-S as the Focus mode.** You then select a specific focus point, and the camera locks focus on that point when you press the shutter button halfway. Focus remains locked on your subject even if you reframe the shot after you press the button halfway. (It helps to remember the *s* factor: for *s*till subjects, *S*ingle Point, and AF-*S*.)

✔ **For moving subjects, set the AF-Area mode to Dynamic Area and the Focus mode to AF-C.** You still begin by selecting a focus point, but if your subject moves after you press the shutter button halfway to establish focus, the camera looks to the other focus points for focusing information. (Think *motion, dynamic, continuous.*) Remember to reframe as needed to keep your subject within the boundaries of the 11 autofocus points, though.

Again, though, you get full control over the Focus mode only in the P, S, A, and M exposure modes. In the other modes, you have only two choices — either MF (manual focus) or AF-A.

Using autofocus lock

When you set your camera's Focus mode to AF-C (continuous-servo autofocus), pressing and holding the shutter button halfway initiates autofocus. But focusing is continually adjusted while you hold the shutter button halfway, so the focusing distance may change if the subject moves out of the active autofocus point or you reframe the shot before you take the picture. The same is true if you use AF-A mode (auto-servo autofocus) and the camera senses movement in front of the lens, in which case it shifts to AF-C mode and operates as I just described. Either way, the upshot is that you can't control the exact focusing distance the camera ultimately uses.

Should you want to lock focus at a specific distance, you have a couple options:

✔ **Focus manually.**

✔ **Change the Focus mode to AF-S (single-servo autofocus).** In this mode, focus is locked when you press and hold the shutter button halfway.

✔ **Lock focus with the AE-L/AF-L button.** First set focus by pressing the shutter button halfway. When the focus is established at the distance you want, press and hold the AE-L/AF-L button, located near the viewfinder. Focus remains set as long as you hold down the button, even if you release the shutter button.

Keep in mind, though, that by default, pressing the AE-L/AF-L button also locks in autoexposure. (Chapter 7 explains.) You can change this behavior, however, setting the button to lock just one or the other. Chapter 11 explains this option as well as a couple other ways to customize the button's function.

For my money, manual focusing is by far the easiest solution; the next section offers more advice on that topic.

Focusing Manually

Some subjects confuse even the most sophisticated autofocusing systems, causing the camera's autofocus motor to spend a long time "hunting" for its focus point. Animals behind fences, reflective objects, water, and low-contrast subjects are just some of the autofocus troublemakers. Autofocus systems also struggle in dim lighting, although that difficulty is often offset on the D5100 by the AF-assist lamp, which shoots out a beam of light to help the camera find its focusing target.

When you encounter situations that cause an autofocus hang-up, you can try adjusting the autofocus options discussed earlier in this chapter. But often, it's simply easier and faster to switch to manual focusing. For best results, follow these manual-focusing steps:

1. **Adjust the viewfinder to your eyesight.**

   Chapter 1 shows you how to take this critical step. If you don't adjust the viewfinder, scenes that are in focus may appear blurry and vice versa.

2. **Set the focus switch on the lens to M.**

   This step assumes that you're using a lens like the D5100 kit lens (refer to Figure 8-1).

   With the kit lens, as well as some other compatible lenses, the camera automatically changes the Focus mode to MF as soon as you set the lens switch to M. For other lenses, check the lens instruction manual for details about what you need to do to focus manually.

3. **Select a focus point.**

   Use the same technique as when selecting a point during autofocusing: Looking through the viewfinder, press the Multi Selector right, left, up, or down until the point you want to use flashes red.

During autofocusing, the selected focus point tells the camera what part of the frame to use when establishing focus. And technically speaking, you don't *have* to choose a focus point for manual focusing — the camera will set the focus according to the position that you set by turning the focusing ring. However, choosing a focus point is still a good idea, for two reasons: First, even though you're focusing manually, the camera provides some feedback to you know if focus is correct, and that feedback is based on your selected focus point. Second, if you use spot metering, an exposure option covered in Chapter 7, exposure is based on the selected focus point.

4. **Frame the shot so that your subject is under your selected focus point.**

5. **Press and hold the shutter button halfway to initiate exposure metering.**

    Adjust exposure as needed; see Chapter 7 for help.

6. **Rotate the focusing ring on the lens to bring the subject into focus.**

    When the camera thinks focus is set on the object under your focus point, the green focus lamp in the lower-left corner of the viewfinder lights, just as it does during autofocusing.

7. **Press the shutter button the rest of the way to take the shot.**

Correcting lens distortion

If you take a lot of pictures with wide-angle lenses, you may notice that vertical structures in the scene sometimes appear to bend outward from the center of the image. This is known as *barrel distortion.* On the flip side of the coin, shooting with a long telephoto lens sometimes causes those verticals to bow inward, which is known as *pincushion distortion.*

The Retouch menu on your camera has a post-capture Distortion Control filter you can apply to try to correct both problems. (See Chapter 10 for help.) But the D5100 also has an Auto Distortion Control feature that attempts to correct the image as you're shooting. It only works with certain types of lenses (specifically, those that Nikon classifies as type G and D), but is worth trying if your lens is compatible. To activate the option, just set the Auto Distortion Control on the Shooting Menu to On, as shown in the figure here.

When you use this feature, understand that some of the area you see in your viewfinder may not be visible in the final photo because the anti-distortion manipulation requires some cropping of the scene. So after activating the feature, take some test shots and examine the pictures carefully. If you're not happy with the results, return to the menu and change the setting back to Off.

SHOOTING MENU	
Reset shooting menu	--
Storage folder	D5100
Image quality	FINE
Image size	▫
White balance	AUTO
Set Picture Control	▣SD
Manage Picture Control	--
Auto distortion control	ON

I know that when you first start working with an SLR-style camera, focusing manually is intimidating. But if you practice a little, you'll find that it's really no big deal and saves you the time and aggravation of trying to bend the autofocus system to your will when it has "issues."

In addition to the green focus lamp, the D5100 offers another manual focusing aid to help you feel more confident, too: You can swap out the viewfinder's exposure meter with a *rangefinder,* which uses a similar, meter-like display, as shown in Figure 8-8, to indicate whether focus is set on the object in the selected focus point. If bars appear to the left of the 0, as shown in the left example in Figure 8-8, focus is set in front of the subject; if the bars are to the right, as in the middle example, focus is slightly behind the subject. The more bars you see, the greater the focusing error. As you twist the focusing ring, the rangefinder updates to help you get focus on track. When you see a single bar on either side of the 0, you're good to go.

Focus front of subject	Focus behind subject	Unable to focus

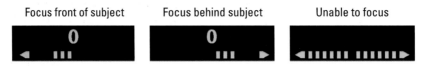

Figure 8-8: The rangefinder offers manual-focusing assistance.

Before I tell you how to activate this feature, I want to point out a couple issues:

- You can use the rangefinder in any exposure mode except M (manual exposure). In M mode, the viewfinder always displays the exposure meter.

- In the other exposure modes, you can continue to view the exposure meter in the Shooting Info display, even with the rangefinder enabled. See Chapter 7 for how to interpret the meter in exposure modes other than M.

- Your lens must offer a maximum aperture (f-stop number) of f/5.6 or lower. To understand f-stops, head to Chapter 7. The kit lens sold with the D5100 meets this qualification.

- With subjects that confuse the camera's autofocus system, the rangefinder may not work well either; it's based on the same system. If the system can't find the focusing target, you see the rangefinder display shown on the right in Figure 8-8.

- The rangefinder is automatically replaced by the normal exposure meter if you switch back to autofocusing, but reappears when you return to manual focus.

Personally, I leave the rangefinder off and just rely on the focus indicator lamp and my eyes to verify focus. I shoot in the S and A exposure modes frequently, and I find it a pain to monitor exposure in the Shooting Info display rather than in the viewfinder. That's not a recommendation to you either way — it's just how I prefer to work. If you want to try the rangefinder, set the Mode dial to any setting but M and then head for Autofocus submenu of the Custom Setting menu. Change the Rangefinder option from Off to On, as shown in Figure 8-9, to enable the feature.

a Autofocus	
a1 AF-C priority selection	
a2 Built-in AF-assist illuminator	OFF
a3 Rangefinder	ON
b1 EV steps for exposure cntrl.	1/3
c1 Shutter-release button AE-L	OFF
c2 Auto off timers	
c3 Self-timer	--
c4 Remote on duration	1m

Figure 8-9: Enable the rangefinder via the Custom Setting menu.

Manipulating Depth of Field

Getting familiar with the concept of *depth of field* is one of the biggest steps you can take to becoming a more artful photographer. I introduce you to depth of field in Chapters 3 and 7; here's a summary in case you missed those pages:

- ✓ *Depth of field* refers to the distance over which objects in a photograph appear sharply focused.

- ✓ With a shallow, or small, depth of field, distant objects appear more softly focused than the main subject.

- ✓ With a large depth of field, the zone of sharp focus extends to include objects at a distance from your subject.

Which arrangement works best depends entirely on your creative vision and your subject. In portraits, for example, a classic technique is to use a shallow depth of field, as shown in the photo in Figure 8-10. This approach increases emphasis on the subject while diminishing the impact of the background. But for the photo in Figure 8-11, I wanted to emphasize that the foreground

Aperture, f/5.6; Focal length, 90mm

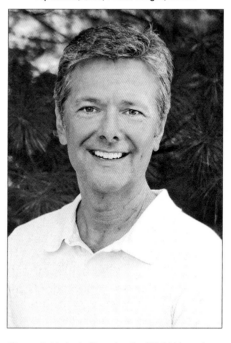

Figure 8-10: A shallow depth of field blurs the background and draws added attention to the subject.

figures were in St. Peter's Square, at the Vatican, so I used a large depth of field, which kept the background buildings sharply focused and gave them equal weight in the scene.

So exactly how do you adjust depth of field? You have three points of control: aperture, focal length, and camera-to-subject distance, as follows:

Aperture, f/14; Focal length, 42mm

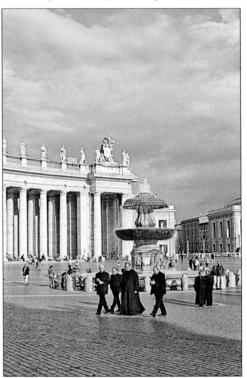

Figure 8-11: A large depth of field keeps both foreground and background subjects in focus.

- ✓ **Aperture setting (f-stop):** The aperture is one of three main exposure settings, all explained fully in Chapter 7. Depth of field increases as you stop down the aperture (by choosing a higher f-stop number). For shallow depth of field, open the aperture (by choosing a lower f-stop number). Figure 8-12 offers an example; in the f/22 version, focus is sharp all the way through the frame; in the f/13 version, focus softens as the distance from the center lure increases. I snapped both images using the same focal length and camera-to-subject distance, setting focus on the red front of center lure.

- ✓ **Lens focal length:** In lay terms, *focal length* determines what the lens "sees." As you increase focal length, measured in millimeters, the angle of view narrows, objects appear larger in the frame, and — the important point for this discussion — depth of field decreases. Additionally, the spatial relationship of objects changes as you adjust focal length. As an example, Figure 8-13 compares the same scene shot at a focal length of 127mm and 183mm. I used the same aperture, f/5.6, for both examples.

Aperture, f/22; Focal length, 92mm

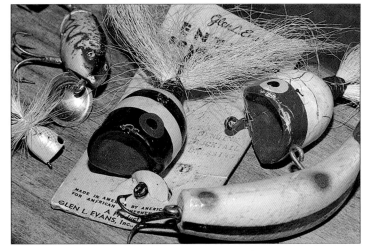

Aperture, f/13; Focal length, 92mm

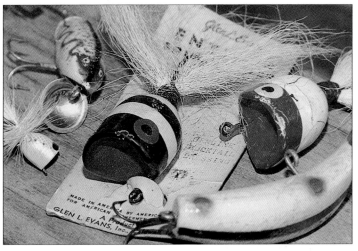

Figure 8-12: A lower f-stop number (wider aperture) decreases depth of field.

Aperture, f/5.6; Focal length, 127mm

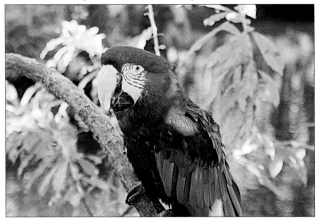

Aperture, f/5.6; Focal length, 183mm

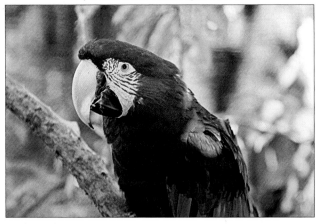

Figure 8-13: Zooming to a longer focal length also reduces depth of field.

Whether you have any focal length flexibility depends on your lens: If you have a zoom lens, you can adjust the focal length — just zoom in or out. (The D5100 kit lens, for example, offers a focal-length range of 18–55mm.) If you don't have a zoom lens, the focal length is fixed, so scratch this means of manipulating depth of field.

For more technical details about focal length and your D5100, see the sidebar "Fun facts about focal length," later in this chapter.

✔ **Camera-to-subject distance:** As you move the lens closer to your subject, depth of field decreases. This assumes that you don't zoom in or out to reframe the picture, thereby changing the focal length. If you do, depth of field is affected by both the camera position and focal length.

Together, these three factors determine the maximum and minimum depth of field that you can achieve, as illustrated by my clever artwork in Figure 8-14 and summed up in the following list:

✔ **To produce the shallowest depth of field:** Open the aperture as wide as possible (the lowest f-stop number), zoom in to the maximum focal length of your lens, and get as close as possible to your subject.

When you combine a very large aperture — f/2.0, for example — you can wind up with an extremely shallow depth of field if you also use a long focal length, are very close to your subject, or both. In fact, in a portrait in which one subject is only a foot or so in front of the other, the depth of field may not be sufficient to keep both people sharply focused. So always shoot a test image and then use the playback zoom feature to check focus on all subjects in the frame. See Chapter 5 to find out how.

✔ **To produce maximum depth of field:** Stop down the aperture to the highest possible f-stop number, zoom out to the shortest focal length your lens offers, and move farther from your subject.

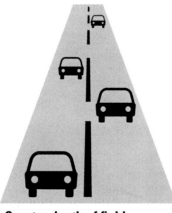 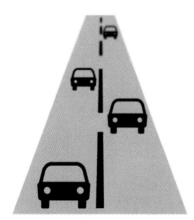

Greater depth of field:
Select higher f-stop
Decrease focal length (zoom out)
Move farther from subject

Shorter depth of field:
Select lower f-stop
Increase focal length (zoom in)
Move closer to subject

Figure 8-14: Your f-stop, focal length, and shooting distance determine depth of field.

Just to avoid a possible point of confusion that has arisen in some of the classes I teach: When I say *zoom in,* some students think that I mean to twist the zoom barrel so that it moves *in* toward the camera body. But in fact, the phrase *zoom in* means to zoom to a longer focal length, which produces the visual effect of bringing your subject closer. This requires twisting the zoom barrel of the lens so that it extends farther *out* from the camera. And the phrase *zoom out* refers to the opposite maneuver: I'm talking about widening your view of the subject by zooming to a shorter focal length, which requires moving the lens barrel *in* toward the camera body.

Here are a few additional tips and tricks related to depth of field:

- ✔ **Aperture-priority autoexposure (A) mode enables you to easily control depth of field.** In this mode, detailed fully in Chapter 7, you set the f-stop, and the camera selects the appropriate shutter speed to produce a good exposure. The range of aperture settings you can access depends on your lens.

  Even in aperture-priority mode, keep an eye on shutter speed as well. To maintain the same exposure, shutter speed must change in tandem with aperture, and you may encounter a situation where the shutter speed is too slow to permit hand-holding of the camera. Lenses that offer optical image stabilization, or Vibration Reduction (VR lenses, in the Nikon world), enable most people to use a slower shutter speed than normal, but double-check your results just to be sure. Or use a tripod for extra security. Of course, all this assumes that you have dialed in a specific ISO Sensitivity setting; if you instead are using Auto ISO adjustment, the camera may adjust the ISO setting instead of shutter speed. (Chapter 7 explores the whole aperture/shutter speed/ISO relationship.)

- ✔ **Some Scene modes are designed to produce a particular depth of field.** Portrait and Close Up modes are designed to produce shallow depth of field, for example, and Landscape mode is designed for large depth of field. (Chapter 3 offers a list of all the available Scene modes.) You can't adjust aperture in these modes, however, so you're limited to the setting the camera chooses. In addition, the extent to which the camera can select an appropriate f-stop depends on the lighting conditions. If you're shooting in Landscape mode at dusk, for example, the camera may have to open the aperture to a wide setting to produce a good exposure.

- ✔ **For greater background blurring, move the subject farther from the background.** The extent to which background focus shifts as you adjust depth of field also is affected by the distance between the subject and the background. For increased background blurring, move the subject farther in front of the background.

Fun facts about focal length

Every lens can be characterized by its *focal length,* or in the case of a zoom lens, the range of focal lengths it offers. Measured in millimeters, focal length determines the camera's angle of view, the apparent size and distance of objects in the scene, and depth of field. According to photography tradition, a focal length of 50mm is described as a "normal" lens. Most point-and-shoot cameras feature this focal length, which is a medium-range lens that works well for the type of snapshots that users of those kinds of cameras are likely to shoot.

A lens with a focal length under 35mm is characterized as a *wide-angle* lens because at that focal length, the camera has a wide angle of view and produces a large depth of field, making it good for landscape photography. A short focal length also has the effect of making objects seem smaller and farther away. At the other end of the spectrum, a lens with a focal length longer than 80mm is considered a *telephoto* lens and often referred to as a *long lens.* With a long lens, angle of view narrows, depth of field decreases, and faraway subjects appear closer and larger, which is ideal for wildlife and sports photographers.

Note, however, that the focal lengths stated here and elsewhere in the book are so-called *35mm equivalent* focal lengths. Here's the deal: For reasons that aren't really important, when you put a standard lens on most digital cameras, including your D5100, the available frame area is reduced, as if you took a picture on a camera that uses 35mm film negatives (the kind you've probably been using for years) and then cropped it.

This so-called *crop factor* varies depending on the digital camera, which is why the photo industry adopted the 35mm-equivalent measuring stick as a standard. With the D5100, the cropping factor is roughly 1.5. So the 18–55mm kit lens, for example, actually captures the approximate area you would get from a 27–83mm lens on a 35mm film camera. In the figure here, for example, the red outline indicates the image area that results from the 1.5 crop factor.

Note that although the area the lens can capture changes when you move a lens from a 35mm film camera to a digital body, depth of field isn't affected, nor are the spatial relationships between objects in the frame. So when lens shopping, you gauge those two characteristics of the lens by looking at the stated focal length — no digital-to-film conversion math is required.

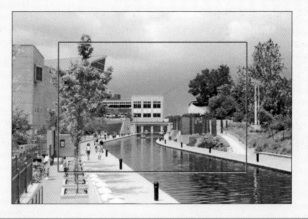

Controlling Color

Compared with understanding some aspects of digital photography —
resolution, aperture and shutter speed, depth of field, and so on — making
sense of your camera's color options is easy-breezy. First, color problems
aren't all that common, and when they are, they're usually simple to fix with
a quick shift of your D5100's White Balance control. And getting a grip on
color requires learning only a couple new terms, an unusual state of affairs
for an endeavor that often seems more like high-tech science than art.

The rest of this chapter explains the aforementioned White Balance control,
plus a couple menu options that enable you to fine-tune the way your camera
renders colors. For information on how to use the Retouch menu's color
options to alter colors of existing pictures, see Chapter 10.

Correcting colors with white balance

Every light source emits a particular color cast. The old-fashioned fluorescent lights found in most public restrooms, for example, put out a
bluish-greenish light, which is why we all look so sickly when we view our
reflections in the mirrors in those restrooms. And if you think that your
beloved looks especially attractive by candle-
light, you aren't imagining things: Candlelight
casts a warm, yellow-red glow that is flattering
to the skin.

Science-y types measure the color of light,
officially known as *color temperature,* on the
Kelvin scale, which is named after its creator.
You can see the Kelvin scale in Figure 8-15.

When photographers talk about "warm light"
and "cool light," though, they aren't refer-
ring to the position on the Kelvin scale — or
at least not in the way most people think of
temperatures, with a higher number meaning
hotter. Instead, the terms describe the visual
appearance of the light. Warm light, produced
by candles and incandescent lights, falls in the
red-yellow spectrum you see at the bottom of
the Kelvin scale in Figure 8-15; cool light, in the
blue spectrum, appears in the upper part of the
Kelvin scale.

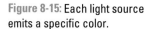

Kelvin	Light source
8000	Snow, water, shade
	Overcast skies
	Flash
5000	Bright sunshine
	Fluorescent bulbs
3000	Tungsten lights / Incandescent bulbs
2000	Candlelight

Figure 8-15: Each light source
emits a specific color.

At any rate, most people don't notice these fluctuating colors of light because human eyes automatically compensate for them. Except in very extreme lighting conditions, we perceive a white tablecloth as white no matter whether it's lit by candlelight, fluorescent light, or regular houselights.

Similarly, a digital camera compensates for different colors of light through white balancing. Simply put, *white balancing* neutralizes light so that whites are always white, which in turn ensures that other colors are rendered accurately. If the camera senses warm light, it shifts colors slightly to the cool side of the color spectrum; in cool light, the camera shifts colors the opposite direction.

The good news is that, as with your eyes, your camera's Auto White Balance setting tackles this process remarkably well in most situations, which means that you can usually ignore it and concentrate on other aspects of your picture. But if your scene is lit by two or more light sources that cast different colors, the white balance sensor can get confused, producing an unwanted color cast like the one you see in the left image in Figure 8-16.

I shot this product image in my home studio using tungsten photo lights, which produce light with a color temperature similar to regular household incandescent bulbs. The problem is that the windows in that room also permit some pretty strong daylight to filter through. In Auto White Balance mode, the camera reacted to that daylight — which has a cool color cast — and applied too much warming, giving my original image a yellow tint. No problem: I just switched the White Balance mode from Auto to the Incandescent setting. The right image in Figure 8-16 shows the corrected colors.

 There's one little problem with white balancing as it's implemented on your D5100, though. You can't make this kind of manual white balance selection if you shoot in the fully automatic exposure modes. So if you spy color problems in your camera monitor, switch to P, S, A, or M exposure mode. (Chapter 7 details all four modes.)

Note, too, that unlike the autofocusing features discussed in the first part of this chapter, the White Balance setting is available during Live View photography as well as viewfinder photography. Your setting also affects colors in any movies you record. See Chapter 4 for complete details about Live View and movie shooting.

The next section explains precisely how to make a simple white balance correction; following that, you can explore some advanced white balance options.

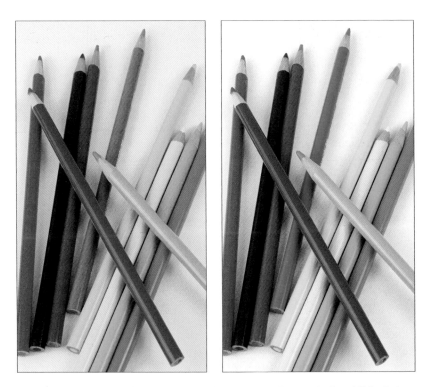

Figure 8-16: Multiple light sources resulted in a yellow color cast in Auto White Balance mode (left); switching to the Incandescent setting solved the problem (right).

Changing the White Balance setting

The current White Balance setting appears in the Shooting Info screen, as shown in Figure 8-17. Settings other than Auto are represented by the icons you see in Table 8-1. During Live View and movie shooting, an icon representing the setting appears in the top-right corner of the monitor; again, details about Live View and movie shooting await in Chapter 4.

White Balance setting

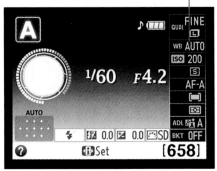

Figure 8-17: This icon represents the current White Balance setting.

Table 8-1	Manual White Balance Settings
Symbol	**Light Source**
	Incandescent
	Fluorescent
	Direct sunlight
	Flash
	Cloudy
	Shade
PRE	Preset

You can adjust the White Balance setting in a few ways:

✏ **Quick Settings screen:** Remember, you can get to this screen by pressing the Info Edit button (shown in the margin here). Press once if the Shooting Info screen is already visible; otherwise, press twice. After highlighting the White Balance option, as shown on the left in Figure 8-18, press OK to display the menu shown on the right. Highlight the desired setting, and press OK.

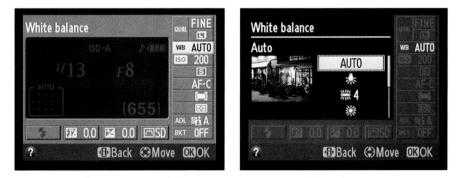

Figure 8-18: You can modify white balance through the Quick Settings display.

✔ **Shooting menu:** You also can adjust the White Balance setting through the Shooting menu, as shown in Figure 8-19. Going this route gives you access to some additional White Balance settings; details momentarily.

✔ **Fn (Function) button plus Command dial:** Through a menu option covered in Chapter 11, you can set the Fn button on the side of the camera to bring up the White Balance setting directly. You then rotate the Command dial while pressing the button to cycle through the available White Balance settings. If you set the Fn button to this role, however, it no longer serves its default purpose, which is to set the camera to the Self-Timer Release mode for your next shot.

SHOOTING MENU			White balance	
Reset shooting menu	--		AUTO Auto	OK
Storage folder	D5100		☀ Incandescent	
Image quality	FINE		☀ Fluorescent	
Image size	▢		☀ Direct sunlight	
White balance	AUTO		⚡ Flash	
Set Picture Control	⬚SD		☁ Cloudy	
Manage Picture Control	--		⬚ Shade	
Auto distortion control	ON		⊙Adjust	

Figure 8-19: To uncover additional White Balance options, hit the Shooting menu.

Okay, now for the aforementioned details about using the Shooting menu to adjust the White Balance setting. Via the menus, you can accomplish the following additional white balance goals:

✔ **Fine-tune the settings:** If you choose any setting but Fluorescent, pressing the Multi Selector right takes you to a screen where you can fine-tune the setting, a process I explain in the next section.

✔ **Select a specific type of fluorescent bulb:** When you choose Fluorescent from the menu, as shown on the left in Figure 8-20, pressing the Multi Selector right displays the second screen in the figure, where you can select a specific type of bulb. Select the option that most closely matches your bulbs and then press OK. Or, to go to the fine-tuning screen, press the Multi Selector right.

After you select a fluorescent bulb type, that option is always used when you change white balance through the Shooting Info display (as outlined previously) and choose the Fluorescent White Balance setting. Again, you can change the bulb type only through the Shooting menu.

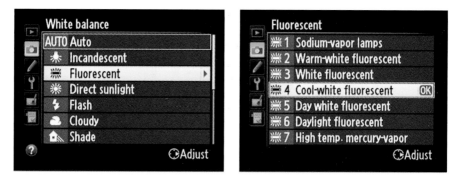

Figure 8-20: If you adjust white balance through the Shooting menu, you can select a specific type of fluorescent bulb.

> ✔ **Create a custom white balance preset:** Selecting the PRE option enables you to create and store a precise, customized White Balance setting, as explained in the upcoming "Creating white balance presets" section, in this chapter. This setting is the fastest way to achieve accurate colors when your scene is lit by multiple light sources that have differing color temperatures.

Your selected White Balance setting remains in force for the P, S, A, and M exposure modes until you change it. So you may want to get in the habit of resetting the option to the Auto setting after you finish shooting whatever subject it was that caused you to switch to manual white balance mode.

Fine-tuning White Balance settings

You can fine-tune any White Balance setting except a custom preset that you create through the PRE option. Make the adjustment as spelled out in these steps:

1. **Display the Shooting menu, highlight White Balance, and press OK.**

2. **Highlight the White Balance setting you want to adjust, as shown on the left in Figure 8-21, and press the Multi Selector right.**

   You're taken to a screen where you can do your fine-tuning, as shown on the right in Figure 8-21.

   If you select Fluorescent, you first go to a screen where you select a specific type of bulb, as covered in the preceding section. After you highlight your choice, press the Multi Selector right again to get to the fine-tuning screen.

3. **Fine-tune the setting by using the Multi Selector to move the white balance shift marker in the color grid.**

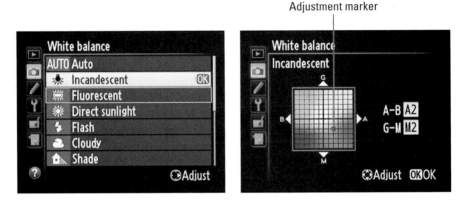

Figure 8-21: Press the Multi Selector right to get to the fine-tuning screen.

The grid is set up around two color pairs: Green and Magenta, represented by G and M; and Blue and Amber, represented by B and A. By pressing the Multi Selector, you can move the adjustment marker — that little black box labeled in Figure 8-21 — around the grid.

As you move the marker, the A–B and G–M boxes on the right side of the screen show you the current amount of color shift. A value of 0 indicates the default amount of color compensation applied by the selected White Balance setting. In Figure 8-21, for example, I moved the marker two levels toward amber and two levels toward magenta to specify that I wanted colors to be a tad warmer.

4. **Press OK to complete the adjustment.**

After you adjust a White Balance setting, an asterisk appears next to the icon representing the setting on the Shooting menu, as shown in Figure 8-22. You see an asterisk next to the White Balance setting in the Shooting Info display as well.

SHOOTING MENU	
Reset shooting menu	--
Storage folder	D5100
Image quality	FINE
Image size	▢
White balance	☀*
Set Picture Control	SD
Manage Picture Control	--
Auto distortion control	ON

Figure 8-22: The asterisk indicates that you applied a fine-tuning adjustment to the White Balance setting.

Creating white balance presets

If none of the standard White Balance settings do the trick and you don't want to fool with fine-tuning them, take advantage of the PRE (Preset Manual) feature. This option enables you to do two things:

- ✔ Base white balance on a direct measurement of the actual lighting conditions.
- ✔ Match white balance to an existing photo.

The next two sections provide you with the step-by-step instructions.

Setting white balance with direct measurement

To use this technique, you need a piece of card stock that's either neutral gray or absolute white — not eggshell white, sand white, or any other close-but-not-perfect white. (You can buy reference cards made just for this purpose in many camera stores for less than $20.)

Position the reference card so that it receives the same lighting you'll use for your photo. Then take these steps:

1. **Set the camera to the P, S, A, or M exposure mode.**

   If the exposure meter reports that your image will be under- or overexposed at the current exposure settings, make the necessary adjustments now. (Chapter 7 tells you how.) Otherwise, the camera can't create your custom white balance preset.

2. **Frame your shot so that the reference card completely fills the viewfinder.**

3. **From the Shooting menu, select White Balance, press OK, and select the PRE Preset Manual White Balance setting, as shown on the left in Figure 8-23.**

4. **Press the Multi Selector right, select Measure, as shown on the right in the figure, and press OK.**

   A warning appears, asking you whether you want to overwrite existing data.

5. **Select Yes and press OK.**

   You see another message, this time telling you to take your picture. You have about six seconds to do so. (The letters PRE flash in the viewfinder and Shooting Info display to let you know the camera's ready to record your white balance reference image.)

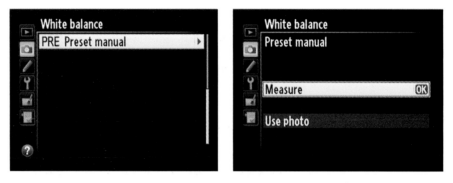

Figure 8-23: Select these options to set white balance by measuring a white or gray card.

6. Take the reference shot.

> If the camera is successful at recording the white balance data, the letters *Gd* flash in the viewfinder and the message "Data Acquired" appears in the Shooting Information display. If the camera couldn't set the custom white balance, you instead see the message *No Gd* in the viewfinder, and a message in the Shooting Information display urges you to try again. Try adjusting your lighting before doing so.

After you complete the process, the camera automatically sets the White Balance option to PRE so you can begin using your preset. You see the letters PRE in the White Balance area of the Shooting Info display, as shown in Figure 8-24.

Any time you want to select and use the preset, switch to the PRE White Balance setting, either via the Shooting menu or Quick Settings screen. Your custom setting is stored in the camera until you override it with a new preset.

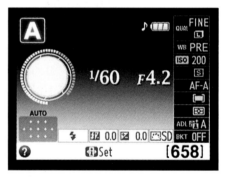

Figure 8-24: Select the PRE Preset Manual option to use your custom White Balance setting.

By the way, if you do set the Fn button to invoke the White Balance setting, a trick I explain in Chapter 11, you gain a related timesaving feature: If you press and hold the button for a few seconds while the PRE setting is in force, the camera automatically sets itself up to record a new preset reference shot. After the letters PRE start flashing in the viewfinder or Shooting Info screen, just snap your reference picture.

Matching white balance to an existing photo

Suppose that you're the marketing manager for a small business, and one of your jobs is to shoot portraits of the company big-wigs for the annual report. You build a small studio just for that purpose, complete with a couple photography lights and a nice, conservative beige backdrop.

Of course, the big-wigs can't all come to get their pictures taken in the same month, let alone on the same day. But you have to make sure that the colors in that beige backdrop remain consistent for each shot, no matter how much time passes between photo sessions. This scenario is one possible use for an advanced White Balance feature that enables you to base white balance on an existing photo.

Basing white balance on an existing photo works well only in strictly controlled lighting situations, where the color temperature of your lights is consistent from day to day. Otherwise, the White Balance setting that produces color accuracy when you shoot Big Boss Number One may add an ugly color cast to the one you snap of Big Boss Number Two.

To give this option a try, follow these steps:

1. **Copy the picture that you want to use as the reference photo to your camera memory card, if it isn't already stored there.**

   You can copy the picture to the card using a card reader and whatever method you usually use to transfer files from one drive to another. Assuming that you're using the default folder names, copy the file to the 100D5100 folder, inside the main DCIM folder.

2. **Open the Shooting menu, highlight White Balance, and press OK.**

3. **Select PRE Preset Manual and press the Multi Selector right.**

   The screen shown on the left in Figure 8-25 appears.

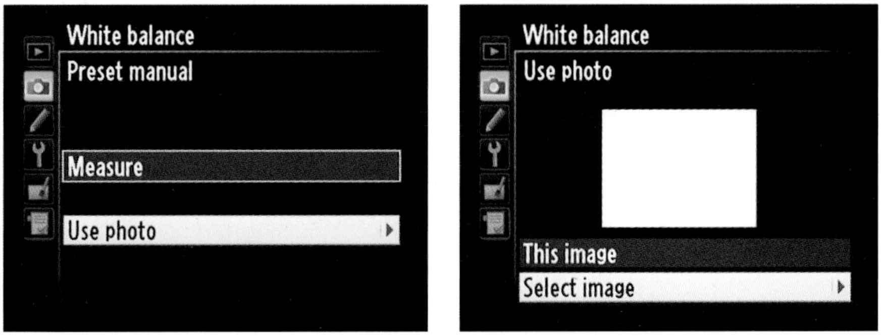

Figure 8-25: You can create a white balance preset based on an existing photo.

4. **Highlight Use Photo and press OK.**

The options shown on the right in Figure 8-25 appear. If you haven't yet used the photo option to store a preset, you see an empty white box in the middle of the screen, as shown in the figure. If you previously selected a photo to use as a preset reference, the thumbnail for that image appears instead.

5. **Select the photo you want to use as your reference image.**

If the photo you want to use is already displayed on the screen, highlight This Image and press OK. Otherwise, highlight Select Image and then press the Multi Selector right to access screens that let you navigate to the photo you want to use as a basis for white balance. Press OK to return to the screen shown on the right in Figure 8-25. Your selected photo appears on the screen.

6. **Highlight This Image and press OK to set the preset white balance based on the selected photo.**

Whenever you want to base white balance on your selected photo, just set the White Balance setting to the PRE option.

Bracketing white balance

Chapter 7 introduces you to your camera's automatic bracketing feature, which enables you to easily record the same image at several different exposure settings. In addition to being able to bracket autoexposure and Active D-Lighting settings, you can use the feature to bracket white balance.

Note a couple of things about this feature:

- ✓ **You must set the Mode dial to P, S, A, or M.** You can't take advantage of auto bracketing in the other exposure modes.

- ✓ **You can bracket only JPEG shots.** You can't use white balance bracketing if you set the camera's Image Quality setting to either Raw (NEF) or any of the RAW+JPEG options. And frankly, there isn't any need to do so because you can precisely tune colors of Raw files when you process them in your Raw converter. Chapter 6 has details on Raw processing.

- ✓ **You take just one picture to record each bracketed series.** Each time you press the shutter button, the camera records a single image and then makes the bracketed copies, each at a different White Balance setting. One frame is always captured with no white balance adjustment.

- ✓ **You can apply white balance bracketing only along the blue-to-amber axis of the fine-tuning color grid.** You can't shift colors along the green-to-magenta axis, as you can when tweaking a specific White Balance setting. (For a reminder of this feature, see the earlier section "Fine-tuning White Balance settings.")

✔ **For each bracketed series, you get one "neutral" shot, one shifted toward amber, and one shifted toward blue.** By *neutral,* I mean that the image is recorded at the current White Balance setting, without any bracketing adjustment.

✔ **You can shift colors a maximum of three steps between frames.** As an example of the range of color shift you can create, I used white balance bracketing to record the three candle photos in Figure 8-26. For the blue and amber versions, I set the bracketing to shift colors the maximum three steps. As you can see, even at that max setting, the color differences between the shots are subtle. In this photo, I find the shift most noticeable in the color of the backdrop.

Neutral   Amber +3   Blue +3

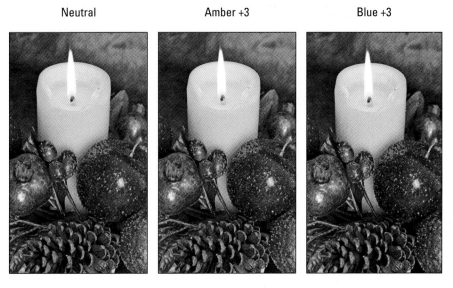

Figure 8-26: I used white balance bracketing to record three variations on the subject.

To try white balance bracketing, take these steps:

1. **Set your camera to the P, S, A, or M exposure mode.**

2. **Set the Image Quality setting to one of the JPEG options (Fine, Normal, or Basic).**

   You can adjust the setting through the Shooting menu or Quick Settings screen. (See Chapter 2 for a full explanation of the JPEG options.)

3. **Display the Custom Setting menu, select the Bracketing/Flash sub-menu, and press OK.**

4. **Select Auto Bracketing Set, as shown on the left in Figure 8-27, and press OK.**

   You see the screen shown on the right in the figure.

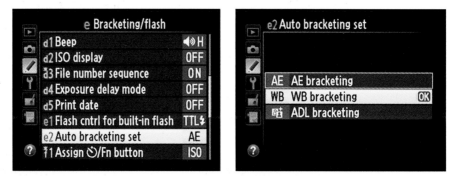

Figure 8-27: Your first step is to set the Auto Bracketing Set option to WB Bracketing.

5. **Select WB Bracketing and press OK.**

6. **Use the Quick Settings screen to set the amount of color shift you want for your bracketed images.**

    After displaying the Shooting Information screen, press the Info Edit button to get to Quick Settings mode. Then use the Multi Selector to highlight the BKT option, as shown on the left in Figure 8-28.

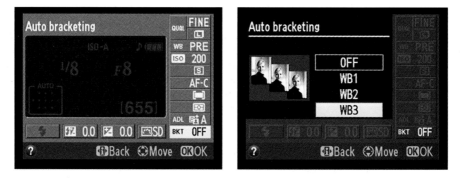

Figure 8-28: Select the amount of color shift through the Quick Settings screen.

7. **Press OK to display the WB Bracketing menu shown on the right in Figure 8-28.**

8. **Highlight the desired increment.**

   Again, WB1 is the smallest increment between color temperatures, and WB3 has the greatest increment between color temperatures.

   The Shooting Information display shows bracketing indicators, as shown in Figure 8-29, reminding you that white balance bracketing is in force.

9. **Take the picture.**

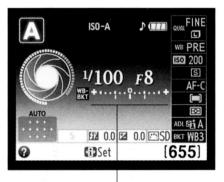

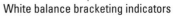

White balance bracketing indicators

Figure 8-29: These markings remind you that white balance bracketing is enabled.

Again, each shutter button press actually produces three images; The first and third shots are the adjusted shots. In the camera metadata, you see A (1, 2, or 3) for the first shot and B (1, 2, or 3) for the last shot. The code tells you whether the image has an amber (A) or blue (B) bias and the level of adjustment you selected when setting your bracketing amount.

Your bracketing option remains in effect even after you shut off the camera. When you're finished taking the pictures that need bracketing, remember to disable bracketing. Just revisit the Quick Settings screen and then set the BKT option to Off, as shown on the left in Figure 8-28.

Choosing a Color Space: sRGB versus Adobe RGB

By default, your camera captures images using the *sRGB color mode,* which simply refers to an industry-standard spectrum of colors. (The *s* is for *standard,* and the *RGB* is for *red, green, blue,* which are the primary colors in the digital color world.) The sRGB color mode was created to help ensure color consistency as an image moves from camera (or scanner) to monitor and printer; the idea was to create a spectrum of colors that all these devices can reproduce.

However, the sRGB color spectrum leaves out some colors that *can* be reproduced in print and onscreen, at least by some devices. So as an alternative, your camera also enables you to shoot in the Adobe RGB color mode, which includes a larger spectrum (or *gamut*) of colors. Figure 8-30 offers an illustration of the two spectrums.

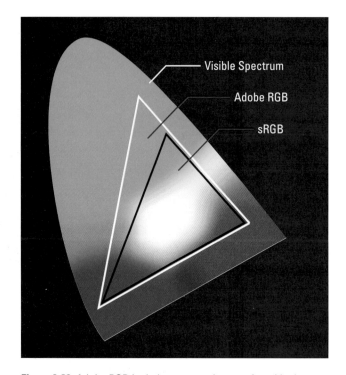

Figure 8-30: Adobe RGB includes some colors not found in the sRGB spectrum but requires some color-management savvy to use to its full advantage.

Some colors in the Adobe RGB spectrum can't be reproduced in print. (The printer just substitutes the closest printable color, if necessary.) Still, I usually shoot in Adobe RGB mode because I see no reason to limit myself to a smaller spectrum from the get-go.

However, just because I use Adobe RGB doesn't mean that it's right for you. First, if you plan to print and share your photos without making any adjustments in your photo editor, you're usually better off sticking with sRGB because most printers and web browsers are designed around that color space. Second, know that to retain all your original Adobe RGB colors when you work with your photos, your editing software must support that color space — not all programs do. You also must be willing to study the whole topic of digital color a little bit because you need to use some specific settings to avoid really mucking up the color works.

If you want to go with Adobe RGB instead of sRGB, visit the Shooting menu and highlight the Color Space option, as shown on the left in Figure 8-31. Press OK to display the screen shown on the right in the figure. Select Adobe RGB and press OK again.

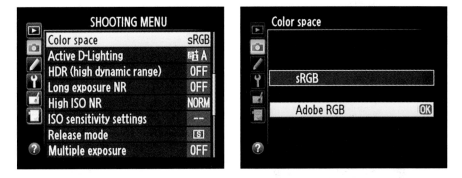

Figure 8-31: Change the Color Space setting via the Shooting menu.

 You can tell whether you captured an image in the Adobe RGB format by looking at its filename: Adobe RGB images start with an underscore, as in _DSC0627.jpg. For pictures captured in the sRGB color space, the underscore appears in the middle of the filename, as in DSC_0627.jpg. See Chapter 5 for more tips on decoding picture filenames.

Taking a Quick Look at Picture Controls

A feature that Nikon calls *Picture Controls* offers one more way to tweak image sharpening, color, and contrast when you shoot in the P, S, A, and M exposure modes and choose one of the JPEG options for the Image Quality setting. (Chapter 2 explains the Image Quality setting.)

 Sharpening, in case you're new to the digital meaning of the term, refers to a software process that adjusts contrast in a way that creates the illusion of slightly sharper focus. I emphasize, "slightly sharper focus." Sharpening produces a subtle *tweak,* and it's not a fix for poor focus.

When you shoot in the advanced exposure modes — P, S, A, and M — you can choose from the following Picture Controls, represented in the menus and on the Shooting Information screen by the two-letter codes in parentheses.

(Figure 8-32 shows you where to find the two-letter code in the Shooting Info display.) In the other exposure modes, the camera selects the Picture Control setting for you.

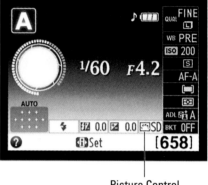

Picture Control

Figure 8-32: This two-letter code represents the Picture Control setting.

- **Standard (SD):** The default setting, this option captures the image normally — that is, using the characteristics that Nikon offers up as suitable for the majority of subjects.

- **Neutral (NL):** At this setting, the camera doesn't enhance color, contrast, and sharpening as much as in the other modes. The setting is designed for people who want to precisely manipulate these picture characteristics in a photo editor. By not overworking colors, sharpening, and so on when producing your original file, the camera delivers an original that gives you more latitude in the digital darkroom.

- **Vivid (VI):** In this mode, the camera amps up color saturation, contrast, and sharpening.

- **Monochrome (MC):** This setting produces black-and-white photos. Only in the digital world, they're called *grayscale images* because a true black-and-white image contains only black and white, with no shades of gray.

I'm not keen on creating grayscale images this way. I prefer to shoot in full color and then do my own grayscale conversion in my photo editor. That technique just gives you more control over the look of your black-and-white photos. Assuming that you work with a decent photo editor, you can control what original tones are emphasized in your grayscale version, for example. Additionally, keep in mind that you can always convert a color image to grayscale, but you can't go the other direction. You can create a black-and-white copy of your color image right in the camera, in fact; Chapter 10 shows you how.

- **Portrait (PT):** This mode tweaks colors and sharpening in a way that is designed to produce nice skin texture and pleasing skin tones. (If you shoot in the Portrait or Night Portrait Scene modes, the camera selects this Picture Control for you.)

- **Landscape (LS):** This mode emphasizes blues and greens. As you might expect, it's the mode used by the Landscape Scene mode.

The extent to which Picture Controls affect your image depends on the subject as well as the exposure settings you choose and the lighting conditions. But Figure 8-33 gives you a general idea of what to expect. As you can see, the differences between the Picture Controls are pretty subtle, with the exception of the Monochrome setting.

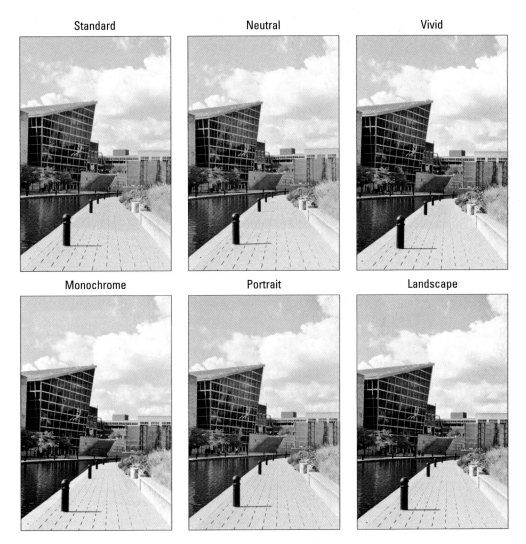

Figure 8-33: Picture Controls apply preset adjustments to color, sharpening, and other photo characteristics to images you shoot in the JPEG file format.

You can adjust the setting through the Quick Settings display, as shown in Figure 8-34, or the Shooting menu, as shown in Figure 8-35.

 At least while you're new to the camera, I recommend that you stick with the default Picture Control setting, for two reasons. First, you have way more important camera settings to worry about — aperture, shutter speed, autofocus, and all the rest. Why add one more setting to your list, especially when the impact of changing it is minimal?

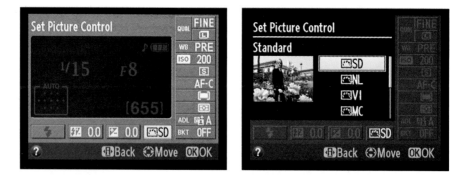

Figure 8-34: The fastest way to select a Picture Control is through the Quick Settings screen.

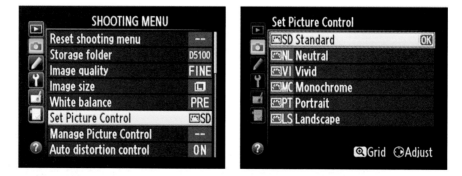

Figure 8-35: But going through the Shooting menu provides access to settings that let you tweak the results of each Picture Control.

Second, if you really want to mess with the characteristics that the Picture Control options affect, you're much better off shooting in the Raw (NEF) format and then making those adjustments on a picture-by-picture basis in your Raw converter. In Nikon ViewNX 2, you can even assign any of the existing Picture Controls to your Raw files and then compare how each one affects the image. The camera does tag your Raw file with whatever Picture Control is active when you take the shot, but the image adjustments are in no way set in stone, or even in sand — you can tweak your photo at will. (The selected Picture Control does affect the JPEG preview that's used to display the Raw image thumbnails in ViewNX 2 and other browsers.)

However, in the interest of full disclosure, I should alert you to a feature that may make Picture Controls a little more useful to some people: You can modify any Picture Control to more closely render a scene the way you envision it. So, for example, if you like the bold colors of Landscape mode but don't think the effect goes far enough, you can adjust the setting to amp up colors even more.

To reserve page space in this book for functions that experience tells me will be the most useful to the most readers, I opted not to provide full details about customizing Picture Controls. But the following steps provide a quick overview of the process so that if you encounter the menu screens that contain the related options, you'll have some idea what you're seeing. So here are the basics:

1. **Set the Mode dial to P, S, A, or M.**

   These are the only modes that let you select or modify a Picture Control.

2. **Display the Shooting menu, choose Set Picture Control, and press OK.**

3. **Highlight the Picture Control you want to modify.**

   For example, I highlighted the Standard setting on the left screen in Figure 8-36.

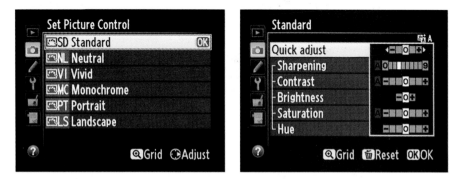

Figure 8-36: After selecting a Picture Control, press right to display options for adjusting its effect on your pictures.

4. **Press the Multi Selector right.**

You see the screen shown on the right in Figure 8-36, containing sliders that you use to modify the Picture Control. Which options you can adjust depend on your selected Picture Control.

5. **Highlight a picture characteristic and then press the Multi Selector right or left to adjust the setting.**

A couple tips:

- Some Picture Controls offer a Quick Adjust setting, which enables you to easily increase or decrease the overall effect of the Picture Control. A positive value produces a more exaggerated effect; set the slider to 0 to return to the default setting.

- The large vertical line in the slider bar indicates the current setting for the option.

- The little line under the slider bar represents the default setting for the selected Picture Control.

- Reset all the options to their defaults by pressing the Delete button.

- To display a grid that lets you see how your selected Picture Control compares with the others in terms of color saturation and contrast, as shown in Figure 8-37, press and hold the Zoom In button. (I vote this screen most likely to confound new camera users who stumble across it. Note that the Standard and Portrait settings are identical in terms of contrast and saturation, so the P for Portrait doesn't appear in the grid unless you selected that Picture Control initially.

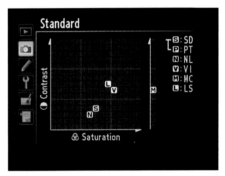

Figure 8-37: Press the Zoom In button to display a grid that ranks each Picture Style according to its level of saturation and contrast.

You can't change any settings via the grid — it's for informational purposes only. However, if you display the grid from the first Set Picture Control menu (the left screen in Figure 8-36), you can press the Multi Selector up or down to select a different Picture Control. You then can press right to access the Picture Control adjustment screen.

6. Press OK to save your changes and exit the adjustment screen.

As when you fine-tune a White Balance setting, an asterisk appears next to the edited Picture Style in the menu and Shooting Information screen to remind you that you have adjusted it.

Again, these steps are intended just as a starting point for those who are interested in playing with Picture Controls. Complete details on each of the Picture Control adjustment options are found in the electronic version of the camera manual, stored on one of the two CDs that shipped with your camera. (The other CD contains the Nikon software.) You can read the manual in Adobe Acrobat or any other program that can open PDF files. The paper manual contains only basic operating instructions, and the Picture Control editing functions didn't make the cut.

9

Putting It All Together

*E*arlier chapters of this book break down each and every picture-taking feature on your D5100, describing in detail how the various controls affect exposure, picture quality, focus, color, and the like. This chapter pulls together all that information to help you set up your camera for specific types of photography.

Keep in mind, though, that there are no hard-and-fast rules as to the "right way" to shoot a portrait, a landscape, or whatever. So feel free to wander off on your own, tweaking this exposure setting or adjusting that focus control, to discover your own creative vision. Experimentation is part of the fun of photography, after all — and thanks to your camera monitor and the Delete button, it's an easy, completely free proposition.

Recapping Basic Picture Settings

Your subject, creative goals, and lighting conditions determine which settings you should use for some picture-taking options, such as aperture and shutter speed. I offer my take on those options throughout this chapter. But for many basic options, I recommend the same settings for almost every shooting scenario. Table 9-1 shows you those recommendations and also lists the chapter where you can find details about each setting.

Table 9-1	All-Purpose Picture-Taking Settings	
Option	*Recommended Setting*	*Chapter*
Exposure mode	P, S, A, or M	7
Image Quality	JPEG Fine or Raw (NEF)	2
Image Size	Large or medium	2
White Balance	Auto	8
ISO Sensitivity	100	7
Focus mode	For autofocusing: still subjects, AF-S; moving subjects, AF-C. For manual focus, MF	8
AF-Area mode	Still subjects, Single Point; moving subjects, Dynamic Area	8
Release mode	Action photos: Continuous; all others: Single Frame	2
Metering	Matrix	7
Active D-Lighting	Off	7

One key point: Instructions in this chapter assume that you set the exposure mode to P, S, A, or M, as indicated in the table. These modes, detailed in Chapter 7, are the only ones that give you access to the entire cadre of D5100 features. In most cases, I recommend using S (shutter-priority autoexposure) when controlling motion blur is important, and A (aperture-priority autoexposure) when controlling depth of field is important. These two modes let you concentrate on one side of the exposure equation and let the camera handle the other. Of course, if you're comfortable making both the aperture and shutter speed decisions, you may prefer to work in M (manual) exposure mode instead. P (programmed autoexposure) is my last choice because it makes choosing a specific aperture or shutter speed more cumbersome.

I don't recommend the fully automated modes — Auto, Auto Flash Off, and Scene — because they don't permit you to access certain settings that can be critical to capturing good shots of certain subjects. For help using the automated modes, visit Chapter 3.

Finally, this chapter discusses choices for normal, through-the-viewfinder photography; Chapter 4 guides you through the options available for Live View photography and movie recording. (For Live View photography, however, most settings work the same as discussed here, with the exception of the autofocus options.)

Shooting Still Portraits

By *still portrait,* I mean that your subject isn't moving. For subjects who aren't keen on sitting still long enough to have their picture taken, skip to the next section and use the techniques given for action photography instead.

Assuming that you do have a subject willing to pose, the classic portraiture approach is to keep the subject sharply focused while throwing the background into soft focus. This artistic choice emphasizes the subject and helps diminish the impact of any distracting background objects in cases where you can't control the setting. The following steps show you how to achieve this look:

1. **Set the Mode dial to A (aperture-priority autoexposure) and select the lowest f-stop value possible.**

   As Chapter 7 explains, a low f-stop setting opens the aperture, which not only allows more light to enter the camera but also shortens *depth of field,* or the range of sharp focus. So dialing in a low f-stop value is the first step in softening your portrait background.

   I recommend aperture-priority mode when depth of field is a primary concern because you can control the f-stop while relying on the camera to select the shutter speed that will properly expose the image. Just rotate the Command dial to select your desired f-stop. (You do need to pay attention to shutter speed also, however, to make sure that it's not so slow that any movement of the subject or camera will blur the image.)

   You can monitor the current f-stop and shutter speed in the viewfinder and Shooting Information display, as shown in Figure 9-1.

2. **To further soften the background, zoom in, get closer, and put more distance between the subject and background.**

   As covered in Chapter 8, zooming in to a longer focal length also reduces depth of field, as does moving physically closer to your subject. And the greater the distance between the subject and background, the more the background blurs. (A good rule is to place the subject at least an arm's length away from the background.) See Chapter 8 for information about calculating the effective focal lengths of lenses mounted on the D5100.

   A lens with a focal length of 85–120mm is ideal for a classic head and shoulders portrait. You should avoid using a much shorter focal length (a wider-angle lens) for portraits. They can cause features to appear distorted — sort of like how people look when you view them through a security peephole in a door.

Shutter speed   f-stop

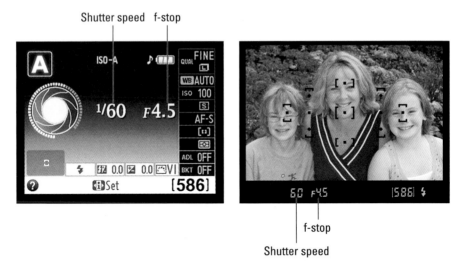

f-stop

Shutter speed

Figure 9-1: You can monitor aperture (f-stop) and shutter speed settings in the displays.

3. For indoor portraits, shoot flashfree if possible.

Shooting by available light rather than flash produces softer illumination and avoids the problem of red-eye. To get enough light to go flashfree, turn on room lights or, during daylight, pose your subject next to a sunny window, as I did for the image in Figure 9-2.

In the A exposure mode, simply keeping the built-in flash unit closed disables the flash. If flash is unavoidable, see my list of flash tips at the end of the steps to get better results.

4. For outdoor portraits, use a flash if possible.

Even in daylight, a flash adds a beneficial pop of light to subjects' faces, as illustrated in Figure 9-3. A flash is especially important when the background is brighter than the subjects, as in this example.

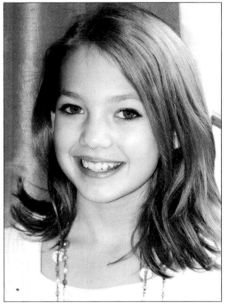

Figure 9-2: For more pleasing indoor portraits, shoot by available light instead of using flash.

No flash

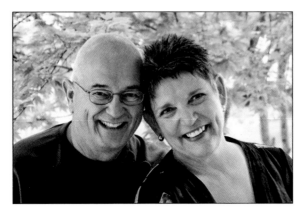

Fill flash

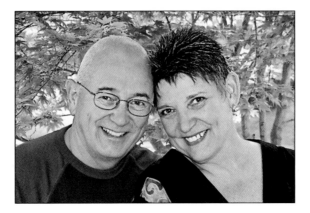

Figure 9-3: To properly illuminate the face in outdoor portraits, use fill flash.

In the A exposure mode, press the Flash button on the side of the camera to enable the built-in flash. For daytime portraits, use the Fill Flash setting. (That's the regular, basic Flash mode.) For nighttime images, try red-eye reduction or slow-sync flash; again, see the flash tips at the end of these steps to use either mode most effectively.

The top shutter speed for flash photography on the D5100 is 1/200 second, so in bright light, you may need to stop down the aperture to avoid overexposing the photo. Doing so, of course, brings the background into sharper focus. So try to move the subject into a shaded area instead.

5. Press and hold the shutter button halfway to initiate exposure metering and autofocusing.

If the camera has trouble finding the correct focusing distance, simply set your lens to manual focus mode and then twist the focusing ring to set focus. See Chapter 8 for help with focusing.

6. Press the shutter button the rest of the way to capture the image.

Again, these steps just give you a starting point for taking better portraits. A few other tips can also improve your people pics:

- **Pay attention to the background.** Scan the entire frame looking for intrusive objects that may distract the eye from the subject. If necessary, reposition the subject against a more flattering backdrop. Inside, a softly textured wall works well; outdoors, trees and shrubs can provide nice backdrops as long as they aren't so ornate or colorful that they diminish the subject (for example, a magnolia tree laden with blooms).

- **Pay attention to white balance if your subject is lit by both flash and ambient light.** Any time you shoot in mixed lighting, the result may be colors that are slightly warmer or cooler (bluer) than neutral. A warming effect typically looks nice in portraits, giving the skin a subtle glow. But if you aren't happy with the result, see Chapter 8 to find out how to fine-tune white balance.

- **When flash is unavoidable, try these tricks to produce better results.** The following techniques can help solve flash-related issues:

  - *Indoors, turn on as many room lights as possible.* With more ambient light, you reduce the flash power that's needed to expose the picture. This step also causes the pupils to constrict, further reducing the chances of red-eye. (Pay heed to my white balance warning, however.) As an added benefit, the smaller pupil allows more of the subject's iris to be visible in the portrait, so you see more eye color.

  - *Try using a Flash mode that enables red-eye reduction or slow-sync flash.* If you choose the first option, warn your subject to expect both a preliminary pop of light from the AF-assist lamp, which constricts pupils, and the actual flash. And remember that slow-sync flash modes use a slower-than-normal shutter speed, which produces softer lighting and brighter backgrounds than normal flash. (Chapter 7 explains the various Flash modes.)

    Take a look at Figure 9-4 for an example of how slow-sync flash can really improve an indoor portrait. When I used regular flash, the shutter speed was 1/60 second. At that speed, the camera has little time to soak up any ambient light. As a result, the scene is lit primarily by the flash. That caused two problems: The strong flash created some "hot spots" on the subject's skin, and the window frame is much more prominent because of the contrast between it and the darker bushes outside the window. Although it was daylight when I took the picture, the skies were overcast, so at 1/60 second, the exterior appears dark.

In the slow-sync example, shot at 1/4 second, the exposure time was long enough to permit the ambient light to brighten the exteriors to the point that the window frame almost blends into the background. And because much less flash power was needed to expose the subject, the lighting is much more flattering. In this case, the bright background also helps to set the subject apart because of her dark hair and shirt. If the subject had been a pale blonde, this setup wouldn't have worked as well, of course. Again, too, note the warming effect that can occur when you use Auto White Balance and shoot in a combination of flash and daylight.

Don't forget that a slower-than-normal shutter speed means an increased risk of blur due to camera shake. So use a tripod or otherwise steady the camera. Remind your subjects to stay absolutely still, too, because they'll appear blurry if they move during the exposure. I was fortunate to have both a tripod and a cooperative subject for my examples, but I probably wouldn't try slow-sync for portraits of young children or pets.

Regular fill flash, 1/60 second   Slow-sync flash, 1/4 second

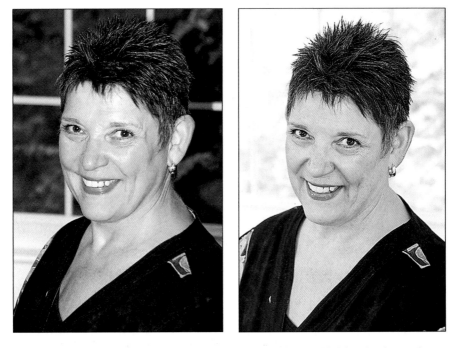

Figure 9-4: Slow-sync flash produces softer, more even lighting and brighter backgrounds.

- *For professional results, use an external flash with a rotating flash head.* Then aim the flash head upward so that the flash light bounces off the ceiling and falls softly down onto the subject. An external flash isn't cheap, but the results make the purchase worthwhile if you shoot lots of portraits. Compare the two portraits in Figure 9-5 for an illustration. In the first example, the built-in flash resulted in strong shadowing behind the subject and harsh, concentrated light. To produce the better result on the right, I used the Nikon Speedlight SB-600 and bounced the light off the ceiling. I also moved the subject a few feet farther in front of the background to create more background blur.

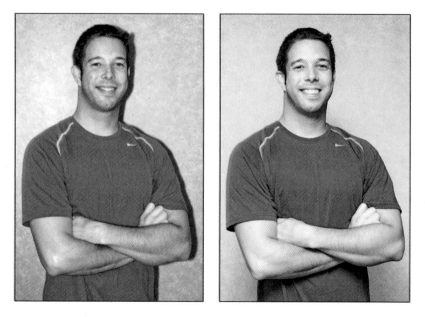

Figure 9-5: To eliminate harsh lighting and strong shadows (left), I used bounce flash and moved the subject farther from the background (right).

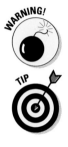

Make sure that the ceiling or other surface you use to bounce the light is white; otherwise, the flash light will pick up the color of the surface and influence the color of your subject.

- *Invest in a flash diffuser to further soften the light.* Whether you use the built-in flash or an external flash, attaching a diffuser is also a good idea. A *diffuser* is simply a piece of translucent plastic or fabric that you place over the flash to soften and spread the light — much like sheer curtains diffuse window light. Diffusers come in lots of different designs, including small, fold-flat models that fit over the built-in flash.

✍ **Frame the subject loosely to allow for later cropping to a variety of frame sizes.** Your D5100 produces images that have an aspect ratio of 3:2. That means that your portrait perfectly fits a 4-x-6-inch print size but will require cropping to print at any other proportions, such as 5 x 7 or 8 x 10. Chapter 6 talks more about this issue.

Capturing action

A fast shutter speed is the key to capturing a blur-free shot of any moving subject, whether it's a flower in the breeze, a spinning Ferris wheel, or, as in the case of Figure 9-6, a racing cyclist.

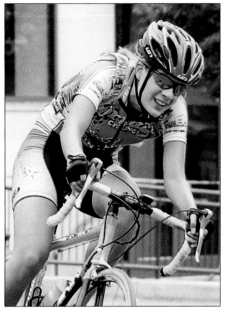

Along with the basic capture settings outlined in Table 9-1, try the techniques in the following steps to photograph a subject in motion:

1. **Set the Mode dial to S (shutter-priority autoexposure).**

   In this mode, you control the shutter speed, and the camera takes care of choosing an aperture setting that will produce a good exposure.

2. **Rotate the Command dial to select the shutter speed.**

Figure 9-6: Use a high shutter speed to freeze motion.

   (Refer to Figure 9-1 to locate shutter speed in the viewfinder and Shooting Information display.) After you select the shutter speed, the camera selects an aperture (f-stop) to match.

What shutter speed should you choose? Well, it depends on the speed at which your subject is moving, so you need to experiment. But generally speaking, 1/320 second should be plenty for all but the fastest subjects (race cars, boats, and so on). For very slow subjects, you can even go as low as 1/250 or 1/125 second. My subject in Figure 9-6 was zipping along at a pretty fast pace, so I set the shutter speed to 1/500 second. Remember, though, that when you increase shutter speed, the camera opens the aperture to maintain the same exposure. At low f-stop numbers, depth of field becomes shorter, so you have to be more careful to keep your subject within the sharp-focus zone as you compose and focus the shot.

You also can take an entirely different approach to capturing action: Instead of choosing a fast shutter speed, select a speed slow enough to blur the moving objects, which can create a heightened sense of motion and, in scenes that feature very colorful subjects, cool abstract images. I took this approach when shooting the carnival ride featured in Figure 9-7, for example. For the left image, I set the shutter speed to 1/30 second; for the right version, I slowed things down to 1/5 second. In both cases, I used a tripod, but because nearly everything in the frame was moving, the entirety of both photos is blurry — the 1/5 second version is simply more blurry because of the slower shutter.

| 1/30 second | 1/5 second |

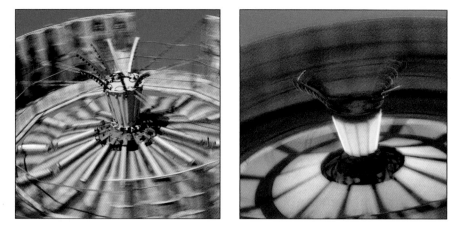

Figure 9-7: Using a shutter speed slow enough to blur moving objects can be a fun creative choice, too.

3. **In dim lighting, raise the ISO setting if necessary to allow a fast shutter speed.**

   Unless you're shooting in bright daylight, you may not be able to use a fast shutter speed at a low ISO, even if the camera opens the aperture as far as possible. If auto ISO override is in force, ISO may go up automatically when you increase the shutter speed — Chapter 7 has details on that feature. Raising the ISO does increase the possibility of noise, but a noisy shot is better than a blurry shot.

   Why not add flash to brighten the scene? Well, adding flash is a bit tricky for action shots, unfortunately. First, the flash needs time to recycle between shots, so try to go without if you want to capture images at a fast pace. Second, the built-in flash has limited range — so don't waste your time if your subject isn't close by. And third, remember that the fastest shutter speed you can use with flash is 1/200 second, which may not be high enough to capture a quickly moving subject without blur.

4. **For rapid-fire shooting, set the Release mode to Continuous.**

In that mode, you can capture multiple images with a single press of the shutter button. As long as you hold down the button, the camera continues to record images, at a rate of up to four frames per second. Here again, though, you need to go flashfree; you can't use this Release mode with flash.

5. **Select speed-oriented focusing options.**

For fastest shooting, try manual focusing: It eliminates the time the camera needs to lock focus when you use autofocusing. If you do use autofocus, try these two autofocus settings for best performance:

- Set the AF-Area mode to Dynamic Area.
- Set the Focus mode to AF-C (continuous-servo autofocus).

At these settings, the camera sets focus initially on your selected focus point but then looks to the surrounding points for focusing information if you subject moves away from the selected one. Focus is adjusted continuously until you take the shot. Remember that by default, the camera won't release the shutter before focus is achieved; you can over-rule that limitation through the AF-C Priority Selection option on the Custom Setting menu if you like. Chapter 8 has the details.

6. **Compose the subject to allow for movement across the frame.**

Frame your shot a little wider than you normally might so that you lessen the risk that your subject will move out of the frame before you record the image. You can always crop to a tighter composition later. (I used this approach for my cyclist image — the original shot includes a lot of background that I later cropped away.) It's also a good idea to leave more room in front of the subject than behind it. This makes it obvious that your subject is going somewhere.

Using these techniques should give you a better chance of capturing any fast-moving subject. But action-shooting strategies also are helpful for shooting candid portraits of kids and pets. Even if they aren't currently running, leaping, or otherwise cavorting, snapping a shot before they do move is often tough. So if an interaction catches your eye, set your camera into action mode and fire off a series of shots as fast as you can.

Capturing scenic vistas

Providing specific capture settings for landscape photography is tricky because there's no single best approach to capturing a beautiful stretch of countryside, a city skyline, or other vast subject. Take depth of field, for example: One person's idea of a super cityscape might be to keep all buildings in the scene sharply focused. But another photographer might prefer to shoot the same scene so that a foreground building is sharply focused while the others are less so, thus drawing the eye to that first building.

That said, I can offer a few tips to help you photograph a landscape the way *you* see it:

- **Shoot in aperture-priority autoexposure mode (A) so that you can control depth of field.** If you want extreme depth of field so that both near and distant objects are sharply focused, as in Figure 9-8, select a high f-stop value. I used an aperture of f/18 for this shot. For short depth of field, use a low value.

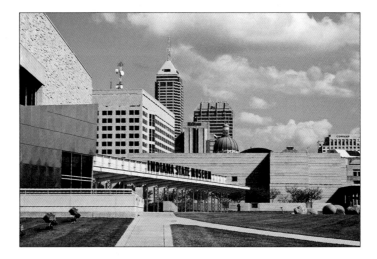

Figure 9-8: Use a high f-stop value to keep foreground and background sharply focused.

- **If the exposure requires a slow shutter, use a tripod to avoid blurring.** The downside to a high f-stop is that you need a slower shutter speed to produce a good exposure. If the shutter speed drops below what you can comfortably handhold, use a tripod to avoid picture-blurring camera shake. Remember that when you use a tripod, Nikon recommends that you turn off Vibration Reduction if you're using the kit lens. Just set the VR switch on the lens to the Off position.

  No tripod handy? Look for any solid surface on which you can steady the camera. You can increase the ISO Sensitivity setting to allow a faster shutter, too, but that option brings with it the chances of increased image noise. See Chapter 7 for details.

- **For dramatic waterfall shots, consider using a slow shutter to create that "misty" look.** The slow shutter blurs the water, giving it a soft, romantic appearance, as shown in Figure 9-9. Again, use a tripod to ensure that the rest of the scene doesn't also blur due to camera shake.

In very bright light, you may overexpose the image at a very slow shutter, even if you stop the aperture all the way down and select the camera's lowest ISO setting. As a solution, consider investing in a *neutral density filter* for your lens. This type of filter works something like sunglasses for your camera: It simply reduces the amount of light that passes through the lens, without affecting image colors, so that you can use a slower shutter than would otherwise be possible.

✔ **At sunrise or sunset, base exposure on the sky.** The foreground will be dark, but you can usually brighten it in a photo editor if needed. If you base exposure on the foreground, on the other hand, the sky will become so bright that all the color will be washed out — a problem you usually can't fix after

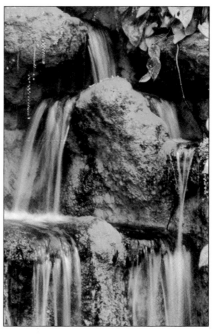

Figure 9-9: For misty waterfalls, use a slow shutter speed and a tripod.

the fact. You can also invest in a *graduated* neutral density filter, which is a filter that's clear on one side and dark on the other. You orient the filter so that the dark half falls over the sky and the clear side over the dimly lit portion of the scene. This setup enables you to better expose the foreground without blowing out the sky colors.

Experiment with adjusting the Active D-Lighting setting as well, and also give the HDR feature a whirl; both enable you to create an image that contains a greater range of brightness values than is normally possible. Chapter 7 explains both features.

✔ **For cool nighttime city pics, experiment with slow shutter.** Assuming that cars or other vehicles are moving through the scene, the result is neon trails of light like those you see in the foreground of the image in Figure 9-10. Shutter speed for this image was about ten seconds.

Instead of changing the shutter speed manually between each shot, try *bulb* mode. Available only in M (manual) exposure mode, this option records an image for as long as you hold down the shutter button. So just take a series of images, holding down the button for different lengths of time for each shot. In bulb mode, you also can exceed the standard maximum exposure time of 30 seconds.

✔ **For the best lighting, shoot during the *magic hours*.** That's the term photographers use for early morning and late afternoon, when the light cast by the sun is soft and warm, giving everything that beautiful, gently warmed look.

Can't wait for the perfect light? Tweak your camera's White Balance setting, using the instructions laid out in Chapter 8, to simulate the color of magic-hour light.

✔ **In tricky light, bracket exposures.** *Bracketing* simply means to take the same picture at several different exposure settings to increase the odds that at least one of them will capture the scene the way you envision. Bracketing is especially a good idea in difficult lighting situations, such as sunrise and sunset. Chapter 7 shows you how to set up automatic exposure bracketing.

✔ **When shooting fireworks, use manual exposure, manual focus, and a tripod.** Fireworks require a long exposure, and trying to handhold your camera simply isn't going to work. If using a zoom lens, zoom out to the shortest focal length (widest angle). Switch to manual focusing and set focus at infinity (the farthest focus point possible on your lens). Set the exposure mode to manual, choose a relatively high f-stop setting — say, f/16 or so — and start at a shutter speed of one to five seconds. From there, it's simply a matter of experimenting with different shutter speeds. Also play with the timing of the shutter release, starting some exposures at the moment the fireworks are shot up, some at the moment they burst open, and so on. For the example featured in Figure 9-11, I used a shutter speed of about five seconds and began the exposure as the rocket was going up — that's what creates the "corkscrew" of light that rises up through the frame.

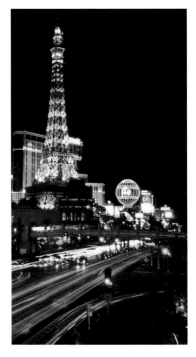

Figure 9-10: A slow shutter also creates neon light trails in city-street scenes.

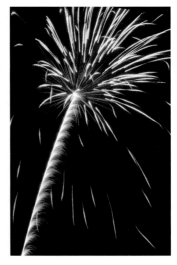

Figure 9-11: I used a shutter speed of five seconds to capture this fireworks shot.

Again, for an easy way to vary exposure time between shots, try using the Bulb shutter speed. This technique enables you to experiment with shutter speed more easily because you don't have to use the Command dial to adjust the setting between each shot. Remember that this option is available only in the M (manual) exposure mode; it's the setting one step below the slowest shutter speed (30 seconds).

Capturing dynamic close-ups

For great close-up shots, try these techniques:

✓ **Check your lens manual to find out its minimum close-focusing distance.** How "up close and personal" you can get to your subject depends on your lens, not the camera body.

✓ **Take control over depth of field by setting the camera mode to A (aperture-priority autoexposure) mode.** Whether you want a shallow, medium, or extreme depth of field depends on the point of your photo. In classic nature photography, for example, the artistic tradition is a very shallow depth of field, as shown in Figure 9-12, and requires an open aperture (low f-stop value). But if you want the viewer to be able to clearly see all details throughout the frame — for example, if you're shooting a product shot for your company's sales catalog — you need to go the other direction, stopping down the aperture as far as possible.

✓ **Remember that zooming in and getting close to your subject both decrease depth of field.** So back to that product shot: If you need depth of field beyond

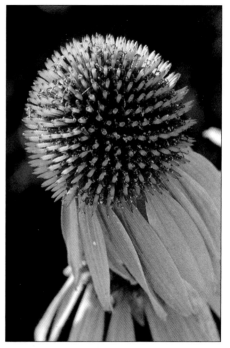

Figure 9-12: Shallow depth of field is a classic technique for close-up floral images.

what you can achieve with the aperture setting, you may need to back away, zoom out, or both. (You can always crop your image to show just the parts of the subject that you want to feature.)

- **When shooting flowers and other nature scenes outdoors, pay attention to shutter speed, too.** Even a slight breeze may cause your subject to move, causing blurring at slow shutter speeds.

- **Use flash for better outdoor lighting.** Just as with portraits, a tiny bit of flash typically improves close-ups when the sun is your primary light source. Again, though, keep in mind that the maximum shutter speed possible when you use the built-in flash is 1/200 second. So in very bright light, you may need to use a high f-stop setting to avoid overexposing the picture. You can also adjust the flash output via the Flash Compensation control. Chapter 7 offers details.

- **When shooting indoors, try not to use flash as your primary light source.** Because you're shooting at close range, the light from your flash may be too harsh even at a low Flash Compensation setting. If flash is inevitable, turn on as many room lights as possible to reduce the flash power that's needed — even a hardware-store shop light can do in a pinch as a lighting source. (Remember that if you have multiple light sources, though, you may need to tweak the White Balance setting.)

- **To really get close to your subject, invest in a macro lens or a set of diopters.** A true macro lens, which enables you to get really, really close to your subjects, is an expensive proposition; expect to pay around $200 or more. But if you enjoy capturing the tiny details in life, it's worth the investment.

  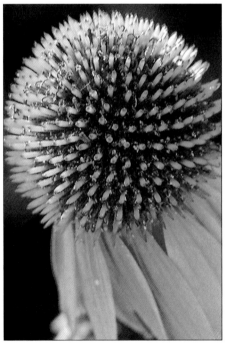

  For a less expensive way to go, you can spend about $40 for a set of *diopters,* which are sort of like reading glasses that you screw onto your existing lens. Diopters come in several strengths — +1, +2, +4, and so on — with a higher number indicating a greater magnifying power. I took this approach to capture the extreme close-up in Figure 9-13, attaching a +2 diopter to my lens. The downfall of diopters, sadly, is that they typically produce images that are very soft around the edges, a problem that doesn't occur with a good macro lens.

  Figure 9-13: To extend your lens's close-focus capability, you can add magnifying diopters.

Part IV
The Part of Tens

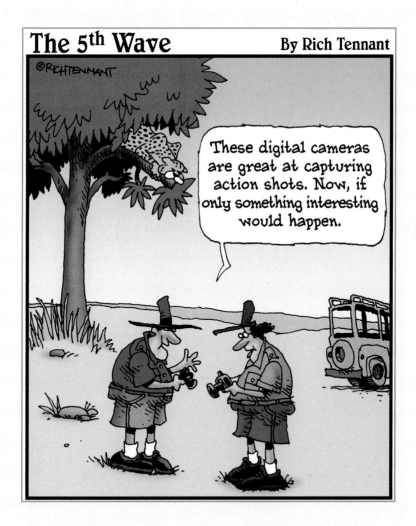

The 5th Wave   By Rich Tennant

These digital cameras are great at capturing action shots. Now, if only something interesting would happen.

In this part . . .

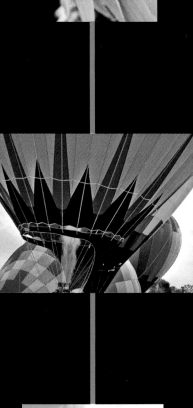

In time-honored *For Dummies* tradition, this part of the book contains additional tidbits of information presented in the always popular "Top Ten" list format. Chapter 10 shows you how to do some minor picture touchups, such as cropping and adjusting exposure, by using tools on your camera's Retouch menu. In addition, I show you how to use the D5100's Effects exposure mode, which enables you to add special effects to photos and movies right at the time you shoot them. Following that, Chapter 11 introduces you to ten camera functions that I consider specialty tools — bonus options that, although not at the top of the list of the features I suggest you study, are nonetheless interesting to explore when you have a free moment or two.

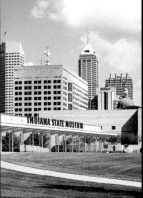

10

Ten Fun (And Practical) Ways to Manipulate Your Photos

*E*very photographer produces a clunker image now and then. When it happens to you, don't be too quick to reach for the Delete button because many common problems are surprisingly easy to fix. In fact, you often can repair your photos right in the camera, thanks to tools found on the Retouch menu.

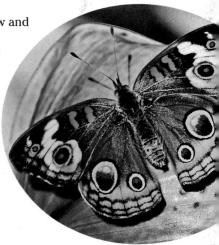

This chapter offers step-by-step recipes for using these photo-repair features and then takes things a step further by introducing special effects that you can create through the Retouch menu or by using the Effects exposure mode. Additionally, the first section of the chapter summarizes tips that relate to all the Retouch menu options.

Applying the Retouch Menu Filters

You can get to most of the Retouch menu features in two ways:

✔ **Display the menu, select the tool you want to use, and press OK.**
You're then presented with thumbnails of your photos. Use the Multi Selector to move the yellow highlight box over the photo you want to adjust and press OK. You next see options related to the selected tool.

The only menu item you can't access this way is Side-By-Side Comparison, explained shortly.

✔ **Switch the camera to playback mode, display your photo in single-frame view, and press OK.** The Retouch menu then appears superimposed over your photo, as shown in Figure 10-1. Select the tool you want to use and press OK again to apply the tool to your picture. I prefer the second method so that's how I approach things in this chapter, but it's entirely a personal choice.

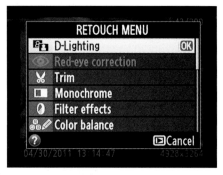

Figure 10-1: In single-frame playback view, press OK to access the Retouch menu tools.

However, you can't use this method to access the Image Overlay menu item. That feature, which combines two photos to create a third, blended image, requires you to use the first method of accessing the menu. You also must start at the Retouch menu to use the Edit Movie option, which I cover in Chapter 4. (All other Retouch menu features work with still photos only.)

A few other critical facts to note before you experiment with the Retouch menu tools:

✔ **Your originals remain intact.** When you apply a correction or enhancement from the Retouch menu, the camera creates a copy of your original photo and makes the changes to the copy only. Your original is preserved. A little icon that looks like the one that represents the Retouch menu appears with the image during playback to let you know that you're not looking at an original photo. The filename also clues you in to a retouched photo: For images created through the Resize menu option (covered in Chapter 6), filenames begin with SSC; for all other retouched images, filenames begin with CSC.

✔ **All menu options work with either JPEG or Raw (NEF) originals except Image Overlay.** Image Overlay works only with Raw files. See Chapter 2 for an explanation of JPEG and Raw.

✔ **Retouched copies for all alterations except Image Overlay are saved in the JPEG file format.** The retouched copy uses the same JPEG quality setting as the original (Fine, Normal, or Basic). For the Image Overlay option, you can choose to store the combined photo in the JPEG or Raw format.

✔ **You can apply each correction to the same picture only once.** The exception, again, is Image Overlay. If you save the composite image in the Raw format, you can combine the composite with a third Raw image. In fact, you can keep combining photos until your memory card is full, if the urge hits you.

✔ **The camera automatically assigns the next available file number to the retouched image.** Make note of the filename of the retouched version so that you can easily track it down later.

✔ **You can compare the original and the retouched version through the Side-by-Side Comparison menu option.** To use this feature, start by displaying either the original or the retouched version in full-frame playback. Then press OK, select Side-by-Side Comparison, as shown on the left in Figure 10-2, and press OK again. You see the original image on one side and the retouched version on the other, as shown in the second screen in the figure. At the top of the screen, labels indicate the Retouch tool that you applied to the photo. (I applied the D-Lighting adjustment to the after image in Figure 10-2.)

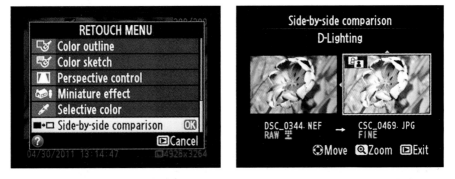

Figure 10-2: Use Side-by-Side Comparison to see whether you prefer the retouched version to the original.

These additional tricks work in Side-by-Side Comparison display:

- If you applied more than one Retouch tool to the picture, press the Multi Selector right and left to display individual thumbnails that show how each tool affected the picture.

- If you create multiple retouched versions of the same original — for example, if you create a monochrome version, save that, and then crop the original image and save that — you use a different technique to compare all the versions. First, press the Multi Selector right or left to surround the after image with the yellow highlight box. Now press the Multi Selector up and down to scroll through all the retouched versions.

- To temporarily view the original or retouched image at full-frame view, use the Multi Selector to highlight its thumbnail and then press and hold the Zoom In button. Release the button to return to Side-by-Side Comparison view.

To exit Side-by-Side Comparison view and return to single-image playback, press the Playback button.

Removing Red-Eye

From my experience, red-eye isn't a major problem with the D5100. Typically, the problem occurs only in very dark lighting, which makes sense: When little ambient light is available, the pupils of the subjects' eyes widen, creating more potential for the flash light to cause red-eye reflection.

If you spot a red-eye problem, however, give the Red-Eye Correction filter a try. After you select the filter from the Retouch menu, as shown on the left in Figure 10-3, one of two things happens: If the camera can't find any red-eye, it displays a message telling you so. But if it does detect red-eye, it applies the removal filter and displays the results in the monitor.

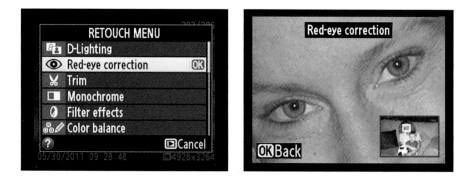

Figure 10-3: An automated red-eye remover is built right into your camera.

After the filter does its thing, press the Zoom In button to magnify the display so that you can check the camera's work, as shown on the right in Figure 10-3. To scroll the display, press the Multi Selector up, down, right, or left. The yellow box in the tiny navigation window in the lower-right corner of the screen indicates the area of the picture that you're currently viewing.

To go forward with the correction, press OK twice. The first OK returns the display to normal magnification; the second creates the retouched copy. To instead cancel the repair, press OK to return to normal magnification and then press the Playback button to cancel the repair.

If the in-camera red-eye repair fails you, most photo-editing programs have red-eye removal tools that you can use to get the job done. Unfortunately, no red-eye remover works on animal eyes. Red-eye removal tools know how to detect and replace only red-eye pixels, and animal eyes typically turn yellow, white, or green in response to a flash. The easiest solution is to use the brush tool found in most photo editors to paint the proper eye colors.

Straightening Tilting Horizon Lines

I seem to have a knack for shooting with the camera slightly misaligned with respect to the horizon line, which means that photos like the one on the left in Figure 10-4 often wind up crooked — in this case, everything tilts down toward the right corner of the frame. Perhaps those who say I have a skewed view of life are right? At any rate, my inability to "shoot straight" makes me especially fond of the Straighten tool on the Retouch menu. With this filter, you can rotate tilting horizons back to the proper angle, as shown in the right image in the figure.

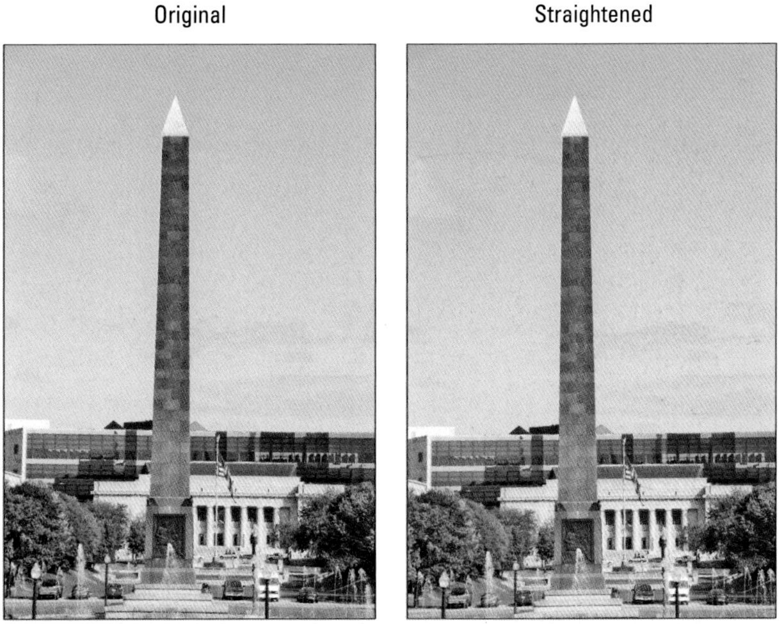

Original   Straightened

Figure 10-4: You can rotate crooked photos back to a level orientation with the Straighten tool.

To achieve this rotation magic, the camera must crop your image and then enlarge the remaining area — that's why the after photo in Figure 10-4 contains slightly less subject matter than the original. (The same cropping occurs if you make this kind of change in a photo editor.) The camera updates the display as you rotate the photo so that you can get an idea of how much of the original scene may be lost.

Here's how to put the tool to work:

1. **Display the photo in single-image playback mode and then press OK to get to the Retouch menu.**

2. **Highlight Straighten, as shown on the left in Figure 10-5, and press OK.**

   You see a screen similar to the one on the right in the figure, with a grid superimposed on your photo to serve as an alignment aid.

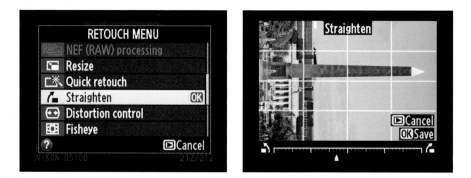

Figure 10-5: Press the Multi Selector right or left to rotate the image in increments of .25 degrees.

3. **To rotate the picture clockwise, press the Multi Selector right.**

   Each press spins the picture by about .25 degrees. You can achieve a maximum rotation of five degrees. The yellow pointer on the little scale under the photo shows you the current amount of rotation.

4. **To rotate in a counterclockwise direction, press the Multi Selector left.**

5. **When things are no longer off-kilter, press OK to create your retouched copy.**

Removing (Or Creating) Lens Distortion

Certain lenses can produce a type of distortion that causes straight lines to appear curved. Wide-angle lenses, for example, often create *barrel distortion,* in which objects at the center of a picture appear to be magnified and pushed forward — as if you wrapped the photo around the outside of a barrel. The effect is perhaps easiest to spot in a rectangular subject like the oil painting in Figure 10-6. Notice that in the original image, on the left, the edges of the painting appear to bow slightly outward. *Pincushion distortion* affects the photo in the opposite way, making center objects appear smaller and farther away.

Slight barrel distortion

After Distortion Control filter

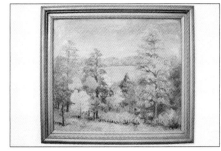 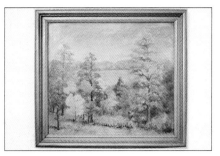

Figure 10-6: Barrel distortion makes straight lines appear to bow outward.

 You can minimize the chances of distortion by researching your lens purchases carefully. Photography magazines and online photography sites regularly measure and report distortion performance in their lens reviews.

If you notice a small amount of distortion, try enabling the Auto Distortion Control option on the Shooting menu. This feature attempts to correct distortion as you take the picture. (Chapter 8 has details.) Or you may prefer to wait until after reviewing your photos and then use the Distortion Control on the Retouch menu to try to fix things. I applied the filter to create the second version of the subject in Figure 10-6, for example. Less helpful, in my opinion, is a related filter, the Fisheye filter, that actually creates distortion in an attempt to replicate the look of a photo taken with a fisheye lens.

 The extent of the in-camera adjustment you can apply is fairly minimal. Additionally, I find it a little difficult to gauge my results on the camera monitor because you can't display any sort of alignment grid over the image to help you find the right degree of correction. For those reasons, I prefer to do this kind of work in my photo editor. Wherever you make the correction, understand that you lose part of your original image area as a result of the distortion correction, just as you do when you apply the Straighten tool, covered earlier in this chapter.

All that said, the first step in applying either filter is to display your photo in single-image playback mode and then press OK to display the Retouch menu. Highlight the filter you want to use (Distortion Control or Fisheye) and press

OK again. From that point, the process depends on which of the two filters you're using:

- **Distortion Control:** Select Distortion Control, as shown on the left in Figure 10-7, and then press OK to see the screen shown on the right. An Auto option is available for some lenses, as long as you didn't apply the Auto Distortion Control feature when taking the picture. As its name implies, the Auto option attempts to automatically apply the right degree of correction. If the Auto option is dimmed or you prefer to do the correction on your own, choose Manual, as shown on the right in the figure. You then see the screen featured in Figure 10-8. The little scale under the image represents the degree and direction of shift that you're applying. Press the Multi Selector right to reduce barrel distortion; press left to reduce pincushioning. Press OK when you're ready to make your corrected copy of the photo.

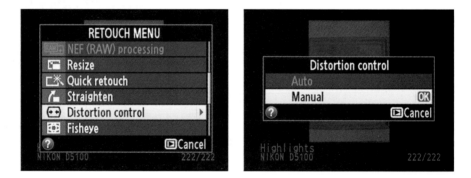

Figure 10-7: Use the Distortion Control filter to reduce barrel or pincushion distortion.

- **Fisheye:** After you highlight the filter name and press OK, you see a screen similar to the one in Figure 10-8, but this time, you see the word Fisheye at the top of the screen, and the scale at the bottom of the image indicates the strength of the distortion effect. Press the Multi Selector right or left to adjust the amount. Then press OK to create the fisheye copy.

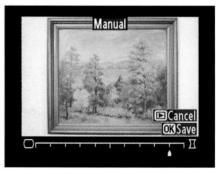

Figure 10-8: Press the Multi Selector right or left to adjust the amount and type of correction.

Correcting Perspective

When you photograph a tall building and tilt the camera up to get it all in the frame, a *convergence* or *keystoning* effect occurs. This effect causes vertical structures to appear to be leaning toward the center of the frame. Buildings sometimes even appear to be falling away from you, as shown in the left image in Figure 10-9. (If the lens is tilting down, verticals instead appear to lean outward, and the building appears to be falling toward you.) Through the Retouch menu's Perspective Control feature, you can right those leaning verticals, as shown in the after photo on the right in Figure 10-9.

Original   After perspective correction

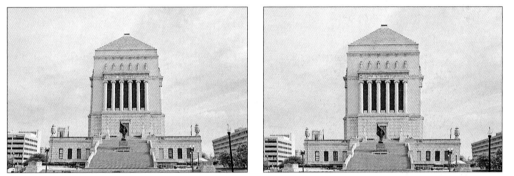

Figure 10-9: The original photo exhibited convergence (left); applying the Perspective Control filter corrected the problem (right).

Note, though, that just like the Straighten tool, you lose some area around the perimeter of your photo as part of the correction process. So when you're shooting this type of subject, frame loosely — that way, you ensure that you don't sacrifice an important part of the scene due to the correction.

To try out the feature, follow these steps:

1. **Display your photo in single-image view and press OK to bring the Retouch menu to life.**

2. **Select Perspective Control and press OK.**

   You see a grid and a horizontal and vertical scale, as shown in Figure 10-10.

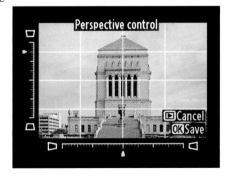

Figure 10-10: Press the Multi Selector to adjust the correction type and amount.

3. **Press the Multi Selector left and right to move the out-of-whack object horizontally.**

4. **Press the Multi Selector up and down to rotate the object toward or away from you.**

5. **Use the guides to get the perspective as close to normal as possible and then press OK to make a copy of the original image with your changes.**

   Depending on the scene, you may not be able to get all structures fully corrected, so just pay attention to the most prominent ones in the scene. For severe distortion problems, you may be able to get better results in your photo editor; in some programs, you can pull and push each side of the image around independently of the others, which enables you to more freely shift perspective than is possible with the type of tool provided in the camera.

Cropping (Trimming) Your Photo

To *crop* a photo simply means to trim away some of its perimeter. Cropping away excess background can often improve an image, as illustrated by Figures 10-11 and 10-12. When shooting this scene, I couldn't get close enough to the ducks to fill the frame with them, so I simply cropped it after the fact to achieve the desired composition.

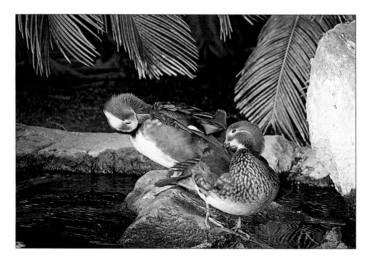

Figure 10-11: The original contains too much extraneous background.

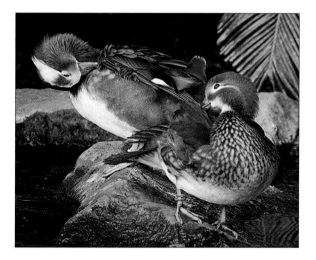

Figure 10-12: Cropping creates a better composition and eliminates background clutter.

With the Trim function on the Retouch menu, you can crop a photo right in the camera. Note a few things about this feature:

✓ You can crop your photo to five different aspect ratios: 3:2, which maintains the original proportions and matches that of a 4-x-6-inch print; 4:3, the proportions of a standard computer monitor or television (that is, not a widescreen model); 5:4, which gives you the same proportions as an 8-x-10-inch print; 1:1, which results in a square photo; and 16:9, which is the same aspect ratio as a widescreen monitor or television. If your purpose for cropping is to prepare your image for a frame size that doesn't match any of these aspect ratios, crop in your photo software instead.

✓ For each aspect ratio, you can choose from a variety of crop sizes, which depend on the size of your original. The sizes are stated in pixel terms, such as 3840 x 2560. If you're cropping in advance of printing the image, remember to aim for at least 200 pixels per linear inch of the print — 800 x 1200 pixels for a 4 x 6 print, for example. See Chapter 6 for more details about printing.

✓ If you captured the original photo using the Raw or Raw+JPEG Image Quality setting, the cropped version is saved as a JPEG Fine image. For other JPEG images, the crop version has the same Image Quality level as the original.

✓ After you apply the Trim function, you can't apply any other fixes from the Retouch menu. So make cropping the last of your retouching steps.

Keeping those caveats in mind, trim your image as follows:

1. **Display your photo in single-image view and press OK to launch the Retouch menu.**

2. **Select Trim and press OK.**

   You see the screen shown in Figure 10-13. The yellow highlight box indicates the current cropping frame. Anything outside the frame is set to be trimmed away.

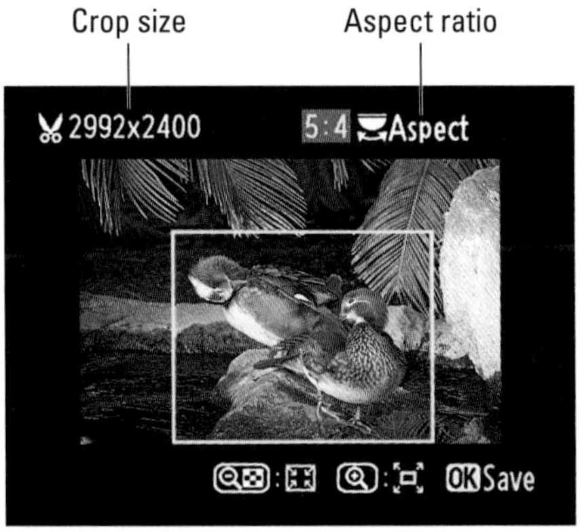

3. **Rotate the Command dial to change the crop aspect ratio.**

   The selected aspect ratio appears in the upper-right corner of the screen, as shown in Figure 10-13.

4. **Adjust the cropping frame size and placement as needed.**

   The current crop size appears in the upper-left corner of the screen. You can adjust the size and placement of the cropping frame like so:

Crop size   Aspect ratio

Figure 10-13: Rotate the Command dial to change the proportions of the crop box.

- *Reduce the size of the cropping frame.* Press and release the Zoom Out button. Each press of the button further reduces the crop size.

- *Enlarge the cropping frame.* Press the Zoom In button to expand the crop boundary and leave more of your image intact.

- *Reposition the cropping frame.* Press the Multi Selector up, down, right, and left to shift the frame position.

5. **Press OK to create your cropped copy of the original image.**

Manipulating Exposure and Color

Chapters 7 and 8 discuss the bazillion exposure and color controls on the D5100. But trust me, even someone who's a pro at using all those controls sometimes produces images that are just a little off. For major problems, using a photo-editing program to make corrections is usually the answer, but for images that need just a little exposure or color tweak, try these four tools:

✏ **D-Lighting:** Chapter 7 explains Active D-Lighting, a feature that brightens too-dark shadows in a way that leaves highlight details intact. You can apply a similar adjustment after you take a picture by choosing the D-Lighting filter on the Retouch menu. I used the filter on the photo in Figure 10-14, where strong backlighting left the balloon underexposed in the original image.

Original image   D-Lighting, High

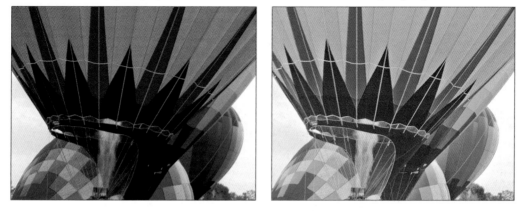

Figure 10-14: An underexposed photo (left) gets help from the D-Lighting filter (right).

When you choose the D-Lighting filter, you see before-and-after views of the image, as shown in Figure 10-15. Press the Multi Selector up or down to set the strength of the adjustment to Low, Normal, or High. I used High for the balloon image. To get a closer view of the adjusted photo, press and hold the Zoom In button. Release the button to return to the two-thumbnail display.

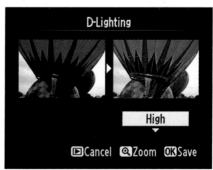

Figure 10-15: Press the Multi Selector up or down to vary the strength of the correction.

You can't apply D-Lighting to a picture taken using the Monochrome Picture Control, introduced in Chapter 8. Nor does D-Lighting work on any pictures to which you've applied the Quick Retouch filter, covered next, or the Monochrome filter, detailed a little later in this chapter.

✔ **Quick Retouch:** This filter increases contrast and color saturation and, if your subject is backlit, also applies a D-Lighting adjustment to restore some shadow detail that otherwise might be lost. In other words, Quick Retouch is sort of like D-Lighting on steroids.

Figure 10-16 illustrates the difference between the two filters. The first example shows my original, a close-up shot of a tree bud about to emerge. I applied the D-Lighting filter to the second example, which brightened the darkest areas of the image. In the final example, I applied the Quick Retouch filter. Again, shadows got a slight bump up the brightness scale. But Quick Retouch also increased color saturation and adjusted the overall image to expand the tonal range across the entire brightness spectrum, from very dark to very bright. In this photo, the saturation change is most noticeable in the yellows and reds of the tree bud. (The sky color may initially appear to be less saturated, but in fact, it's just a lighter hue than the original, thanks to the contrast adjustment.)

As with D-Lighting, you can choose from three levels of Quick Retouch correction. And the same restrictions apply: You can't apply the filter to monochrome images or on pictures that you adjusted via D-Lighting. (However, you can create two retouched copies of your original image, applying

Original

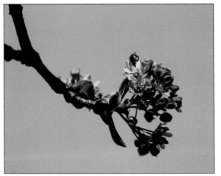

D-Lighting

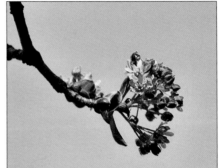

Quick Retouch

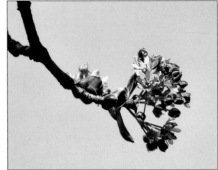

Figure 10-16: Quick Retouch adjusts saturation and contrast and, if necessary, also applies a D-Lighting correction.

D-Lighting to one and Quick Retouch to the other. You then can use the Side-by-Side Comparison feature, explained at the beginning of this chapter, to see which version you prefer.)

✔ **Filter Effects:** Shown in Figure 10-17, the Filter Effects option offers filters that are designed to mimic the results produced by traditional lens filters. The first five are color-manipulation filters. The other two, Cross Screen and Soft (not shown in the figure), are special-effects filters; you can read about both later in this chapter.)

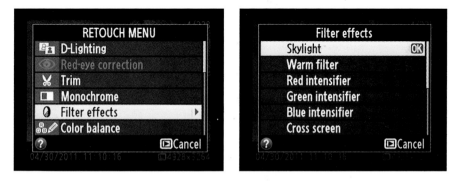

Figure 10-17: You can choose from filter effects that mimic traditional lens filters.

The color filters work like so:

- *Skylight filter:* This filter reduces the amount of blue in an image. The result is a very subtle warming effect.

- *Warm filter:* This one produces a warming effect that's just a bit stronger than the Skylight filter.

- *Color intensifiers:* You can boost the intensity of reds, greens, or blues individually by applying these filters. When you choose these filters, you can press the Multi Selector up or down to control the strength of the adjustment.

As an example, Figure 10-18 shows you an original image and three adjusted versions. As you can see, the Skylight and Warm filters are both very subtle; in this image, the effects are most noticeable in the sky. The fourth example shows a variation created by using the Color Balance filter, explained next, and shifting colors toward the cool (bluish) side of the color spectrum.

✏ **Color Balance:** Offering more flexibility than the Filter Effects options, this filter enables you to shift colors toward any part of the color spectrum. For example, shifting colors toward the cooler — bluer — spectrum produced the fourth example in Figure 10-18.

When you choose the filter from the Retouch menu, you see the screen shown in Figure 10-19. The important control here is the color grid in the lower-left corner. You shift image colors by using the Multi Selector to move the tiny black square (labeled _Color shift marker_ in the figure) around the grid. Press up to make the image greener, press right to make it redder, and so on. In the figure, I positioned the marker to strengthen blue tones, for example.

Original image

Skylight filter

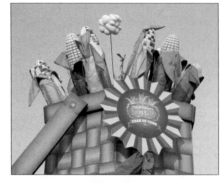 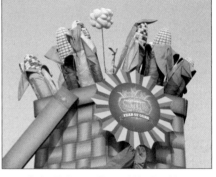

Warm filter

Color Balance filter, shifted to blue

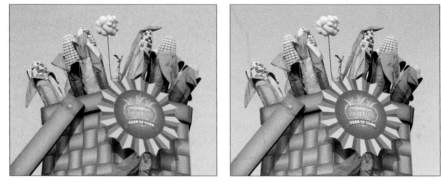

Figure 10-18: Here you see the results of applying two Filter Effects adjustments and a Color Balance shift.

The histograms on the right side of the display show you the resulting impact on overall image brightness as well as on the individual red, green, and blue brightness values — a bit of information that's helpful if you're experienced in the science of reading histograms. (Chapter 5 gives you an introduction.)

Press the Zoom In button to magnify the image and display the usual picture-in-picture zoom navigation thumbnail. Then press the AE-L/AF-L button to toggle between that thumbnail and the color-balance control box. When the thumbnail is active, pressing the Multi Selector scrolls the display; when the control box is active, pressing the Multi Selector adjusts color balance. Use the Zoom Out button to reduce the magnification.

Color shift marker

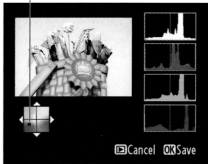

Figure 10-19: Press the Multi Selector to move the color shift marker and adjust color balance.

Creating Monochrome Images

With the Monochrome Picture Control feature covered in Chapter 8, you can shoot black-and-white photos. As an alternative, you can create a black-and-white copy of an existing color photo by applying the Monochrome option on the Retouch menu. You can also create sepia and *cyanotype* (blue and white) images via the Monochrome option. Figure 10-20 shows you examples of all three effects.

I prefer to convert my color photos to monochrome images in my photo editor; going that route simply offers more control, not to mention it's easier to preview your results on a large computer monitor than on the camera monitor. Still, I know that not everyone's as much of a photo-editing geek as I am, and there's certainly no harm in trying the in-camera filter. Just select Monochrome from the Retouch menu, press OK, select the type of monochrome image you want to create (black and white, sepia, or cyanotype) and press OK again. For the Sepia and Cyanotype options, you then see a screen that asks you to set the intensity of the tint; press the Multi Selector up and down to do so and then give OK one final tap.

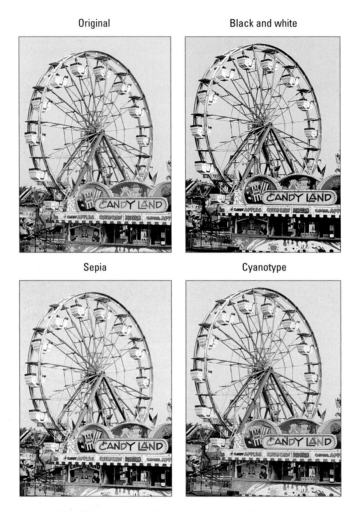

Figure 10-20: You can create three monochrome effects through the Retouch menu.

Playing with Special Effects

For photographers who want to alter reality beyond what you can achieve with the tools mentioned so far, the Retouch menu offers a number of more dramatic special-effects filters. And through the Effects exposure mode, you can add certain effects at the moment you capture the image — you don't have to shoot the picture and then tweak it through the Retouch menu. The Effects exposure mode also enables you to record movies using special effects.

The next section describes the remaining Retouch menu effects; following that, I show you how to take advantage of the Effects exposure mode.

Retouch menu special-effects filters

For some easy special-effects fun, experiment with these Retouch menu filters:

✓ **Cross Screen:** The Cross Screen filter adds a starburst effect to the brightest part of your image, as shown in Figure 10-21. To try it, select Filter Effects from the Retouch menu and then scroll down to the Cross Screen option, as shown on the left in Figure 10-22.

Original   Cross Screen filter applied

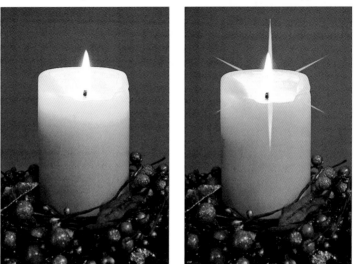

Figure 10-21: The Cross Screen filter adds a starburst effect to the brightest parts of the photo.

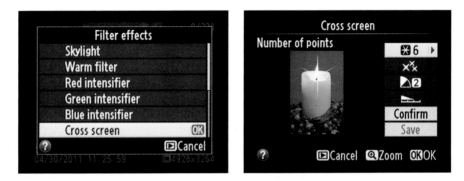

Figure 10-22: You can play with four filter settings to tweak the effect.

When you choose the filter, a column of options appears on the right side of the screen, as shown on the right in Figure 10-22. From top to bottom, the options enable you to adjust the number of points on the star, the intensity of the effect, the length of the star's rays, and the angle of the effect. Just use the Multi Selector to highlight an option (the label at the top of the screen tells you the name of the current option) and then press right to display the available settings. Highlight your choice and press OK. To update the preview after changing a filter setting, highlight Confirm and press OK. When you're happy with the effect, choose Save and press OK.

The number of starbursts the filter applies depends on your image. You can't change that number; the camera automatically adds the twinkle effect wherever it finds very bright objects. If you want to control the exact placement of the starbursts, forgo the in-camera filter and find out whether your photo software offers a more flexible star-filter effect. Or you can create the effect manually by painting the starburst strokes onto the image in a photo editor.

It's also important to frame your original image with a little extra "head room" around the object that will get the starburst, as I did in my examples. Otherwise, there isn't room in the picture for the effect.

✔ **Soft:** Also found on the Filter Effects menu, the Soft filter blurs your photo to give it a dreamy look, as shown in Figure 10-23. You can choose from three levels of blur: Low, Normal, and High; I used High for the example. Squint hard enough, and you can almost see a Monet in the making.

✔ **Color Outline:** Select this Retouch menu option to create a black-and-white line drawing based on a photo, as illustrated in Figure 10-24. This is a fun project to do with kids — you can, in essence, create a custom coloring-book page that they can then fill in with watercolors, crayons, or markers.

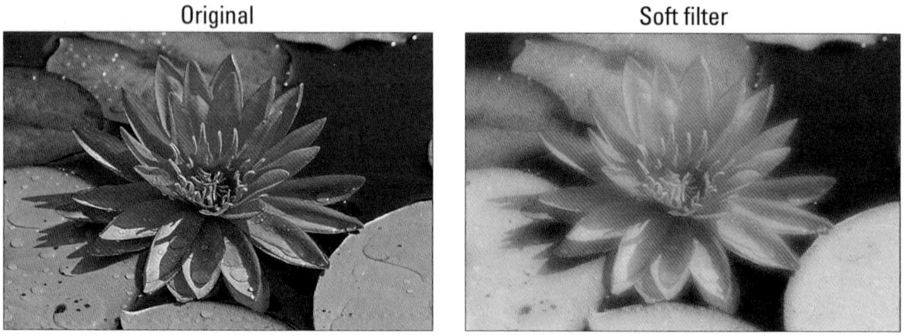

Original   Soft filter

Figure 10-23: I used the Soft filter at the High setting to create the second image here.

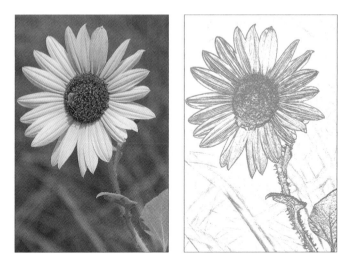

Figure 10-24: Use Color Outline to create a black-and-white line drawing out of a photo.

✔ **Color Sketch:** This filter also creates a sketch of your photo, but this time with a result similar to a drawing done in colored pencils. I used the filter on the architectural image shown in Figure 10-25, for example. When you select the effect, you can play with two options: Vividness, which affects the boldness of the colors; and Outlines, which determines the thickness of outlines. Highlight an option and press the Multi Selector right or left to adjust the setting. Press OK when you create a look you like.

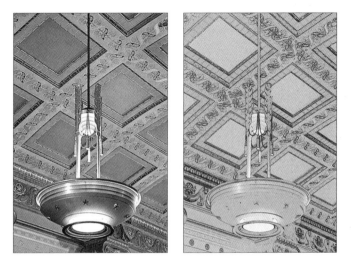

Figure 10-25: Color Sketch produces this type of effect.

✔ **Miniature Effect:** Have you ever seen an architect's small-scale models of planned developments? The ones complete with tiny trees and even people? The Miniature Effect attempts to create a photographic equivalent by applying a strong blur to all but one portion of a landscape, as shown in Figure 10-26. The left photo is the original; the right shows the result of applying the filter. For this example, I set the focus point on the part of the street occupied by the cars.

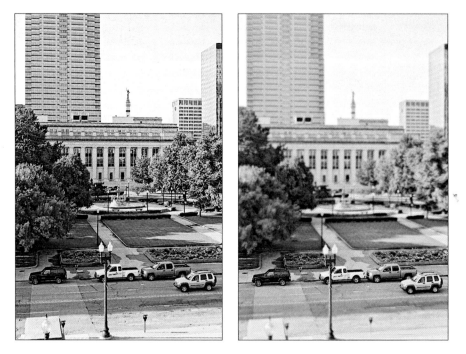

Figure 10-26: The Miniature Effect throws all but a small portion of a scene into very soft focus.

This look is based on an effect that you can create by using a *tilt-shift* lens. This type of lens can also capture pictures of tall buildings without the converging vertical lines that occur when you shoot with a normal lens.

The Miniature Effect works best if you shoot your subject from a high angle — otherwise, you don't get the miniaturization result. To try it, choose Miniature Effect from the Retouch menu and press OK to display a preview like the one shown in Figure 10-27. Then experiment with the effect as follows:

- Use the Multi Selector to position the yellow box over the area you want to keep in sharp focus.

- To rotate the focus box 90 degrees, press the Zoom Out button.

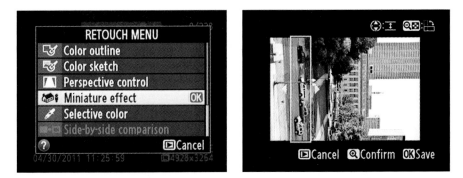

Figure 10-27: Use the Multi Selector to position the yellow rectangle over the area you want to keep in sharp focus.

- To preview the effect, press the Zoom In button.

- When you get a result you like, press OK to save a copy of the original with the effect applied.

✔ **Selective Color:** This effect enables you to *desaturate* (remove color from) parts of a photo while leaving specific colors intact. For example, in Figure 10-28, I desaturated everything but the yellows and peaches in the rose. The result lends additional drama to your subject because the eye goes first to the areas of color, and distracting background colors are eliminated.

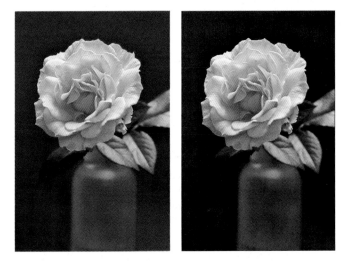

Figure 10-28: I used the Selective Color filter to desaturate everything but the rose petals.

When you choose the filter from the Retouch menu, you see a screen similar to the one on the left in Figure 10-29. Here, you can select up to three colors to retain and specify how much a color can vary from the selected one and still be retained. Make your wishes known as follows:

- *Select the first color to be retained:* Using the Multi Selector, move the yellow highlight box over the color. Then press the AE-L/AF-L button to tag that color, which appears in the left color swatch at the top of the screen, as shown on the right in Figure 10-30.

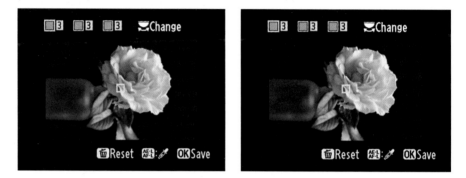

Figure 10-29: To select a color you want to keep, move the yellow box over it and press the AE-L/AF-L button.

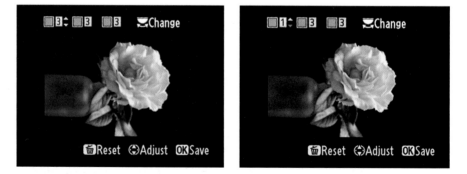

Figure 10-30: Rotate the Command dial to display a preview and activate the range value box (left); press the Multi Selector up and down to adjust the color range (right).

- *Set the range of the selected color:* Rotate the Command dial to display a preview of the desaturated image and highlight the number box to the right of the color swatch, as shown on the left in Figure 10-30. Then press the Multi Selector up or down to choose a value from 1 to 7. The higher the number, the more a pixel can vary in color from the selected hue and still be retained.

At a low value, only pixels that are very similar to the one you selected are retained. The display updates to show you the impact of the setting; for example, lowering the value to 1 turned some of the rose petals to gray, as shown on the right in Figure 10-30.

- *Choose one or two additional colors:* Rotate the Command dial to highlight the second color swatch box. Then repeat the selection process: Move the yellow highlight box over the color and press the AE-L/AF-L button to select that color. Rotate the Command dial to display the preview and activate the range value box; press the Multi Selector up and down to set the range. To choose a third color, lather, rinse, and repeat.

- *Fine-tune your settings:* You can keep rotating the Command dial to cycle through the color swatch boxes and range values, adjusting each as necessary.

- *Reset a color swatch box:* To empty a selected swatch box, press the Delete button. You can then move the yellow highlight box over a new color and press the AE-L/AF-L button to select it.

    To reset all the swatch boxes, hold down the Delete button until you see a message asking whether you want to get rid of all selected colors. Highlight Yes and press OK.

- *Save a copy of the image with the effect applied:* Press OK.

Shooting in Effects mode

When you set the Mode dial to Effects, as shown in Figure 10-31, you can apply special effects on the fly: That is, the effect is added as the camera writes the picture to the memory card.

For still photos, I prefer to capture my originals sans effect and then go through the Retouch menu to alter them. That way, I wind up with one normal image and one with the effect applied, just in case I decide I prefer the unaltered photo to the effects version. Shooting in the Effects mode also brings up another problem: In order to create the effects, the camera puts most picture-taking controls, such as White Balance and Metering mode, off limits, just as it does when you shoot in the Auto, Auto Flash Off, and Scene modes.

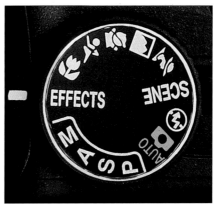

Figure 10-31: Effects mode lets you apply special effects to movies and still photos.

However, Effects mode does offer some artistic filters not available through the Retouch menu. In addition, it enables you to add effects to movies, which isn't possible through the Retouch menu. So even though I suspect that you won't find use for the Effects mode very often, I'd be remiss if I didn't spend a little time discussing it.

As soon as you set the Mode dial to Effects, an icon representing the currently selected effect appears in the top-left corner of the Shooting Info screen, as shown on the left in Figure 10-32. Rotate the Command dial to cycle through the available effects, as shown on the right in the figure, just as you do when selecting a scene type when shooting in the Scene exposure mode. (See Chapter 3 for details on Scene mode shooting.)

Effects icon

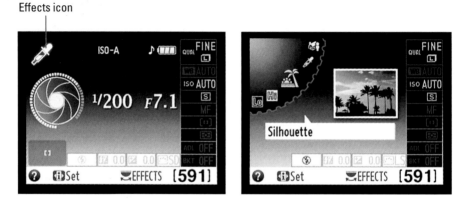

Figure 10-32: Rotate the Command dial to cycle through the available effects.

Although the Shooting Info display offers a little illustration to show you what each effect does, you don't have to rely on that artwork: Instead, set the camera to Live View mode. The monitor then shows a live preview of each effect as you select it. In Figure 10-33, for example, the Color Sketch effect is active. Again, you can cycle through the effects by rotating the Command dial; the icon representing the effect appears in the upper-left corner of the screen.

Either way, you can choose from the following effects:

Effects icon

Figure 10-33: You can preview the effects in Live View mode.

✔ **Night Vision:** Use this setting in low-light situations to produce a black-and-white image that resembles what you see with night-vision goggles. Selecting the effect gives the camera permission to increase the ISO setting beyond the top setting normally available — Hi 2, or ISO 25600. As Chapter 7 explains, a high ISO produces noise, and, thus, the grainy look of the effect. Figure 10-34 has an example. How high the ISO climbs and, thus, how much noise becomes visible, depends on the ambient light.

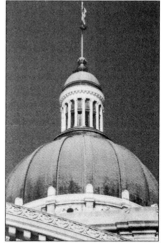

Figure 10-34: The Night Vision effect creates an exceptionally noisy black-and-white image.

A few other critical points to note:

- *Autofocusing is available only in Live View mode.* For viewfinder photography, you must focus manually. Remember to set the lens switch to the M position before turning the focusing ring! See Chapter 4 for details about Live View autofocusing.

- *Flash is disabled, as is the AF-assist lamp.* The whole idea is to create a picture taken in little light, after all.

- *Use a tripod to avoid blur.* A slow shutter speed is needed to capture the image in dark conditions, and you must be careful to avoid camera movement during the exposure. If your subject is moving, however, it could appear blurry even if the camera is on a tripod.

✔ **Color Sketch:** This produces the same effect as the Color Sketch filter on the Retouch menu. And, if you engage Live View when the effect is selected, you can adjust the same options available through the Retouch menu: Vividness and Color Outlines. First, press OK to display the options; then press the Multi Selector up or down to highlight the option you want to change, and press right or left to adjust the value for that option. Press OK again to hide the options and return to shooting. The camera remembers your settings and uses them any time you select the Color Sketch effect until you change them again.

If you're interested in this filter, it's best to compose the image using the viewfinder and then switch to Live View. When the effect is selected, the Live View display updates very slowly, making it a pain to play with composition using the monitor.

Movies recorded using this effect play back as a series of still images rather than a standard movie. Also note that autofocusing during recording is disabled.

✔ **Miniature Effect:** This one is also a double of the one on the Retouch menu; Figure 10-26 shows an example of the result.

You must set the camera to Live View mode in order to position the box that specifies the part of the scene that will remain in sharp focus. After switching to Live View, position the rectangular focus frame over the area that you want to keep in focus. Then press OK to display horizontal markings that indicate the width of the sharp-focus region, as shown in Figure 10-35. Press the Multi Selector up and down to adjust the width of the in-focus region; press right or left to change the orientation of the box. When you achieve the look you want, press OK again.

Focus zone markings

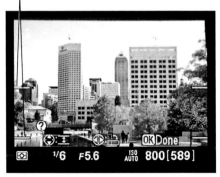

Figure 10-35: You must engage Live View to adjust the in-focus zone when using the Miniature Effect setting.

A few other limitations also apply: Flash is disabled, as is the AF-assist lamp. If you use the Continuous Release mode, the frames per second rate is reduced. For movies, sound recording is disabled, and movies play back at high speed. (The high-speed playback means that a movie that contains about 45 minutes of footage is compressed into a three-minute clip, for example.)

✏ **Selective Color:** Use this effect to create an image in which all but one to three colors are desaturated, just as when you use the Selective Color option on the Retouch menu. Figure 10-28 has an example.

To choose the colors you want to retain and specify the range of similar colors that are included, you must use Live View. You see the normal three color swatch boxes and their accompanying value boxes at the top of the screen, but the process of choosing the colors and setting the range is a little different than when you go through the Retouch menu. Use these tactics instead:

- *Access the color options:* Press OK.

- *Choose a color to retain:* Frame the image so that the little white selection box, labeled in Figure 10-36, is over the color you want to preserve. Then press the Multi Selector up.

- *Set the color range:* After setting the color, press the Multi Selector up or down to adjust the color range value. A higher value retains a broader spectrum of similar shades as the one you chose.

- *Choose additional color to retain:* Rotate the Command dial to select the second color swatch box and repeat the process of choosing a color and setting its range value.

- *Deselect a color:* Change your mind about retaining one of your chosen colors? Rotate the Command dial to highlight its color swatch and then press the Delete button. Or hold down the button for a few seconds to delete all your selected colors.

After setting your color preferences, press OK to lock in your decisions and hide the options. The camera will use those settings any time you choose the Selective Color effect until you specify new settings.

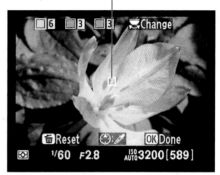

Color selection box

Figure 10-36: Frame your subject so that the white box is over a color you want to keep; then press the Multi Selector up to select that color.

✔ **Silhouette:** Choosing this setting ensures that backlit subjects will be captured as dark silhouettes against a bright background, as shown in Figure 10-37. To help ensure that the subject is dark, flash is disabled. If you want your subject instead to be properly exposed, Chapter 7 has some tips for dealing with back lighting.

✔ **High Key:** A *high key* photo is dominated by white or very light areas, such as a white china cup resting on a white doily in front of a sunny window. This setting is designed to produce a good exposure for this type of scene, which the camera otherwise tends to underexpose in response to all the high brightness values. Flash is disabled.

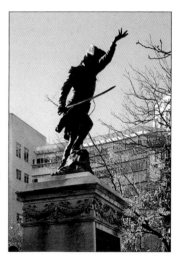

Figure 10-37: The Silhouette effect purposely underexposes backlit subjects.

How does the name relate to the characteristics of the picture? Well, photographers refer to the dominant tones — or brightness values — as the *key tones.* In most photos, the *midtones,* or areas of medium brightness, are the key tones. In a high key image, the majority of tones are at the high end of the brightness scale.

✔ **Low Key:** The opposite of a high key photo, a low key photo is dominated by shadows. Use this mode to prevent the camera from brightening the scene too much and thereby losing the dark and dramatic nature of the image. Flash is disabled.

After selecting an effect, you can exit Live View to take your picture using the viewfinder if you prefer. Or, to record a movie, remain in Live View mode and just press the red movie-record button to stop and start recording.

For four effects — Night Vision, Miniature Effect, Selective Color, and Color Sketch — still photos are always captured as a JPEG Fine file, even if you set the Image Quality setting to Raw (NEF). If the Image Quality option is set to Raw+JPEG, only the JPEG version gets the effect. Check out Chapter 2 for an explanation of all this JPEG and Raw (NEF) stuff.

Two Roads to a Multi-Image Exposure

The D5100 offers two features that enable you to combine multiple photographs into one:

- **Multiple Exposure (Shooting menu):** With this option, you can combine your next two to three shots. After you enable the option and take your shots, the camera merges them into one file. The shots used to create the composite aren't recorded and saved separately. The Multiple Exposure option isn't available in Live View mode.

- **Image Overlay (Retouch menu):** This option enables you to merge two existing Raw images. I used this option to combine a photo of a werewolf friend, shown on the top left in Figure 10-38, with a nighttime garden scene, shown on the top right. The result is the ghostly image shown beneath the two originals. Oooh, scary!

On the surface, both options sound kind of cool. The problem is that you can't control the opacity or positioning of the individual images in the combined photo. For example, my overlay picture would have been more successful if I could move the werewolf to the left in the combined image so that he and the lantern aren't blended. And I'd also prefer to keep the background of image 2 at full opacity in the overlay image rather than getting a 50/50 mix of that background and the one in image 1, which only creates a fuzzy looking background in this particular example.

However, there is one effect that you can create successfully with either option: a "two views" composite like the one in Figure 10-39. For this image, I used Image Overlay to combine the front and rear views of the antique match striker, shown at the top of the figure, into the composite on the bottom.

For this trick to work, the background in both images must be the same solid color (black seems to be best), and you must compose your photos so that the subjects don't overlap in the combined photo, as shown here. Otherwise, you get the ghostly portrait effect like what you see in Figure 10-38.

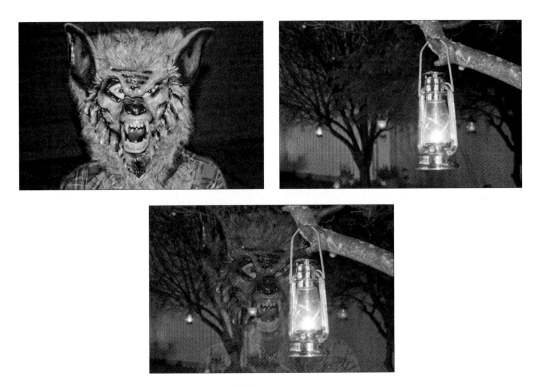

Figure 10-38: Image Overlay merges two Raw (NEF) photos into one.

To be honest, I don't use Image Overlay or Multiple Exposure for the purpose of serious photo compositing. I prefer to do this kind of work in my photo-editing software, where I have more control over the blend. Understand, too, that neither feature is designed to produce an HDR (high dynamic range) image, which lifts different brightness ranges from different images to create the composite. For HDR, you need software that can do tone mapping, not just whole-image blending. (See the Chapter 7 section related to exposure bracketing for more about HDR, including the built-in HDR tool on the Shooting menu.)

In the interest of reserving space in this book for features that I think you will find much more useful, I leave you to explore these two on your own. The electronic version of the camera manual (found on a CD that ships you're your camera) explains the steps involved in using each of them. Again, though, I think that you'll find photo compositing much easier and much more flexible if you do the job in your photo-editing software.

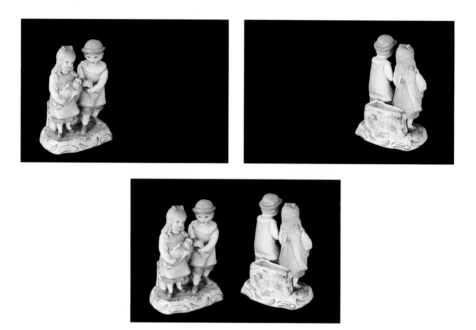

Figure 10-39: If you want each subject to appear solid, use a black background and position the subjects so that they don't overlap.

Ten Special-Purpose Features to Explore on a Rainy Day

Consider this chapter the literary equivalent of the end of one of those late-night infomercial offers — the part where the host exclaims, "But wait! There's more!"

The ten features covered in these pages fit the category of "interesting bonus." They aren't the sort of features that drive people to choose one camera over another, and they may come in handy only for certain users, on certain occasions. Still, they're included at no extra charge with your camera purchase, so check 'em out when you have a few spare moments. Who knows; you may discover that one of these bonus features is actually a hidden gem that provides just the solution you need for one of your photography problems.

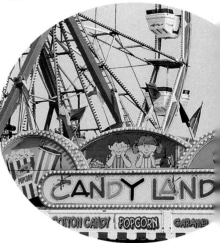

Changing the Look of the Shooting Information Display

By default, the Shooting Information screen appears as shown in the left example in Figure 11-1. The circular graphic is a representation of the aperture setting; the aperture "opening" — the gold area in the center of the graphic — grows or shrinks when you adjust the f-stop setting. (Chapter 7 explains apertures and f-stops fully.)

Graphic display   Classic display

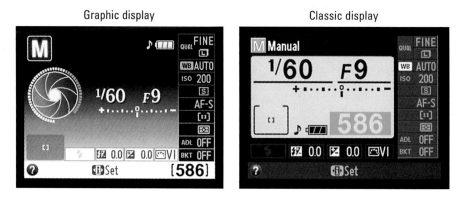

Figure 11-1: You can alter the display style of the Shooting Information screen.

When you no longer need the graphic reminder of the f-stop's impact on the aperture size, you may prefer to switch from the default screen display style to the simpler design shown on the right in the figure. To do so, select the Info Display Format option on the Setup menu, featured in Figure 11-2. You can choose from two styles, Graphic (the default) and Classic (the simpler display), and for each style, you can select from three background colors: black, blue, and orange.

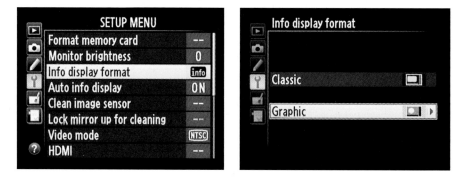

Figure 11-2: Modify the display through this Setup menu option.

Keeping the Shooting Information Display Hidden

Just below the Info Display Format option on the Setup menu, the Auto Info Display option offers another way to customize the Shooting Information display. When this option is set to On, as it is by default, the Shooting Info screen appears when you press the shutter button halfway and release it.

And, if you disable Image Review (an option covered in Chapter 5), the screen also appears after you take a picture.

Turn off the Auto Info Display option, as shown in Figure 11-3, and the screen appears briefly when you first turn on the camera, but after that, you must press the Info button or the Info Edit button to display it. Instructions in this book assume that you stick with the default setting (On). But because the monitor is one of the biggest drains of battery power, you may want to set the option to Off if you have a lot of shooting left to do and your battery is running low.

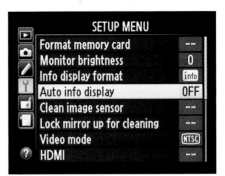

Figure 11-3: Turn off this option to prevent the Shooting Information display from appearing automatically.

Cleaning the Image Sensor

Your D5100 is set up at the factory to perform an internal cleaning routine each time you turn the camera on or off. This cleaning system is designed to keep the image sensor — that's the part of the camera that actually captures the image — free of dust and dirt. If you notice symptoms of a dirty sensor — specks that appear at the same place in all your photos, for example — despite this routine cleaning, you have two potential solutions:

✓ **Run the internal cleaning system again.** By choosing the Clean Image Sensor menu item and then selecting Clean Now, as shown in Figure 11-4, you can perform a cleaning at any time. Nikon recommends that you set the camera on a solid surface, base down, when you perform the cleaning. Don't try to perform the cleaning several times in a row, by the way — if you do, the camera will temporarily disable the function to protect itself.

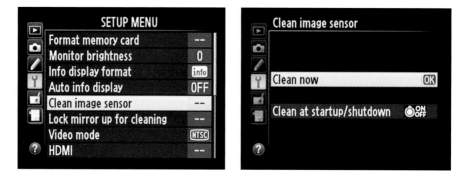

Figure 11-4: If your images display signs of a dirty sensor, try choosing these menu options to run the internal cleaning mechanism.

The other option available through the Clean Image Sensor item, called Clean At, enables you to specify whether you want the camera to change from the default setting (cleaning at startup and shutdown) to clean only at startup, only at shutdown, or never. I suggest that you stick with the default, however.

✓ **Perform a physical cleaning of the sensor.** If running the internal cleaning routine isn't sufficient, you may need to do a manual cleaning of the sensor. I recommend that you take your camera to a camera specialist to have this job done — you can easily damage the sensor permanently if you're not an expert at the procedure. But if you know what you're doing and want to tackle the task yourself, you need to take two steps in order to get to the sensor.

First, make sure the battery is fully charged. Then select the Lock Mirror Up for Cleaning option on the Setup menu, visible in Figure 11-5. Press OK and then select Start and press OK again to raise the mirror (in the camera's optical path) so that you can get to the sensor. If the menu item is dimmed, you skipped step one: The menu command is dimmed unless the battery is fully charged.

One other note about this command: It's provided only for cleaning purposes. You can't lock up the mirror to ensure shake-free long exposures as you can with some cameras; in fact, you can't take pictures on the D5100 while the mirror lock-up option is enabled.

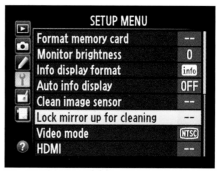

Figure 11-5: The Lock Mirror Up for Cleaning option is provided to enable a technician to rid the image sensor of dirt.

Annotate Your Images

Through the Image Comment feature on the Setup menu, you can add text comments to your picture files. Suppose, for example, that you're traveling on vacation and visiting a different destination every day. You can annotate all the pictures you take on a particular outing with the name of the location or attraction. You can then view the comments either in Nikon ViewNX 2, which ships free with your camera, or Capture NX 2, which you must buy separately. The comments also appear in some other photo programs that enable you to view metadata.

Here's how the Image Comment feature works:

1. **Display the Setup menu and highlight Image Comment, as shown on the left in Figure 11-6.**

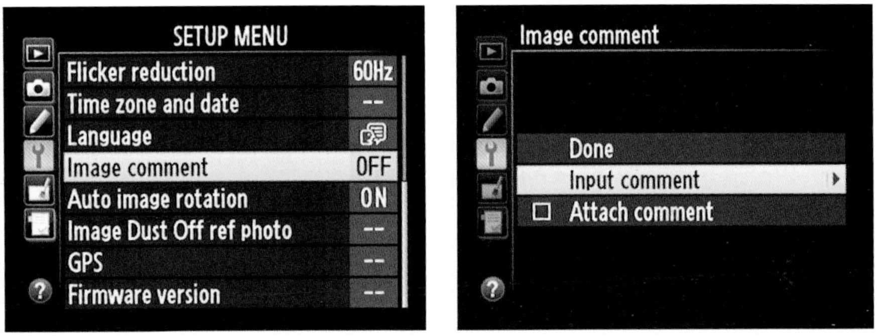

![Setup menu screens showing the SETUP MENU with Image comment highlighted, and the Image comment screen with Done, Input comment, and Attach comment options.]

Figure 11-6: You can tag pictures with text comments that you can view in Nikon ViewNX 2.

2. **Press OK to display the right screen in the figure.**

3. **Highlight Input Comment and press the Multi Selector right.**

   A keyboard-type screen appears, as shown in Figure 11-7.

4. **Use the Multi Selector to high-light the first letter of the text you want to add.**

   Note that if you scroll the display, you can access lowercase letters in addition to the uppercase ones shown on the initial screen.

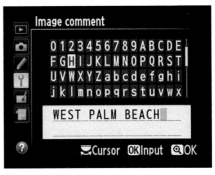

Figure 11-7: Highlight a letter and press the OK button to enter it into the comment box.

5. **Press OK to enter that letter into the display box at the bottom of the screen.**

6. **Keep highlighting letters and pressing OK to continue entering your comment.**

   Your comment can be up to 36 characters long.

   To move the text cursor, rotate the Command dial in the direction you want to shift the cursor.

   To delete a letter, move the cursor under the offending letter and then press the Delete button.

7. **To save the comment, press the Zoom In button.**

   You return to the Image Comment menu.

8. **Highlight Attach Comment, as shown on the left in Figure 11-8, and press the Multi Selector right to put a check mark in the box.**

   The check mark turns on the Image Comment feature.

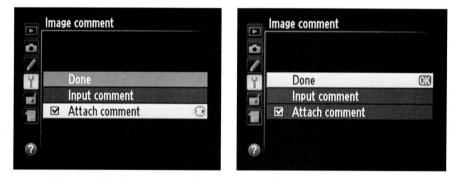

Figure 11-8: Don't forget to highlight Done and press OK to make your changes "stick."

9. **Highlight Done, as shown on the right in Figure 11-8, and press OK to wrap up.**

   You return to the Setup menu. The Image Comment menu item is set to On.

The camera applies your comment to all pictures you take after turning on Image Comment. To disable the feature, revisit the Image Comment menu, highlight Attach Comment, and press the Multi Selector right to toggle the check mark off. Select Done and press OK to make your decision official.

To view comments in Nikon ViewNX 2, display the Metadata tab. Choose Window⇨Edit to display the panel that runs down the right side of the program window, and then click the Metadata triangle, labeled in Figure 11-9. The Image Comment text appears in the File Info 2 section of the tab, as shown in Figure 11-9. (If the panel is closed, click the little triangle next to File Info 2.) See Chapter 6 for more details about using ViewNX.

Click to display/hide metadata   Image comment

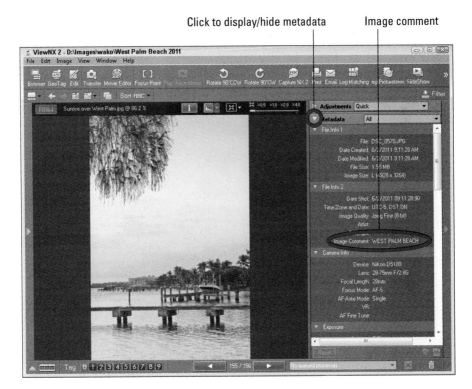

Figure 11-9: Comments appear with other metadata in Nikon ViewNX.

Creating Your Own Menu

Keeping track of how to access all the D5100's options can be a challenge, especially when it comes to those that you adjust through menus. To make things a little easier, you can build a custom menu that holds up to 20 of the options you use most frequently. Check it out:

1. Display the My Menu menu, as shown on the left in Figure 11-10.

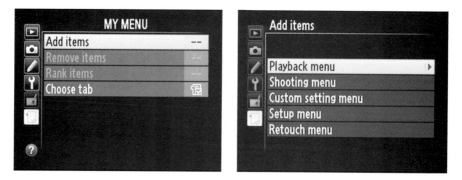

Figure 11-10: You can create a custom menu to hold up to 20 of the settings you access most often.

If the Recent Settings menu appears instead, scroll to the end of the menu, select Choose Tab, press OK, select My Menu, and press OK again. The My Menu screen then appears.

2. Highlight Add Items and press OK.

You see a list of the five main camera menus, as shown on the right in Figure 11-10.

3. Highlight a menu that contains an option you want to add to your custom menu and then press the Multi Selector right.

You see a list of all available options on that menu, as shown on the left in Figure 11-11.

A few items can't be added to a custom menu. A little box with a slash through it appears next to those items.

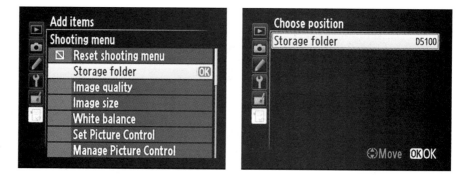

Figure 11-11: Highlight a menu item and press OK to add it to your custom menu.

4. To add an item to your custom menu, highlight it and press OK.

You see the Choose Position screen, as shown on the right in Figure 11-11, where you can change the order of your menu items. For now, just press OK to return to the My Menu screen; you can set up the order of your menu items later. (See the bulleted list following these steps.) The menu item you just added appears at the top of the My Menu screen.

5. Repeat Steps 2–4 to add more items to your menu.

When you get to Step 3, a check mark appears next to any item that's already on your menu.

After creating your custom menu, access it by pressing the Menu button and choosing the Recent Settings/My Menu screen. (If you want to switch to the Recent Settings menu, select Choose Tab and then select Recent Settings.)

You can reorder and remove menu items as follows:

✔ **Change the order of menu options:** Display the My Menu screen and highlight Rank Items, as shown on the left in Figure 11-12. You see a screen that lists all your menu items in their current order. Highlight a menu item, as shown on the right in the figure, press OK, and then use the Multi Selector to move it up or down the list. Press OK to lock in the new position of the menu item. When you're happy with the order of the menu items, press the Multi Selector left to return to the My Menu screen.

✔ **Remove menu items:** Again, head for the My Menu screen. Select Remove Items and press OK. You see a list of all the current menu items, with an empty box next to each item. To remove an item, highlight it and press the Multi Selector right. A check mark appears in that item's box. After tagging all the items you want to remove, highlight Done and press OK. You see a confirmation screen asking permission to remove the item; press OK to go forward.

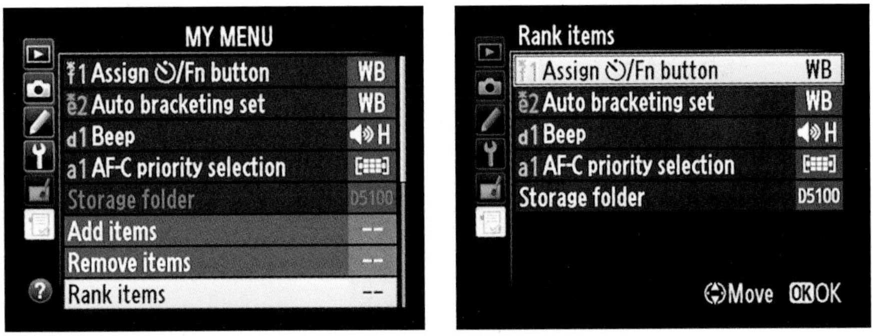

Figure 11-12: Choose Rank Items to change the order of menu items.

Creating Custom Image Folders

By default, your camera initially stores all your images in one folder, which it names 100D5100. Folders have a storage limit of 9999 images; when you exceed that number, the camera creates a new folder, assigning a name that indicates the folder number — 101D5100, 102D5100, and so on.

If you choose, however, you can create your own, custom-named folders. For example, perhaps you sometimes use your camera for business and sometimes for personal use. To keep your images separate, you can set up one folder named DULL and one named FUN — or perhaps something less incriminating, such as WORK and HOME.

Whatever your folder-naming idea, you create custom folders like so:

1. **Display the Shooting menu and highlight Storage Folder, as shown on the left in Figure 11-13.**

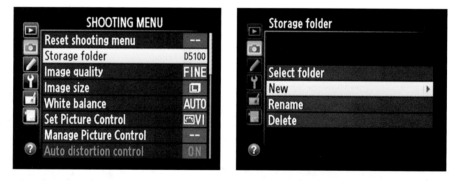

Figure 11-13: You can create custom folders to organize your images right on the camera.

2. **Press OK to display the screen shown on the right in Figure 11-13.**

3. **Highlight New and press the Multi Selector right.**

   You see a keyboard-style screen similar to the one used to create image comments, as described at the start of the chapter. The folder-naming version appears in Figure 11-14.

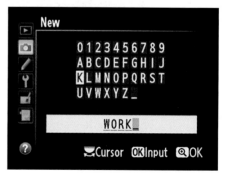

Figure 11-14: Folder names can contain up to five characters.

4. **Enter a folder name up to five characters long.**

   Use these techniques:

   - *To enter a letter,* highlight it by using the Multi Selector and then press OK.
   - *To move the text cursor,* press and rotate the Command dial in the direction you want to move the cursor.

   - *To delete a letter,* place the cursor under it and press the Delete button.

5. **After entering your folder name, press the Zoom In button.**

   You return to the Shooting menu, and the folder you just created is automatically selected as the active folder.

If you take advantage of this option, remember to specify where you want your pictures stored each time you shoot: Select Storage Folder from the Shooting menu and press OK to display the screen shown on the left in Figure 11-15. Highlight Select Folder and press the Multi Selector right to display a list of all your folders, as shown on the right. Highlight the folder that you want to use and press OK. Your choice also affects which images you can view in playback mode; see Chapter 5 to find out how to select the folder you want to view.

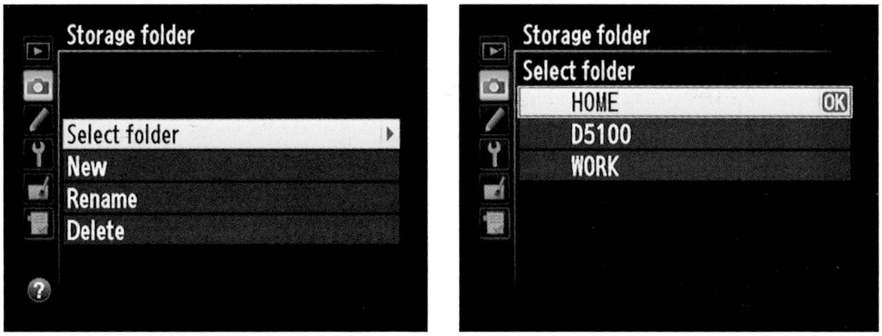

Figure 11-15: Remember to specify where you want to store new images.

If necessary, you can rename a custom folder by using the Rename option on the Active Folder screen. (See the left screen in Figure 11-15.) The Delete option on the same screen enables you to get rid of all empty folders on the memory card.

Assigning a Duty to the Function Button

Tucked away on the left-front side of the camera, just under the Flash button, the Function (Fn) button is set by default to activate Self-Timer shooting temporarily for your next picture. But if you don't use that function often, you may want to assign some other purpose to the button.

You establish the button's behavior via the Assign Fn Button option, found on the Controls submenu of the Custom Setting menu and shown on the left in Figure 11-16. After highlighting the option, press OK to display the screen shown on the right in the figure. Here's a quick description of the possible settings.

f Controls	
d1 Beep	🔊 H
d2 ISO display	OFF
d3 File number sequence	ON
d4 Exposure delay mode	OFF
d5 Print date	OFF
e1 Flash cntrl for built-in flash	TTL⚡
e2 Auto bracketing set	WB
f1 Assign ⏱/Fn button	⏱

f1 Assign ⏱/Fn button	
⏱ Self-timer	OK
🖷 Release mode	
QUAL Image quality/size	
ISO ISO sensitivity	
WB White balance	
🖼 Active D-Lighting	
HDR HDR mode	
+RAW + NEF (RAW)	

Figure 11-16: You can assign any number of jobs to the Function button.

- **Self-Timer:** The default option actives Self-Timer shooting with the current specified time delay. The Self-Timer mode applies only to your next shot, however.

- **Release mode:** Pressing the Fn button while turning the Command dial lets you change the Release mode.

- **Image Quality/Size:** Pressing the Fn button while turning the Command dial cycles through the available Image Quality and Image Size settings.

- **ISO Sensitivity:** Pressing the button while turning the Command dial changes the ISO setting.

- **White Balance:** Pressing the button while turning the Command dial cycles through the available White Balance settings (available only when the Mode dial is set to P, S, A, or M).

- **Active D-Lighting:** Pressing the button while turning the Command dial changes the Active D-Lighting setting (again, only in P, S, A, and M exposure modes).

✔ **HDR mode:** Pressing the button enables the HDR option for your next shot. See Chapter 7 for more about HDR.

✔ **+ NEF (RAW):** This setting relates to the Image Quality option, introduced in Chapter 2. If you set that option to JPEG Basic, Fine, or Normal and then press the Fn button, the camera records two copies of the next pictures you shoot: a JPEG version plus a second image in the NEF format. Press the button again or turn off the camera to stop recording the Raw (NEF) version.

✔ **Auto bracketing:** Pressing the Fn button while turning the Command dial lets you select a bracketing increment for AEB (automatic exposure bracketing) or white-balance bracketing. For ADL (Active D-Lighting) bracketing, you can use the button and Command dial to turn bracketing on and off. Bracketing, explained at the end of Chapter 7, is possible only in the P, S, A, or M exposure mode.

After selecting the function you want to assign, press OK to lock in your choice.

Changing the Function of the AE-L/AF-L Button

 Set just to the right of the viewfinder, the AE-L/AF-L button enables you to lock focus and exposure settings when you shoot in autoexposure and autofocus modes, as explored in Chapters 7 and 8.

Normally, autofocus and autoexposure are locked when you press the button, and they remain locked as long as you keep your finger on the button. But you can change the button's behavior. To access the available options, open the Custom Setting menu, navigate to the Controls submenu, press OK, and then highlight Assign AE-L/AF-L Button, as shown on the left in Figure 11-17. Press OK to display the options shown on the right in the figure.

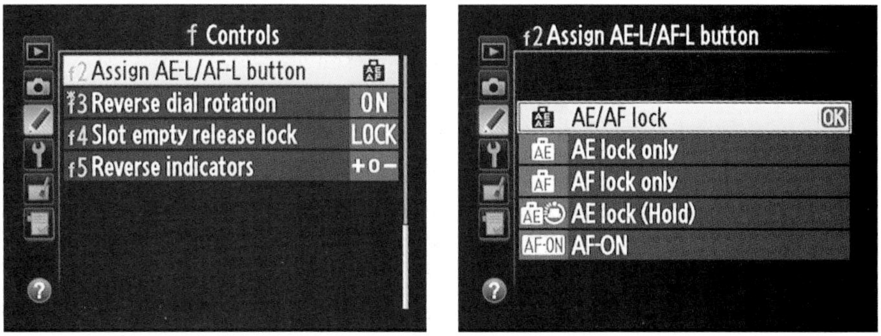

Figure 11-17: You can set the AE-L/AF-L button to lock autoexposure only if you prefer.

The options produce these results:

- ✓ **AE/AF Lock:** This is the default setting. Focus and exposure remain locked as long as you press the button.

- ✓ **AE Lock Only:** Autoexposure is locked as long as you press the button; autofocus isn't affected. (You can still lock focus by pressing the shutter button halfway.)

- ✓ **AF Lock Only:** Focus remains locked as long as you press the button. Exposure isn't affected.

- ✓ **AE Lock (Hold):** This one locks exposure only with a single press of the button. The exposure lock remains in force until you press the button again or the exposure meters turn off.

- ✓ **AF-On**: Pressing the button activates the camera's autofocus mechanism. If you choose this option, you can't lock autofocus by pressing the shutter button halfway.

After highlighting the option you want to use, press OK.

The information that I give in this book with regard to using autofocus and autoexposure assumes that you stick with the default setting. So if you change the button's function, remember to amend my instructions accordingly.

Using the Shutter Button to Lock Exposure and Focus

The Timers/AE Lock section of the Custom Setting menu offers a third button tweak called Shutter-Release Button AE-Lock, as shown in Figure 11-18. This option determines whether pressing the shutter button halfway locks focus only or locks both focus and exposure.

At the default setting, Off, you lock focus only when you press the shutter button halfway. Exposure is adjusted continually up to the time you take the shot. If you change the setting to On, your half-press of the shutter button locks both focus and exposure.

c Timers/AE lock	
a1 AF-C priority selection	▣
a2 Built-in AF-assist illuminator	OFF
a3 Rangefinder	ON
b1 EV steps for exposure cntrl.	1/3
c1 Shutter-release button AE-L	ON
c2 Auto off timers	⏱✎
c3 Self-timer	--
c4 Remote on duration	1m

Figure 11-18: If you turn on this option, pressing the shutter button halfway locks exposure and focus.

As with the AE-L/AF-L button adjustment described in the preceding section, I recommend that you leave this option set to the default while you're working with this book. Otherwise, your camera won't behave as described here (or in the camera manual, for that matter). If you encounter a situation that calls for locking exposure and focus together, you can always use the AE-L/AF-L button. Chapter 7 provides details.

Reversing the Command Dial Orientation

When you shoot in the P, S, A, or M exposure modes, you rotate the Command dial to adjust shutter speed and aperture settings. By default, rotating the dial to the right raises the value that's being adjusted: the shutter speed in S mode, for example, or the f-stop in A mode. In M mode, rotating the dial to the right increases the shutter speed, and rotating the dial to the right while you hold down the Exposure Compensation button raises the f-stop value. In P mode, rotating the dial to the right raises the shutter speed and lowers the f-stop.

If that setup seems backward to you, you can tell the camera that you prefer to rotate the dial to the right to lower the values and rotate left to raise them. Just set the Reverse Dial Rotation option to On, as shown in Figure 11-19. Look for the setting in the Controls section of the Custom Setting menu.

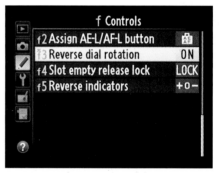

Figure 11-19: For people who like to go left when everyone else goes right, the Reverse Dial Rotation option reverses the orientation of the Command dial.

You also can reverse the orientation of the exposure meter so that the positive end of the meter appears to the right and the negative side to the left. The command to make that change is called Reverse Indicators and also lives on the Custom Setting menu. Chapter 7 explains more about reading the exposure meter.

Index